Europe as Ideological Resource

Europe as Ideological Resource

European Integration and Far-Right Legitimation in France and Italy

Marta Lorimer

Great Clarendon Street, Oxford, OX2 6DP,
United Kingdom

Oxford University Press is a department of the University of Oxford.
It furthers the University's objective of excellence in research, scholarship,
and education by publishing worldwide. Oxford is a registered trade mark of
Oxford University Press in the UK and in certain other countries

© Marta Lorimer 2024

The moral rights of the author have been asserted

All rights reserved. No part of this publication may be reproduced, stored in
a retrieval system, or transmitted, in any form or by any means, without the
prior permission in writing of Oxford University Press, or as expressly permitted
by law, by licence or under terms agreed with the appropriate reprographics
rights organization. Enquiries concerning reproduction outside the scope of the
above should be sent to the Rights Department, Oxford University Press, at the
address above

You must not circulate this work in any other form
and you must impose this same condition on any acquirer

Published in the United States of America by Oxford University Press
198 Madison Avenue, New York, NY 10016, United States of America

British Library Cataloguing in Publication Data

Data available

Library of Congress Control Number: 2023944404

ISBN 9780198892366

DOI: 10.1093/oso/9780198892366.001.0001

Printed and bound by
CPI Group (UK) Ltd, Croydon, CR0 4YY

Links to third party websites are provided by Oxford in good faith and
for information only. Oxford disclaims any responsibility for the materials
contained in any third party website referenced in this work.

Acknowledgements

When asked why I decided to study the far right and Europe, I usually tell a story. It starts with a neo-fascist song overheard in a car in Sardinia, goes through a research-led YouTube rabbit hole, and ends with the puzzling discovery of far-right pan-Europeanism. To make sense of that discovery, I did what some curious people faced with a puzzle do: I embarked upon a PhD to find the answers to all of my questions. The book you are reading is based on that PhD.

Writing a PhD was no easy feat, and transforming it into a book was no easier. I have incurred many debts of gratitude along the way. I am thankful to my supervisors Jonathan White and Roger Eatwell for being thoughtful and supportive readers of the many drafts it took to finish the PhD. I am particularly thankful to Jonathan for taking the time to read both the thesis and the first draft of this book. I want to acknowledge my examiners Paul Taggart and Tim Bale. Their comments helped me define how I wanted the book to look. I am also indebted to my late supervisor Maurice Fraser for encouraging me to apply for a PhD in the first place.

Several colleagues graciously agreed to read early drafts of the book's argument and chapters. I am deeply thankful to Léonie de Jonge, Marianna Griffini, Simona Guerra, Lise Herman, Hjalte Lokdam, and Manès Weisskircher for their feedback. I am also grateful to the many friends and colleagues at the LSE European Institute who supported me in the thinking and writing process. I particularly wish to acknowledge Angelos Angelou, Marina Cino Pagliarello, Sean Deel, Cristobal Garibay-Petersen, Kira Gartzou-Katsouyanni, Katerina Glyniadaki, Angelo Martelli, Daphnée Papiasse, and Matilde Rosina for offering welcome breaks from work.

Most of this book was written at LSE, but parts of it were written while I was completing a postdoc at the University of Exeter with Sandra Kröger and Richard Bellamy. I thank them for leaving me the time to work on the book. This book also benefitted from research stays at Sciences Po's *Centre d'Études Européennes* and Forum MIDEM at TU Dresden.

My work would not have been possible without the staff at the BNF in Paris, the Biblioteca Cesare Alfieri in Florence, and at the archives of the Fondazione Ugo Spirito in Rome. I am also deeply grateful to Gianfranco Fini, Jean-Yves Le Gallou, Marco Tarchi, and the four (former) Rassemblement

National members who agreed to speak to me for giving me the reference points I needed to understand the archival material better.

At Oxford University Press, I would like to thank Dominic Byatt and Phoebe Aldridge-Turner for their support, as well as the three anonymous reviewers for their thoughtful comments. This book's argument and two empirical chapters draw on previously published material, and I acknowledge Taylor & Francis for permission to reproduce passages from the following: 'Europe as Ideological Resource: The Case of the Rassemblement National', *Journal of European Public Policy* 27(9), 2020; and 'What Do They Talk about When They Talk about Europe? Euro-Ambivalence in Far Right Ideology', *Ethnic and Racial Studies* 44(11), 2021.

Without the support of my friends and family outside academia, I would never have finished the PhD, let alone the book. While I can't thank each of them individually, I do have to thank my cousins Greta and Julian, my parents Silvia and Dino, and my sister Francesca for reminding me that there is a life outside academia.

Finally, my most heartfelt thank-you goes to Lorenzo. For always being there for nearly eighteen years, I thank him.

Stintino

July 2023

Contents

Introduction	1
1. Europe as ideological resource	25
2. *Europa patria nostra*	58
3. The battle for Europe's freedom	87
4. States of emergency	114
5. For the nation and for Europe	139
Conclusion	166
Appendix	180
Index	188

Introduction

When a haggard group of neo-fascists entered the Italian parliament in 1948, few expected them to hang around for long, let alone join a government. Similar thoughts would have crossed the minds of those following the early steps of a diverse group of French far-right activists uniting for the first time in 1972. Fast-forward to 1994, and the Italian neo-fascists are readying to become junior partners in a coalition government (and will, in due course and after some change, also become government leaders). Fast-forward to 2017, and the leader of the French far-right group is facing her biggest political challenge yet: persuading enough French voters to pick her as their presidential candidate in the second round of the French presidential elections.

The two parties described above are the Movimento Sociale Italiano/Alleanza Nazionale (MSI/AN) and the Rassemblement National (RN, previously Front National). Their parable, however, is reflective of the broader trajectory of the far right in post-war Europe. Parties once considered pariahs entered the mainstream and increasingly found themselves in positions of power. This book tries to understand how these parties went from the margins to the mainstream by focusing specifically on how 'Europe' and what they had to say about it helped them along the way.

Europe might appear as a counterintuitive topic to look at. Political, academic, and media commentaries alike have stressed how deeply critical of European integration far-right parties are, presenting Euroscepticism, or even 'Europhobia', as one of their distinguishing features.[1] Although there is some acknowledgement that the EU has represented an enabling feature in their success, providing them with funding, visibility, and political capital in times when they were ostracized at the domestic level,[2] their positions on European integration have mainly been considered as markers of marginalization. In particular, their strong opposition to the EU project on both ideological and strategic grounds has been approached as a factor standing in

---

[1] Gary Marks and Carole J. Wilson, 'The Past in the Present: A Cleavage Theory of Party Response to European Integration', *British Journal of Political Science* 30, no. 3 (2000): 457.
[2] Emmanuelle Reungoat, 'Mobiliser l'Europe dans la compétition nationale. La fabrique de l'européanisation du Front national', *Politique européenne* 43, no. 1 (2014): 120–162, doi:10.3917/poeu.043.0120.

the way of their access to power because of its fringe, rather than mainstream, character.[3] Euroscepticism's nature as a 'touchstone of dissent',[4] then, would appear not only to hinder the far right's progress in domestic and European political systems by making its access to power more tortuous, but also to entrench its position at the margins.

This book challenges this assessment and demonstrates how the far right's positions on European integration helped them appear more palatable. Its core argument is that as a relatively new and contentious political issue, European integration has functioned as a powerful ideological resource for far-right parties looking for legitimation because it allowed them to refashion their political message in a more acceptable form, while maintaining the allegiance of their core voters and supporters. The argument is developed through an in-depth study of how the Movimento Sociale Italiano/Alleanza Nazionale in Italy and the Rassemblement National in France integrated Europe into their ideological frames, and to what effects. The book centres on four key concepts and discourses these parties associated with Europe: the concept of identity, which enabled them to transnationalize their message and create a positive association between themselves and Europe; the concept of liberty, which made it possible for them to foster an image of actors holding uncontroversial positions; the notion of threat, which helped them justify their measures by promoting the idea that 'desperate times call for desperate measures'; and finally, the concept of national interest, which weaved with the other three, helping them stress commitment to core principles in their ideology even as a new issue was being introduced.

Ever since its re-emergence on the European political scene after the Second World War, scholars have sought to understand how the success and persistence of the far right could be explained. The normalization and spread of its ideas have played a key role in its success, and present one of the key political challenges of our time in Europe and beyond. By understanding how the process of European integration facilitated far-right parties' transition from illegitimate fringe to contenders for public office, this book adds one piece to the puzzle of understanding the process of legitimation and mainstreaming of the far right.

---

[3] Gilles Ivaldi, 'Contesting the EU in Times of Crisis: The Front National and Politics of Euroscepticism in France', *Politics* 38, no. 3 (2018): 286, doi:10.1177/0263395718766787; Sofia Vasilopoulou, *Far Right Parties and Euroscepticism: Patterns of Opposition* (London; New York: Rowman & Littlefield, 2018).

[4] Paul Taggart, 'A Touchstone of Dissent: Euroscepticism in Contemporary Western European Party Systems', *European Journal of Political Research* 33, no. 3 (1998): 363–388, doi:10.1023/A:1006853204101.

Defining far-right ideology

The field of study of the far right is a crowded one. If in the 1980s, the late Klaus von Beyme could lament the absence of perspectives on far-right parties,[5] this has by now become the most studied party family in political science and beyond.[6] Over the years, studies have tackled a variety of issues including the definition and ideological characteristics of far-right parties, the reasons for their success, and their impact on democratic polities and other parties.[7] Revisiting these debates is beyond the scope of this work, but this book's interest in the notion of Europe as an ideological resource does require the identification of a definition of far-right ideology.

Defining what constitutes a far-right party has been terminologically and substantively controversial. Terminologically, scholars have adopted a variety of terms including radical right,[8] extreme right,[9] far right,[10] and variations of populist radical right[11] to identify a similar group of parties. While these disputes are not fully settled, a broadly agreed-upon distinction is that between the 'extreme' and the 'radical' right, with the former term being used to refer

---

[5] Klaus von Beyme, 'Right-Wing Extremism in Post-War Europe', ed. Klaus von Beyme, *West European Politics* 11, no. 2 (1988): 1.

[6] Kai Arzheimer, 'Conceptual Confusion Is Not Always a Bad Thing: The Curious Case of European Radical Right Studies', in *Demokratie Und Entscheidung*, ed. Karl Marker and Michael Roseneck (Wiesbaden: Springer, 2018), 23–40, doi:10.1007/978-3-658-24529-0_3; Cas Mudde, *The Far Right Today* (Cambridge: Polity, 2019); for perspectives from other fields see for example Mabel Berezin, *Illiberal Politics in Neoliberal Times: Culture, Security and Populism in the New Europe* (Cambridge: Cambridge University Press, 2009); Douglas R. Holmes, *Integral Europe: Fast-Capitalism, Multiculturalism, Neofascism* (Princeton: Princeton University Press, 2000); Cynthia Miller-Idriss, *The Extreme Gone Mainstream: Commercialization and Far Right Youth Culture in Germany* (Princeton; Oxford: Princeton University Press, 2017).

[7] For a recent review of the field, see Pietro Castelli Gattinara, 'The Study of the Far Right and Its Three E's: Why Scholarship Must Go beyond Eurocentrism, Electoralism and Externalism', *French Politics* 18 (2020): 314–333, doi:10.1057/s41253-020-00124-8.

[8] David Art, *Inside the Radical Right: The Development of Anti-Immigrant Parties in Western Europe* (Cambridge; New York: Cambridge University Press, 2011); Herbert Kitschelt and Anthony J. McGann, *The Radical Right in Western Europe: A Comparative Analysis* (Ann Arbor: University of Michigan Press, 1995); Jens Rydgren, *The Oxford Handbook of the Radical Right* (New York: Oxford University Press, 2018).

[9] Paul Hainsworth, *The Extreme Right in Western Europe* (New York: Routledge, 2008); Michael Bruter and Sarah Harrison, *Mapping Extreme Right Ideology*, 2011, doi:10.1057/9780230336834; Piero Ignazi, *Extreme Right Parties in Western Europe* (Oxford: Oxford University Press Oxford, 2003), doi:10.1093/0198292259.001.0001; Cas Mudde, *The Ideology of the Extreme Right* (New York: Manchester University Press, 2000).

[10] Vasilopoulou, *Far Right Parties and Euroscepticism: Patterns of Opposition*; Mudde, *The Far Right Today*.

[11] Tjitske Akkerman, Sarah L. de Lange, and Matthijs Rooduijn, *Radical Right-Wing Populist Parties in Western Europe: Into the Mainstream?* (London: Routledge, 2016); Hans-Georg Betz, *Radical Right-Wing Populism in Western Europe* (Basingstoke, Hants: Macmillan, 1994); Lise Esther Herman and James B. Muldoon, *Trumping the Mainstream: The Conquest of Mainstream Democratic Politics by the Populist Radical Right* (London; New York: Routledge, 2019); Cas Mudde, *Populist Radical Right Parties in Europe* (Cambridge: Cambridge University Press, 2007), doi:10.1111/j.1478-9302.2009.00194.x.

to groups and parties that reject the existing constitutional order, and the latter to identify those who broadly accept it.[12] The term 'far right', on the other hand, is mostly used as a shorthand to discuss parties of the extreme and radical right together.[13]

Substantively, scholars have frequently disagreed on the core ideological characteristics of far-right parties. In an early review of existing definitions, for example, Cas Mudde noted that in 26 existing definitions, scholars identified no less than 58 different features of 'right-wing extremism'.[14] Today, a broad consensus exists that a core defining feature of these parties is nationalism. The nation, in fact, constitutes the 'focal point' of their ideology,[15] the 'core concept' serving as the 'coat-hanger'[16] on which other ideological features can be draped. While nationalism is as debated a concept as that of 'far right',[17] definitions will usually encompass two aspects: first, they will identify the nation as the central referent actor, and second, they will observe the need for this group's identity to be expressed politically and/or institutionally. Ernest Gellner, for example, defined nationalism as a political principle 'which holds that the political and national unit should be congruent'.[18] Anthony D. Smith, for his part, described it as 'an ideological movement to attain and maintain autonomy, unity and identity on behalf of a population, some of whose members conceive it to constitute an actual or potential "nation"'.[19] In studies of the far right, far-right nationalism has been further specified as being a specific type of exclusionary nationalism,[20] or, as Mudde puts it, a form of 'nativism' that combines xenophobia and nationalism to present an 'ideology that holds that states should be inhabited exclusively by members of the native group ("the nation"), and that non-native people and

---

[12] For more on the distinction, see Hainsworth, *The Extreme Right in Western Europe*, 8–9.

[13] Andrea L. P. Pirro, 'Far Right: The Significance of an Umbrella Concept', *Nations and Nationalism* 29, no. 1 (January 2023): 101–112, doi:10.1111/nana.12860.

[14] Cas Mudde, 'The War of Words Defining the Extreme Right Party Family', *West European Politics* 19, no. 2 (1996): 225–248.

[15] Michael Minkenberg, *The Radical Right in Eastern Europe: Democracy under Siege?* (New York: Palgrave Macmillan, 2017), 14.

[16] Michael Freeden, 'Ideologies and Conceptual History', *Journal of Political Ideologies* 2, no. 1 (1997): 5, doi:10.1080/13569319708420747.

[17] Ian Adams, *Political Ideology Today* (Manchester; New York: Manchester University Press, 1993), 82ff; Michael Freeden, 'Is Nationalism a Distinct Ideology?', *Political Studies* 46, no. 4 (1998): 748–765, doi:10.1111/1467-9248.00165; Roger Griffin, 'Nationalism', in *Contemporary Political Ideologies*, ed. Roger Eatwell (London; New York: Pinter, 1999), 152–179.

[18] Ernest Gellner, *Nations and Nationalism* (Oxford: Blackwell, 1983), 1.

[19] Anthony D. Smith, *Myths and Memories of the Nation* (New York: Oxford University Press, 1999), 256.

[20] Michael Minkenberg, 'The West European Radical Right as a Collective Actor: Modeling the Impact of Cultural and Structural Variables on Party Formation and Movement Mobilization', *Comparative European Politics* 1, no. 2 (2003): 149–170, doi:10.1057/palgrave.cep.6110017; Roger Eatwell, 'The Rebirth of the "Extreme Right" in Western Europe?', *Parliamentary Affairs* 53 (2000): 407–425, doi:10.1093/pa/53.3.407.

ideas are fundamentally threatening to the homogenous nation-state'.[21] This nativism has at times been framed in racial terms, but in political parties in Europe it is now mostly present in an 'ethno-pluralist' version which strips the insider/outsider divide of its hierarchical character, while maintaining the idea that cultures are fundamentally different and incompatible.[22]

In addition to nationalism, several authors point to authoritarianism as a second defining characteristic of the far right.[23] While not as central as nationalism, it denotes these parties' 'belief in a strictly ordered society, in which infringements of authority are to be punished severely',[24] along with their commitment to the 'promotion of a return to the national/traditional way of life and opposition to immigration and policies promoting multiculturalism, which are seen as eroding national identity, culture and values'.[25]

Many recent definitions also include populism among the key defining features of a specific subset of the far right.[26] Populism draws on a fundamental opposition between 'the (dispossessed) people' and 'the elite', and considers that politics should be the expression of the general and unmediated 'will of the people'.[27] Populism, however, is not a shared feature of all far-right parties, but only of a subset of them. Historically in particular, far-right parties have tended towards elitism rather than populism. This was the case of the MSI studied here, but also of other far-right parties including the Nationaldemokratische Partei Deutschlands (Democratic Party of Germany, NPD), or the Greek Ethniki Politiki Enosis (National Political Union, EPEN), and even of the RN in its early years.[28] Thus, although it is increasingly rare to find non-populist far-right parties, it is best to regard populism as a relevant, but not core, aspect of the party family as a whole.

---

[21] Mudde, *Populist Radical Right Parties in Europe*, 19.
[22] Jens Rydgren, 'The Sociology of the Radical Right', *Annual Review of Sociology* 33, no. 1 (2007): 241–262, doi:10.1146/annurev.soc.33.040406.131752; Aurelien Mondon and Aaron Winter, 'Articulations of Islamophobia: From the Extreme to the Mainstream?', *Ethnic and Racial Studies* 40, no. 13 (2017): 2151–2179, doi:10.1080/01419870.2017.1312008.
[23] Sarah Harrison and Michael Bruter, *Mapping Extreme Right Ideology: An Empirical Geography of the European Extreme Right* (London: Palgrave Macmillan, 2011); Ignazi, *Extreme Right Parties in Western Europe*; Pippa Norris and Ronald Inglehart, *Cultural Backlash: Trump, Brexit, and the Rise of Authoritarian Populism* (Cambridge: Cambridge University Press, 2019); Mudde, *Populist Radical Right Parties in Europe*.
[24] Mudde, *Populist Radical Right Parties in Europe*, 22–23.
[25] Vasilopoulou, *Far Right Parties and Euroscepticism: Patterns of Opposition*, 7.
[26] Rydgren, *The Oxford Handbook of the Radical Right*, 5–6; Damir Skenderovic, *The Radical Right in Switzerland: Continuity and Change, 1945–2000* (New York: Berghahn Books, 2009).
[27] Mudde, *Populist Radical Right Parties in Europe*, 23; for definitions of populism, see e.g. Margaret Canovan, 'Trust the People! Populism and the Two Faces of Democracy', *Political Studies* 67 (1999): 2–16; Ben Stanley, 'The Thin Ideology of Populism', *Journal of Political Ideologies* 13, no. 1 (2008): 95–110, doi:10.1080/13569310701822289; Cristóbal Rovira Kaltwasser et al., *The Oxford Handbook of Populism* (Oxford: Oxford University Press, 2017).
[28] Mudde, *Populist Radical Right Parties in Europe*, 49.

In light of these considerations, this book uses the term 'far right' to refer to political parties whose ideological core is characterized by the combination of nationalism and authoritarianism. Where appropriate, the distinction between the 'extreme' and 'radical' right will be discussed; however, for the purposes of this work, these parties are considered sufficiently similar to be discussed and studied together.

Supporters, sceptics, and beneficiaries: the complex relationship between the far right and Europe

While for obvious geographical reasons Euroscepticism is not usually viewed as a core element of the global far right's ideology, it has increasingly imposed itself as a shared feature of the European members of the far-right party family,[29] and a 'natural' one given its oppositional role[30] and its nationalist ideology.[31] It has also become increasingly clear that even though European integration is not the only factor pushing voters to choose the far right,[32] it is an issue that matters to them and that helps establish linkages between far-right parties and their voters.[33]

Analyses of the relationship between the far right and Europe were conspicuously absent (or barely mentioned) in early monographs on the far right; however, following the EU's multiple crises and the growth of public Euroscepticism, they have acquired more prominence in recent works. Literature on the far right and Europe can be broadly divided into three research

---

[29] Margarita Gómez-Reino Cachafeiro, *Nationalisms in the European Arena: Trajectories of Transnational Party Coordination* (Cham: Palgrave Macmillan, 2018), 63–64; Marks and Wilson, 'The Past in the Present: A Cleavage Theory of Party Response to European Integration', 457.

[30] Taggart, 'A Touchstone of Dissent: Euroscepticism in Contemporary Western European Party Systems'; Benedicte Williams, 'Electoral Strategy Trumps Political Ideology', in *Varieties of Right-Wing Extremism in Europe*, ed. Andrea Mammone, Emmanuel Godin, and Brian Jenkins (Abingdon: Routledge, 2013), 134–148; Nick Sitter, 'The Politics of Opposition and European Integration in Scandinavia: Is Euro-Scepticism a Government–Opposition Dynamic?', *West European Politics* 24, no. 4 (2001): 22–39, doi:10.1080/01402380108425463.

[31] Marks and Wilson, 'The Past in the Present: A Cleavage Theory of Party Response to European Integration', 457; Liesbet Hooghe, Gary Marks, and Carole J. Wilson, 'Does Left/Right Structure Party Positions on European Integration?', *Comparative Political Studies* 35, no. 8 (2002): 965–989, doi:10.1177/001041402236310; Daphne Halikiopoulou, Kyriaki Nanou, and Sofia Vasilopoulou, 'The Paradox of Nationalism: The Common Denominator of Radical Right and Radical Left Euroscepticism', *European Journal of Political Research* 51, no. 4 (2012): 504–539, doi:10.1111/j.1475-6765.2011.02050.x.

[32] Duncan McDonnell and Annika Werner, 'Differently Eurosceptic: radical right populist parties and their supporters', *Journal of European Public Policy*, 26, no.12 (2019:), 1761–1778.

[33] Pablo Ortiz Barquero, Antonia María Ruiz Jiménez, and Manuel Tomás González-Fernández. 'Ideological Voting for Radical Right Parties in Europe'. *Acta Politica* (2021); Margarita Gómez-Reino and Iván Llamazares. 'The Populist Radical Right and European Integration: A Comparative Analysis of Party–Voter Links,' *West European Politics* 36, no. 4 (2013): 794.

streams with different foci. The first focuses on content and consists primarily of works seeking to understand both the historical roots of the relationship between the far right and Europe, and how far-right parties and groups conceive of Europe. The second strand of literature focuses on causes and seeks to answer the question 'how can far-right Euroscepticism be explained?' The third strand of research centres on the actions of far-right parties in the EU's institutions and on the effects of their engagement with European integration.

Understanding the content of far-right positions on Europe and their historical development has been the main goal of the first stream of research. Researchers in this stream have highlighted that the idea of Europe has a long pedigree in far-right thinking and have shown how pan-European ideas led early far-right parties to construct transnational links.[34] These works have also analysed the content of far-right positions on Europe, notably by identifying both its 'Eurosceptic' and its 'Euro-ambivalent' aspects.[35] They have shown how far-right parties have viewed European integration as 'an encroaching, bureaucratic and elitist phenomenon' which undermines 'constructs and values, such as the nation-state, national identity, state sovereignty, deeply embedded roots and national belonging'.[36] At the same time, they have stressed that approaching the far right as a 'homogenous and static Eurosceptic bloc'[37] is incorrect in at least two ways. First, it conflates views of Europe intended as a continent and civilization, and views of the EU as a concrete political project. In fact, as several authors have noted, the far right's positions on Europe are dominated by a tendency to claim an attachment to Europe as a civilization, while vividly opposing the European Union.[38] Second, approaching the far right as a Eurosceptic bloc fails to acknowledge that while far-right parties have converged on anti-EU

---

[34] Robert Roger Griffin, 'Europe for the Europeans. Fascist Myths of the European New Order 1922–1992', *Occasional Paper (No. 1)* 1 (1994): 1–37; Dieter Gosewinkel, 'Europe antilibérale ou Anti-Europe? Les conceptions européennes de l'extrême droite française entre 1940 et 1990', *Politique européenne* 62, no. 4 (2018): 152–179; Tamir Bar-On, 'Fascism to the Nouvelle Droite: The Dream of Pan-European Empire', *Journal of Contemporary European Studies* 16, no. 3 (2008): 327–345, doi:10.1080/14782800802500981; Tamir Bar-On, 'Transnationalism and the French Nouvelle Droite', *Patterns of Prejudice* 45, no. 3 (2011): 199–223, doi:10.1080/0031322X.2011.585013; Andrea Mammone, *Transnational Neofascism in France and Italy, Transnational Neofascism in France & Italy* (Cambridge: Cambridge University Press, 2015).
[35] Marta Lorimer, 'What Do They Talk about When They Talk about Europe? Euro-Ambivalence in Far Right Ideology', *Ethnic and Racial Studies* 44, no. 11 (2021): 2016–2033, doi:10.1080/01419870.2020.1807035.
[36] Hainsworth, *The Extreme Right in Western Europe*, 82.
[37] Dimitri Almeida, 'Europeanized Eurosceptics? Radical Right Parties and European Integration', *Perspectives on European Politics and Society* 11, no. 3 (2010): 244, doi:10.1080/15705854.2010.503031.
[38] Katy Brown, 'When Eurosceptics Become Europhiles: Far-Right Opposition to Turkish Involvement in the European Union', *Identities*, 27, no. 6 (2020): 633–654, doi:10.1080/1070289X.2019.1617530; Rogers Brubaker, 'Between Nationalism and Civilizationism: The European Populist Moment in Comparative Perspective', *Ethnic and Racial Studies* 40, no. 8 (2017): 1191–1226,

positions, they were not originally or uniformly against European integration. This point has been highlighted by Mudde, amongst others. In his study on the far right in Europe, he stressed that many far-right parties started off from pro-EU positions but changed following the end of the Cold War and the signing of the Maastricht Treaty.[39] Dimitri Almeida similarly suggested that in the past, the European Union acted as a counterweight to the Soviet Union in far-right thinking.[40] While the far right's attachment to the European project was never unqualified, as the EU was often seen as being either too influenced by the United States or in need of some kind of reform (for example to reduce the 'democratic deficit'), 'hard' Euroscepticism was not a dominant feature until the 1990s.[41]

Drawing on a wider body of work dedicated to explaining how political parties and voters position themselves on the issue of European integration,[42] the second strand of literature has sought to account for how far-right parties came to oppose the European Union. Research on far-right Euroscepticism has mainly drawn on either ideological or strategic explanations. These explanations need not be seen as antithetical but, rather, as mutually reinforcing or determining different aspects of a party's opposition to EU integration.[43] Proponents of ideological explanations for far-right Euroscepticism have suggested that far-right parties oppose European integration by virtue of their nationalist ideology and their position on key territorial and cultural cleavages.[44] Liesbet Hooghe, Gary Marks, and Carole Wilson, for example, argued that far-right parties 'react against a series of perceived threats to the national community. [. . .] European integration combines several of

doi:10.1080/01419870.2017.1294700; Laurie Beaudonnet and Henio Hoyo Prohuber, 'Being European, the Nationalist Way: Europe in the Discourse of Radical Right Parties', *Party Politics*, March 2023, 13540688231161208, doi:10.1177/13540688231161209; Joseph Cerrone, 'Reconciling National and Supranational Identities: Civilizationism in European Far-Right Discourse', *Perspectives on Politics* 21, no. 3 (2023): 951–966.

[39] Mudde, *Populist Radical Right Parties in Europe*, 182.
[40] Almeida, 'Europeanized Eurosceptics?', 241–244.
[41] On the distinction between 'hard' and 'soft' Euroscepticism, see Aleks Szczerbiak and Paul A. Taggart, *Opposing Europe?: The Comparative Party Politics of Euroscepticism. Volume 2* (Oxford: Oxford University Press, 2008), 2.
[42] For a few examples in a vast literature, see C. E. De Vries, *Euroscepticism and the Future of European Integration* (Oxford: Oxford University Press, 2018), doi:10.1093/oso/9780198793380.001.0001; Petr Kopecky and Cas Mudde, 'The Two Sides of Euroscepticism: Party Positions on European Integration in East Central Europe', *European Union Politics* 3, no. 3 (2002): 297–326; Cécile Leconte, *Understanding Euroscepticism* (Basingstoke; New York: Palgrave Macmillan, 2010); Aleks Szczerbiak and Paul A. Taggart, *Opposing Europe?: The Comparative Party Politics of Euroscepticism* (Oxford: Oxford University Press, 2008).
[43] Catherine E. De Vries and Erica E. Edwards, 'Taking Europe To Its Extremes: Extremist Parties and Public Euroscepticism', *Party Politics* 15, no. 1 (2009): 19, doi:10.1177/1354068808097889; Margarita Gómez-Reino et al., 'The Populist Radical Right and European Integration: A Comparative Analysis of Party–Voter Links', *West European Politics* 36, no. 4 (2013): 794, doi:10.1080/01402382.2013.783354; Szczerbiak and Taggart, *Opposing Europe. Volume 2*, 13–14.
[44] Gómez-Reino Cachafeiro, *Nationalisms in the European Arena*.

these threats and poses one more: it undermines national sovereignty'.⁴⁵ In a similar fashion, Daphne Halikiopoulou, Sofia Vasilopoulou, and Kyriaki Nanou have stressed that far-right parties oppose the EU as a body that threatens the 'autonomy, unity and identity of the nation'.⁴⁶ Researchers inclined towards strategic explanations have argued that far-right parties' position within the domestic political system and their electoral objectives provide them with strategic incentives to support or oppose the EU. Catherine De Vries and Erica Edwards, for example, have argued that these parties benefitted from opposition to the EU by presenting themselves as the only actors that defend the nation from it.⁴⁷ Almeida stressed this point further, suggesting that far-right parties' Euroscepticism is part of a strategy to differentiate themselves from mainstream ones and 'sustain a role as tribunes against the "political establishment"'.⁴⁸ In the most detailed study of far-right Euroscepticism to date, Sofia Vasilopoulou has made strategic claims central to her analysis. While acknowledging the role of ideology in determining the type of Euroscepticism brought forward by the parties, she argued that far-right parties perform a balancing act between interest representation, electoral politics, and party competition in defining their positions on the EU, thereby showing that—depending on their strategic goals and position within the electoral system—they adopted different levels of Euroscepticism.⁴⁹

Whereas the first two strands of literature focused primarily on the content of far-right ideas on Europe and how their Euroscepticism could best be explained, the third strand of research has analysed the far right's behaviour within the European institutions, as well as the advantages they gained from this activity. A key observation emerging from this literature is that the EU has provided far-right parties with a number of ideational and strategic resources which have helped them establish themselves in the political system. Catherine Fieschi has summarized this most clearly when arguing that, 'in spite of their anti-Europeanism, these parties have gained enormously from the solemnity, ritual and political symbolism of the European arena and from the credibility derived through seats in the European Parliament'.⁵⁰

---

⁴⁵ Hooghe, Marks, and Wilson, 'Does Left/Right Structure Party Positions on European Integration?', 976–978.
⁴⁶ Halikiopoulou, Nanou, and Vasilopoulou, 'The Paradox of Nationalism', 510.
⁴⁷ De Vries and Edwards, 'Taking Europe To Its Extremes'.
⁴⁸ Almeida, 'Europeanized Eurosceptics?', 243.
⁴⁹ Vasilopoulou, *Far Right Parties and Euroscepticism*; See also Sofia Vasilopoulou, 'European Ingegration and the Radical Right. Three Patterns of Opposition', *Government and Opposition* 46, no. 2 (2011): 226.
⁵⁰ Catherine Fieschi, 'European Institutions: The Far-Right and Illiberal Politics in a Liberal Context', *Parliamentary Affairs* 53 (2000): 521.

More recently, Alina Polyakova went even further, arguing that the persistence of nationalism and the success of the far right could be read as an unintended consequence of, and a direct response to, the process of European economic integration.[51]

Far right parties have benefitted both electorally and symbolically from European integration. While they have struggled historically to gain representation at the national level, the 'second order' nature of EU elections,[52] coupled with a proportional electoral system, has made it easier for them to win seats in the European Parliament than in their national parliaments.[53] This has come with a number of other advantages because winning seats allowed far-right parties to gain 'legitimacy, resources and patronage' which could then be used to consolidate their results.[54] By participating in European elections and gaining elected office, far-right parties have also been able to share their ideas more widely and voice their concerns in an additional arena. This has given them more visibility and influence on the policy agenda, both at the national and the European level.[55] The rise in salience of European integration, in conjunction with far-right parties' ability to establish a level of 'ownership' of it,[56] has also offered them an opportunity to reinforce the electoral link with their voters and gain new votes by covering positions on integration previously ignored by the mainstream.[57] In a study of the RN, Emmanuelle Reungoat clearly illustrated these dynamics by showing how the EU provided the party with both practical and symbolic resources that

---

[51] Alina Polyakova, *The Dark Side of European Integration: Social Foundations and Cultural Determinants of the Rise of Radical Right Movements in Contemporary Europe* (Stuttgart: ibidem press, 2015).

[52] Karlheinz Reif and Hermann Schmitt, 'Nine Second-Order National Elections—A Conceptual Framework for the Analysis of European Election Results', *European Journal of Political Research* 8, no. 1 (1980): 3–44, doi:10.1111/j.1475-6765.1980.tb00737.x; Simon Hix and Michael Marsh, 'Second-Order Effects plus Pan-European Political Swings: An Analysis of European Parliament Elections across Time', *Electoral Studies* 30, no. 1 (2011): 4–15, doi:10.1016/j.electstud.2010.09.017.

[53] Almeida, 'Europeanized Eurosceptics?', 243–244; Hainsworth, *The Extreme Right in Western Europe*, 83; Emmanuelle Reungoat, 'Changing the Rules, Changing the Winners? The Various Effects of European Election Rules on Party Oppositions to the EU in France', in *The Routledge Handbook of Euroscepticism*, ed. Benjamin Leruth, Nicholas Startin, and Simon Usherwood (London: Routledge, 2018), 155–167.

[54] Pippa Norris, *Radical Right: Voters and Parties in the Electoral Market* (New York: Cambridge University Press, 2005), 255–256.

[55] Julia Schulte-Cloos, 'Do European Parliament Elections Foster Challenger Parties' Success on the National Level?', *European Union Politics* 19, no. 3 (2018): 408–426, doi:10.1177/1465116518773486.

[56] John Petrocik, 'Issue Ownership in Presidential Elections, with a 1980 Case Study', ed. John Petrocik, *American Journal of Political Science* 40, no. 3 (1996): 825; Wouter van der Brug and Joost van Spanje, 'Immigration, Europe, and the 'New' Cultural Dimension', *European Journal of Political Research* 48, no. 3 (2009): 309–334, doi:10.1111/j.1475-6765.2009.00841.x.

[57] Gómez-Reino Cachafeiro, *Nationalisms in the European Arena*, 77; although see also Duncan McDonnell and Annika Werner, 'Differently Eurosceptic: Radical Right Populist Parties and Their Supporters', *Journal of European Public Policy* 26, no. 12 (2019): 1761–1778, doi:10.1080/13501763.2018.1561743 on the limitations of far-right party–voter linkages on the EU issues.

helped it survive and grow. In practical terms, she argued that the EU gave the RN and its MEPs the financial means and institutional framework to gain in political experience and dedicate themselves fully to the profession of politicians. In symbolic terms, Reungoat suggested that, internally, successes in the European arena could be sold to the party membership as a demonstration of the success of the party's ideas, while externally, the European Parliament mandates represented symbols of legitimation by making the party appear less isolated, especially through alliances with like-minded parties abroad.[58]

Far-right parties have not only been passive beneficiaries of the process of European integration, but have also actively sought to use it to their own advantage. This was already apparent in the 'strategic' accounts of far-right opposition to European integration, but has been shown even more clearly in the study of the transnational practices of the far right,[59] with authors such as Nicholas Startin, and Duncan McDonnell and Annika Werner arguing that far-right parties have strategically used transnational collaboration as a legitimacy-enhancing tool.[60] Startin, for example, highlighted how the creation of the short-lived Identity, Tradition and Sovereignty Group in the European Parliament was guided by the belief that collaboration at the EU level would represent 'a clear and transparent confirmation that their parties are able to play by the existing rules of the game within a clear democratic framework, thus allowing them to negate some of the accusations of a broadly hostile media and political class about the group's lack of democratic integrity'.[61] In a similar vein, McDonnell and Werner have shown how concerns about legitimacy and respectability at the national level helped explain why and with whom far-right parties decided to collaborate in the European Parliament.[62]

---

[58] Reungoat, 'Mobiliser l'Europe dans la compétition nationale', 133–136.
[59] Manuela Caiani, 'Radical Right Cross-National Links and International Cooperation', in *The Oxford Handbook of the Radical Right*, ed. Jens Rydgren (New York: Oxford University Press, 2018), 394–411; Gerda Falkner and Georg Plattner, 'EU Policies and Populist Radical Right Parties' Programmatic Claims: Foreign Policy, Anti-Discrimination and the Single Market', *JCMS: Journal of Common Market Studies* 58, no. 3 (May 2020): 723–739, doi:https://doi.org/10.1111/jcms.12963; José Pedro Zúquete, 'The New Frontlines of Right-Wing Nationalism', *Journal of Political Ideologies* 20, no. 1 (2015): 74–78, doi:10.1080/13569317.2015.991492.
[60] Nicholas Startin, 'Where to for the Radical Right in the European Parliament? The Rise and Fall of Transnational Political Cooperation', *Perspectives on European Politics and Society* 11, no. 4 (2010): 429–449, doi:10.1080/15705854.2010.524402; Nicholas Startin, '"Euromondialisme" and the Growth of the Radical Right', in *Routledge Handbook of Euroscepticism*, ed. Benjamin Leruth, Nicholas Startin, and Simon McDougall Usherwood (London: Routledge, 2018): 75–85; Duncan McDonnell and Annika Werner, *International Populism: The Radical Right in the European Parliament* (London: Hurst, 2019).
[61] Startin, 'Where to for the Radical Right in the European Parliament?', 439.
[62] McDonnell and Werner, *International Populism*; Duncan McDonnell and Annika Werner, 'Respectable radicals: why some radical right parties in the European Parliament forsake policy congruence,' *Journal of European Public Policy* 25, no. 5 (2018): 747–763.

In focusing on the legitimizing effects of party practices in Europe, however, this literature has mostly neglected the potential effects of party beliefs about Europe. There are a few noteworthy exceptions. Bartek Pytlas recently studied how far-right parties could 'highjack' Europe from within and use 'counter-European' claims to validate and normalize their political message.[63] Reinhard Heinisch, Duncan McDonnell, and Annika Werner also explored this dimension by looking at how far-right parties could use their positions on Europe for strategic purposes.[64] In particular, they stressed how adopting an 'equivocal Eurosceptic' ideological stance could serve the dual purpose of facilitating both transnational and national collaboration for far-right parties. These works, however, have covered a short time span, and centred mainly on the far right's ambivalent messaging on 'Europe'. As such, they have missed the evolutions over time of the far right's ideological approach to Europe, and fall short when it comes to providing a more holistic assessment of the elements of far-right ideology that contribute to legitimation. Building on these studies and with these limitations in mind, this book explores the question of how far-right parties have benefitted from the process of European integration by exploring the contention that Europe functioned as an 'ideological resource' for them.

An empirically grounded interpretive study of the far right and Europe

The book's analysis of the notion of Europe as an ideological resource is built on three distinctive conceptual and methodological elements. First, the book's primary focus is on ideology and its 'character and effects'.[65] Its aim is not to explain why far-right parties hold the positions they do. Rather, it is interested in how the positions they hold on Europe and how they present them help them construct a more legitimate image. Its approach is also less geared towards testing assumptions as it is towards unfolding the concept of an ideological resource and showing how it works in practice.[66] Concretely,

---

[63] Bartek Pytlas, 'Hijacking Europe: Counter-European Strategies and Radical Right Mainstreaming during the Humanitarian Crisis Debate 2015–16', *Journal of Common Market Studies* 59 (2021): 335–353, doi:10.1111/jcms.13092.

[64] Reinhard Heinisch, Duncan McDonnell, and Annika Werner, 'Equivocal Euroscepticism: How Populist Radical Right Parties Can Have Their EU Cake and Eat It', *Journal of Common Market Studies* 59 (2021): 189–205, doi:10.1111/jcms.13455.

[65] Rochana Bajpai, *Debating Difference Group Rights and Liberal Democracy in India* (New Delhi: Oxford University Press, 2011), 72–73.

[66] For a similar approach, see Jonathan White, *Political Allegiance after European Integration* (Basingstoke; New York: Palgrave Macmillan, 2011), x–xi.

this means that the focus is on identifying ideology-based legitimation mechanisms, rather than on measuring the outcomes of this process. To reach this objective, the book adopts an exploratory approach and interpretive stance aimed at understanding 'meanings, beliefs, and discourses' rather than 'laws and rules, correlations between social categories, or deductive models'.[67] While 'ideology' has a poor reputation in political science and public discourse and is frequently negatively loaded from a normative standpoint,[68] ideologies are conceptualized here in a neutral sense as 'systems of political thinking, loose or rigid, deliberate or unintended, through which individuals and groups construct an understanding of the political world they, or those who preoccupy their thoughts, inhabit, and then act on that understanding'.[69]

Some might understandably be reluctant to separate the identification of legitimation mechanisms and the measurement of their effectiveness; however, the complexities associated with assessing responses to political messages and measuring legitimacy suggest this is a prudent strategy. On the first point, political messages usually have many different addressees, and trying to identify the success of a specific strategy with regard to all of them would prove extremely complicated, especially given the same strategy could have very different effects depending on who is being interpellated. On the second point, the measurement of legitimacy is fraught with difficulty because of the complexity of the concept itself and the difficulty in isolating the various elements that constitute it. Although one might be tempted to measure it with proxies such as vote share, such measures are unsatisfactory as they fail to capture that one could conceivably consider that a party has a right to compete in elections and even govern without, however, voting for it. A party's legitimacy will also rarely be based exclusively on what it says or does. Rather, it will depend on a variety of factors including what other parties do, how the media reacts to them, and the historical and social context they act in. These factors make assessing the success of far-right mechanisms of legitimation a difficult task to achieve, at least within the confines of a single book.

Nevertheless, the fact that an aspect of a phenomenon is complicated to measure should not stop one from studying the parts of it that are amenable

---

[67] Mark Bevir and R. A. W. Rhodes, 'Defending Interpretation', *European Political Science* 5, no. 1 (2006): 70, doi:10.1057/palgrave.eps.2210059.
[68] Willard A. Mullins, 'On the Concept of Ideology in Political Science', *The American Political Science Review* 66, no. 2 (1972): 499–502, doi:10.2307/1957794; Michael Freeden, 'Practising Ideology and Ideological Practices', *Political Studies* 48, no. 2 (2000): 302, doi:10.1111/1467-9248.00261; Malcolm B. Hamilton, 'The Elements of the Concept of Ideology', *Political Studies* 35, no. 1 (1987): 20–21, doi:10.1111/j.1467-9248.1987.tb00186.x.
[69] Michael Freeden, *Ideologies and Political Theory: A Conceptual Approach* (Oxford: Oxford University Press, 1998), 3.

to empirical analysis. The focus of legitimation mechanisms serves precisely that purpose. It puts the researcher on more stable grounds, and makes it possible to empirically identify mechanisms of legitimation with some degree of certainty. Such an approach may also have some predictive value to the extent that it can alert to strategies that political actors have employed in the past and could use when faced with similar issues in the future.

A second defining aspect of this book's approach is that, in line with the interpretive commitment to understand 'how humans conceive of their worlds, the language they use to describe them and other elements constituting that social world',[70] it seeks to understand far-right parties in their own words and interpret them as much as possible according to their own logic. Accordingly, it draws on the rigorous qualitative analysis of over 400 party documents produced between 1978 and 2019 by the MSI/AN and the RN. These documents are analysed by means of morphological and discourse analysis (a complete description of the study's research design and methodology is presented in Chapter 1). Studying these parties in their own words does not entail subscribing to that world view or taking what they say at face value; however, it does mean seeking to understand how they would want to be thought of and, most likely, how many of those who do follow them see them. If one is to understand how to effectively counter and deconstruct their message, it may be worth thinking of what they look like at their best rather than at their worst.

Finally, in approaching Europe as an ideological resource, this book takes a somewhat broad definition of what 'Europe' is. Europe, in fact, is not limited to the political project of the European Union. It has been noted earlier that the far right considers Europe to be something beyond the EU. Europe, in their view, is a specific civilization, characterized by a shared culture. This distinction is not one that has been made exclusively by them; there is a rich body of literature that seeks to understand how one might define 'Europe' and the 'Europeans'.[71] Even joining the European Union requires that a prospective member state persuade the others of its 'Europeanness' and, as the case of Turkey shows, the question is not merely of a geographical nature. In short, because Europe is an extremely 'malleable' concept,[72] it is pertinent to look

---

[70] Peregrine Schwartz-Shea and Dvora Yanow, *Interpretive Research Design: Concepts and Processes* (New York: Routledge, 2012), 52.

[71] Anthony R. Pagden, *The Idea of Europe: From Antiquity to the European Union* (Cambridge, Washington, DC, and New York: Cambridge University Press, 2002); Norman Davies, *Europe: A History* (Oxford; New York; London: Oxford University Press, 1996); Pim den Boer, *The History of the Idea of Europe*, ed. Ole Wæver et al. (Milton Keynes; New York: Open University; Routledge and Kegan Paul, 1995).

[72] Chris Flood, 'Euroscepticism: A Problematic Concept', *UACES 32nd Annual Conference*, 2002, 7.

not only at what far-right parties have to say about the EU, but also at how this relates to the concept of Europe that preceded it, and how European integration enabled them to make broader claims about Europe.

The book makes a four-fold contribution to existing research on the far right and Europe. Theoretically, it advances a novel argument concerning the ideological role of European integration in the legitimation of the far right. Doing so it challenges existing accounts suggesting that opposition to European integration entrenches far-right parties' marginal positions by showing that even strong opposition can be used to produce political benefits. Methodologically, the monograph's in-depth interpretive analysis of material produced over a long time span complements existing works which have either focused on a shorter period of time, or studied 'ideology' in a purely quantitative fashion. From an empirical standpoint, the book draws on a large number of previously unstudied party documents produced by two key parties in the history of the far right. Finally, the book contributes to our understanding of key political issues surrounding the far right. At a time where far-right parties have become a regular presence in the political make-up of most European countries, and even governmental forces in some of them, it is as important as ever to reflect on the causes of their success. Focusing on how the EU may have helped them achieve public legitimacy, this book contributes to the wider debate on how they went from the margins of politics to the mainstream.

Plan of the book

The book's argument that European integration has functioned as a powerful ideological resource for-far right parties is developed both theoretically and empirically throughout the following chapters.

Chapter 1 presents the theoretical argument of the book and details the study's empirical and methodological tenets. It opens by discussing the far right's 'legitimacy deficit', and how these parties sought to address it. It then develops a theoretical account of how European integration contributed to far-right parties' attempts to plug this deficit. Drawing on literature on Europeanization, it introduces the concept of an 'ideological resource', defined as a device that offers political parties an opportunity to revise and reframe their political message. The chapter argues that as a new and relatively contentious political issue, with no clear 'ideological' answer, European integration offers political parties some leeway to determine their positions in a way that may help them appeal both to their core electorate and to a wider public. It then suggests that for far-right parties suffering from a legitimacy deficit, this is particularly important as it creates the space for them to use their positions on Europe to construct a more respectable image without alienating their core support. The concluding section presents the book's empirical strategy based on the in-depth interpretive analysis of over 400 party documents produced between 1978 and 2019 by the Movimento Sociale Italiano/Alleanza Nazionale and the Rassemblement National. The chapter discusses how the empirical analysis combines morphological analysis to identify the key concepts the parties used to define Europe and discourse analysis to tease out the content of each concept, so as to present an account of how the MSI/AN and RN integrated Europe in their world view, and to what effects for their political image.

Chapters 2, 3, 4, and 5 develop the book's argument empirically. The chapters are arranged thematically and each chapter describes the content of the concepts the parties used to define Europe and considers how they fed into their legitimation.

Chapter 2 examines how the MSI/AN and RN employed the concept of identity to define Europe. It shows how since the 1970s, the parties thought of 'Europe' as a distinct civilization, with clear boundaries separating it from foreign 'others'. Both groups claimed to belong to this civilization and initially supported European integration in its name. However, from the mid 1980s onwards, the RN began to develop a 'pro-Europe, anti-EU' message which presented the EU as a violation of Europe's true nature. The MSI/AN, on the other hand, did not adopt a similar position, remaining broadly collaborative in its stance towards EU integration. Claiming to hold a European identity and supporting 'Europe', the chapter argues, made it possible for the parties to refashion their message in a more transnational direction and draw on a form of legitimacy by association which helped them address critiques of them as 'closed' and potentially aggressive nationalists. While the MSI/AN, especially as AN, drew on direct association with the EU as a source of legitimation, the RN distinguished between 'Europe' and the EU and used only the former to construct legitimacy.

Chapter 3 analyses the second concept the MSI/AN and RN employed to define Europe, namely the concept of liberty, intended in their language as a collective form of freedom. It shows how in their early years and in the context of the Cold War, both parties stressed the need for Europe to become free from foreign interference. This came with a call for Europe to become an international power, equipped with a strong common defence and able to project influence beyond its borders. From the early 1990s onwards, the parties parted ways. While the MSI/AN remained committed to its view of

Europe as a foreign policy actor, the RN increasingly appealed to freedom from the constraints imposed by European integration, thus refocusing its discourse on ideas of domestic self-rule. Using the language of freedom and autonomy to define their views on Europe, the chapter argues, presented the parties with an occasion to draw on ideas that were not exclusive to them, but part of a shared way of thinking about politics. This made it possible for them to foster an image as actors holding common, rather than exceptional, positions.

Chapter 4 shows how the MSI and RN, but not AN, employed the concept of threat to further characterize Europe. In the 1970s and 1980s, both political parties presented 'Europe' as endangered by a series of internal and external threats including communism, the USA and the USSR, materialism, demographic decline, and immigration. In the 1990s, the MSI's transformation into AN entailed the abandonment of a rhetoric of emergency. The RN, on the other hand, shifted from being aware of threats to Europe to speaking of the distinct threat posed *by* the EU. The chapter argues that this far-right version of emergency politics made it possible for the parties to validate their own 'exceptional' political action. By identifying a threat, advocating for the need to address it, and identifying themselves as the most appropriate actors to do so, they promoted the idea that given the circumstances, their own 'extreme' positions were a commensurate response to the dangers being faced.

Whereas the previous chapters analysed the individual concepts the parties used to define Europe and the EU, Chapter 5 looks at how the three concepts discussed in the previous chapters, along with the concept of national interest, came together in the parties' approach to the principle, practice, and future of European integration. It argues that each of these concepts can be tied to the parties' core doctrine of nationalism and that their redeployment in the definition of positions on European integration served the purpose of highlighting consistency as a new issue was being introduced. Stressing commitment to core principles in their ideology and presenting themselves as principled actors, the chapter holds, fed into the parties' internal legitimacy because it presented them as credible and trustworthy to their own voters.

The Conclusion summarizes the book's key argument and discusses its broader implications. It considers whether Europe can still function as an ideological resource, and the extent to which Euroscepticism as a term captures the far right's relationship with Europe. It also discusses how the findings from the book help shed light on the phenomenon of far-right 'Euronationalism' and discusses their implications for the European Union. The chapter concludes with a brief discussion of the rise of Fratelli d'Italia (Brothers of Italy, FdI), the successor party to the MSI/AN.

References

Adams, Ian. *Political Ideology Today* (Manchester; New York: Manchester University Press, 1993).

Akkerman, Tjitske, Sarah L. de Lange, and Matthijs Rooduijn. *Radical Right-Wing Populist Parties in Western Europe: Into the Mainstream?* (London: Routledge, 2016).

Almeida, Dimitri. 'Europeanized Eurosceptics? Radical Right Parties and European Integration'. *Perspectives on European Politics and Society* 11, no. 3 (2010): 237–253. https://doi.org/10.1080/15705854.2010.503031.

Art, David. *Inside the Radical Right: The Development of Anti-Immigrant Parties in Western Europe* (Cambridge; New York: Cambridge University Press, 2011).

Arzheimer, Kai. 'Conceptual Confusion Is Not Always a Bad Thing: The Curious Case of European Radical Right Studies'. In *Demokratie Und Entscheidung*, edited by Karl Marker and Michael Roseneck (Wiesbaden: Springer, 2018), 23–40. https://doi.org/10.1007/978-3-658-24529-0_3.

Bajpai, Rochana. *Debating Difference Group Rights and Liberal Democracy in India* (New Delhi: Oxford University Press, 2011).

Bar-On, Tamir. 'Fascism to the Nouvelle Droite: The Dream of Pan-European Empire'. *Journal of Contemporary European Studies* 16, no. 3 (2008): 327–345. https://doi.org/10.1080/14782800802500981.

Bar-On, Tamir. 'Transnationalism and the French Nouvelle Droite'. *Patterns of Prejudice* 45, no. 3 (2011): 199–223. https://doi.org/10.1080/0031322X.2011.585013.

Beaudonnet, Laurie, and Henio Hoyo Prohuber. 'Being European, the Nationalist Way: Europe in the Discourse of Radical Right Parties'. *Party Politics*, March 2023, 13540688231161208. https://doi.org/10.1177/13540688231161209.

Berezin, Mabel. *Illiberal Politics in Neoliberal Times: Culture, Security and Populism in the New Europe* (Cambridge: Cambridge University Press, 2009).

Betz, Hans-Georg. *Radical Right-Wing Populism in Western Europe* (Basingstoke, Hants: Macmillan, 1994).

Bevir, Mark, and R. A. W. Rhodes. 'Defending Interpretation'. *European Political Science* 5, no. 1 (2006): 69. https://doi.org/10.1057/palgrave.eps.2210059.

Beyme, Klaus von (ed.). 'Right-Wing Extremism in Post-War Europe'. *West European Politics* 11, no. 2 (1988): 1.

Boer, Pim den. *The History of the Idea of Europe*. With Ole Wæver and Peter Bugge. Edited by Kevin Wilson and W. J. van der Dussen. MyiLibrary (Milton Keynes; New York: Open University; Routledge and Kegan Paul, 1995).

Brown, Katy. 'When Eurosceptics become Europhiles: far-right opposition to Turkish involvement in the European Union', *Identities* 27, no. 6 (2020): 633–654.

Brubaker, Rogers. 'Between Nationalism and Civilizationism: The European Populist Moment in Comparative Perspective'. *Ethnic and Racial Studies* 40, no. 8 (2017): 1191–1226. https://doi.org/10.1080/01419870.2017.1294700.

Brug, Wouter van der, and Joost van Spanje. 'Immigration, Europe, and the "New" Cultural Dimension'. *European Journal of Political Research* 48, no. 3 (2009): 309–334. https://doi.org/10.1111/j.1475-6765.2009.00841.x.

Bruter, Michael, and Sarah Harrison. *Mapping Extreme Right Ideology*, 2011. https://doi.org/10.1057/9780230336834.

Caiani, Manuela. 'Radical Right Cross-National Links and International Cooperation'. In *The Oxford Handbook of the Radical Right*, edited by Jens Rydgren (New York: Oxford University Press, 2018), 394–411.

Canovan, Margaret. 'Trust the People! Populism and the Two Faces of Democracy'. *Political Studies* 67 (1999): 2–16.

Castelli Gattinara, Pietro. 'The Study of the Far Right and Its Three E's: Why Scholarship Must Go beyond Eurocentrism, Electoralism and Externalism'. *French Politics*, 18 (2020): 314–333.

Cerrone, Joseph. 'Reconciling National and Supranational Identities: Civilizationism in European Far-Right Discourse', *Perspectives on Politics* 21, no. 3 (2023): 951–966.

Davies, Norman. *Europe: A History* (Oxford; New York; London: Oxford University Press, 1996).

De Vries, C. E. *Euroscepticism and the Future of European Integration* (Oxford: Oxford University Press, 2018). https://doi.org/10.1093/oso/9780198793380.001.0001.

De Vries, Catherine E., and Erica E. Edwards. 'Taking Europe to Its Extremes: Extremist Parties and Public Euroscepticism'. *Party Politics* 15, no. 1 (2009): 5–28. https://doi.org/10.1177/1354068808097889.

Eatwell, Roger. 'The Rebirth of the "Extreme Right" in Western Europe?' *Parliamentary Affairs* 53 (2000): 407–425. https://doi.org/10.1093/pa/53.3.407.

Falkner, Gerda, and Georg Plattner. 'EU Policies and Populist Radical Right Parties' Programmatic Claims: Foreign Policy, Anti-Discrimination and the Single Market'. *JCMS: Journal of Common Market Studies* 58, no. 3 (May 2020): 723–739. https://doi.org/10.1111/jcms.12963.

Fieschi, Catherine. 'European Institutions: The Far-Right and Illiberal Politics in a Liberal Context'. *Parliamentary Affairs* 53 (2000): 517–531.

Flood, Chris. 'Euroscepticism: A Problematic Concept'. *UACES 32nd Annual Conference*, 2002.

Freeden, Michael. 'Ideologies and Conceptual History'. *Journal of Political Ideologies* 2, no. 1 (1997): 3–11. https://doi.org/10.1080/13569319708420747.

Freeden, Michael. *Ideologies and Political Theory: A Conceptual Approach* (Oxford: Oxford University Press, 1998).
Freeden, Michael. 'Is Nationalism a Distinct Ideology?' *Political Studies* 46, no. 4 (1998): 748–765. https://doi.org/10.1111/1467-9248.00165.
Freeden, Michael. 'Practising Ideology and Ideological Practices'. *Political Studies* 48, no. 2 (2000): 302–322. https://doi.org/10.1111/1467-9248.00261.
Gellner, Ernest. *Nations and Nationalism* (Oxford: Blackwell, 1983).
Gómez-Reino Cachafeiro, Margarita. *Nationalisms in the European Arena: Trajectories of Transnational Party Coordination* (Cham: Palgrave Macmillan, 2018).
Gómez-Reino, Margarita, and Iván Llamazares. 'The Populist Radical Right and European Integration: A Comparative Analysis of Party–Voter Links'. *West European Politics* 36, no. 4 (2013): 789–816. https://doi.org/10.1080/01402382.2013.783354.
Gosewinkel, Dieter. 'Europe antilibérale ou Anti-Europe? Les conceptions européennes de l'extrême droite française entre 1940 et 1990'. *Politique européenne* 62, no. 4 (2018): 152–179.
Griffin, Robert Roger. 'Europe for the Europeans. Fascist Myths of the European New Order 1922–1992'. *Occasional Paper (No. 1)* 1 (1994): 1–37.
Griffin, Roger. 'Nationalism'. In *Contemporary Political Ideologies*, edited by Roger Eatwell (London; New York: Pinter, 1999), 152–179.
Hainsworth, Paul. *The Extreme Right in Western Europe* (New York: Routledge, 2008).
Halikiopoulou, Daphne, Kyriaki Nanou, and Sofia Vasilopoulou. 'The Paradox of Nationalism: The Common Denominator of Radical Right and Radical Left Euroscepticism'. *European Journal of Political Research* 51, no. 4 (2012): 504–539. https://doi.org/10.1111/j.1475-6765.2011.02050.x.
Hamilton, Malcolm B. 'The Elements of the Concept of Ideology'. *Political Studies* 35, no. 1 (1987): 18–38. https://doi.org/10.1111/j.1467-9248.1987.tb00186.x.
Harrison, Sarah, and Michael Bruter. *Mapping Extreme Right Ideology: An Empirical Geography of the European Extreme Right* (London: Palgrave Macmillan, 2011).
Heinisch, Reinhard, Duncan McDonnell, and Annika Werner. 'Equivocal Euroscepticism: How Populist Radical Right Parties Can Have Their EU Cake and Eat It'. *Journal of Common Market Studies* 59 (2021): 189–205. https://doi.org/10.1111/jcms.13055.
Herman, Lise Esther, and James B. Muldoon. *Trumping the Mainstream: The Conquest of Mainstream Democratic Politics by the Populist Radical Right* (London; New York: Routledge, 2019).
Hix, Simon, and Michael Marsh. 'Second-Order Effects plus Pan-European Political Swings: An Analysis of European Parliament Elections across Time'. *Electoral Studies* 30, no. 1 (2011): 4–15. https://doi.org/10.1016/j.electstud.2010.09.017.

Holmes, Douglas R. *Integral Europe: Fast-Capitalism, Multiculturalism, Neofascism* (Princeton: Princeton University Press, 2000).

Hooghe, Liesbet, Gary Marks, and Carole J. Wilson. 'Does Left/Right Structure Party Positions on European Integration?' *Comparative Political Studies* 35, no. 8 (2002): 965–989. https://doi.org/10.1177/001041402236310.

Ignazi, Piero. *Extreme Right Parties in Western Europe* (Oxford: Oxford University Press Oxford, 2003). https://doi.org/10.1093/0198293259.001.0001.

Ivaldi, Gilles. 'Contesting the EU in Times of Crisis: The Front National and Politics of Euroscepticism in France'. *Politics* 38, no. 3 (2018): 278–294. https://doi.org/10.1177/0263395718766787.

Kitschelt, Herbert, and Anthony J. McGann. *The Radical Right in Western Europe: A Comparative Analysis* (Ann Arbor: University of Michigan Press, 1995).

Kopecky, Petr, and Cas Mudde. 'The Two Sides of Euroscepticism: Party Positions on European Integration in East Central Europe'. *European Union Politics* 3, no. 3 (2002): 297–326.

Leconte, Cécile. *Understanding Euroscepticism* (Basingstoke; New York: Palgrave Macmillan, 2010).

Lorimer, Marta. 'What Do They Talk about When They Talk about Europe? Euro-Ambivalence in Far Right Ideology'. *Ethnic and Racial Studies* 44, no. 11 (2021): 2016–2033. https://doi.org/10.1080/01419870.2020.1807035.

Mammone, Andrea. *Transnational Neofascism in France and Italy. Transnational Neofascism in France & Italy* (Cambridge: Cambridge University Press, 2015).

Marks, Gary, and Carole J. Wilson. 'The Past in the Present: A Cleavage Theory of Party Response to European Integration'. *British Journal of Political Science* 30, no. 3 (2000): 433–459.

McDonnell, Duncan. and Annika Werner, 'Respectable radicals: why some radical right parties in the European Parliament forsake policy congruence,' *Journal of European Public Policy* 25, no. 5 (2018): 747–763.

McDonnell, D., and A. Werner. *International Populism: The Radical Right in the European Parliament* (London: Hurst, 2019).

McDonnell, Duncan, and Annika Werner. 'Differently Eurosceptic: Radical Right Populist Parties and Their Supporters'. *Journal of European Public Policy* 26, no. 12 (2019): 1761–1778. https://doi.org/10.1080/13501763.2018.1561743.

Miller-Idriss, Cynthia. *The Extreme Gone Mainstream: Commercialization and Far Right Youth Culture in Germany* (Princeton; Oxford: Princeton University Press, 2017).

Minkenberg, Michael. 'The West European Radical Right as a Collective Actor: Modeling the Impact of Cultural and Structural Variables on Party Formation and Movement Mobilization'. *Comparative European Politics* 1, no. 2 (2003): 149–170. https://doi.org/10.1057/palgrave.cep.6110017.

Minkenberg, Michael. *The Radical Right in Eastern Europe: Democracy under Siege?* (New York: Palgrave Macmillan, 2017).

Mondon, Aurelien, and Aaron Winter. 'Articulations of Islamophobia: From the Extreme to the Mainstream?' *Ethnic and Racial Studies* 40, no. 13 (2017): 2151–2179. https://doi.org/10.1080/01419870.2017.1312008.

Mudde, Cas. 'The War of Words Defining the Extreme Right Party Family'. *West European Politics* 19, no. n 2 (1996): 225–248.

Mudde, Cas. *The Ideology of the Extreme Right* (New York: Manchester University Press, 2000).

Mudde, Cas. *Populist Radical Right Parties in Europe* (Cambridge: Cambridge University Press, 2007). https://doi.org/10.1111/j.1478-9302.2009.00194.x.

Mudde, Cas. *The Far Right Today* (Cambridge: Polity, 2019).

Mullins, Willard A. 'On the Concept of Ideology in Political Science'. *The American Political Science Review* 66, no. 2 (1972): 498–510. https://doi.org/10.2307/1957794.

Norris, Pippa. *Radical Right: Voters and Parties in the Electoral Market* (New York: Cambridge University Press, 2005).

Norris, Pippa, and Ronald Inglehart. *Cultural Backlash: Trump, Brexit, and the Rise of Authoritarian Populism.* (Cambridge: Cambridge University Press, 2019).

Pagden, Anthony R. *The Idea of Europe: From Antiquity to the European Union* (Cambridge, Washington, DC, and New York: Cambridge University Press, 2002).

Petrocik, John. 'Issue Ownership in Presidential Elections, with a 1980 Case Study'. *American Journal of Political Science* 40, no. 3 (1996): 825.

Pirro, Andrea L. P. 'Far Right: The Significance of an Umbrella Concept'. *Nations and Nationalism* 29, no. 1 (January 2023): 101–112. https://doi.org/10.1111/nana.12860.

Pytlas, Bartek. 'Hijacking Europe: Counter-European Strategies and Radical Right Mainstreaming during the Humanitarian Crisis Debate 2015-16'. *Journal of Common Market Studies* 59 (2021): 335–353. https://doi.org/10.1111/jcms.13092.

Reif, Karlheinz, and Hermann Schmitt. 'Nine Second-Order National Elections—A Conceptual Framework for the Analysis of European Election Results'. *European Journal of Political Research* 8, no. 1 (1980): 3–44. https://doi.org/10.1111/j.1475-6765.1980.tb00737.x.

Reungoat, Emmanuelle. 'Mobiliser l'Europe dans la compétition nationale. La fabrique de l'européanisation du Front national'. *Politique européenne* 43, no. 1 (2014): 120–162. https://doi.org/10.3917/poeu.043.0120.

Reungoat, Emmanuelle. 'Changing the Rules, Changing the Winners? The Various Effects of European Election Rules on Party Oppositions to the EU in France'. In *The Routledge Handbook of Euroscepticism*, edited by Benjamin Leruth, Nicholas Startin, and Simon Mcdougall Usherwood (London: Routledge, 2018), 155–167.

Rovira Kaltwasser, Cristóbal, Paul A. Taggart, Paulina Ochoa Espejo, and Pierre Ostiguy. *The Oxford Handbook of Populism* (Oxford: Oxford University Press, 2017).

Rydgren, Jens. 'The Sociology of the Radical Right'. *Annual Review of Sociology* 33, no. 1 (2007): 241–262. https://doi.org/10.1146/annurev.soc.33.040406.131752.

Rydgren, Jens. *The Oxford Handbook of the Radical Right* (New York: Oxford University Press, 2018).

Schulte-Cloos, Julia. 'Do European Parliament Elections Foster Challenger Parties' Success on the National Level?' *European Union Politics* 19, no. 3 (2018): 408–426. https://doi.org/10.1177/1465116518773486.

Schwartz-Shea, Peregrine, and Dvora Yanow. *Interpretive Research Design: Concepts and Processes* (New York: Routledge, 2012).

Sitter, Nick. 'The Politics of Opposition and European Integration in Scandinavia: Is Euro-Scepticism a Government–Opposition Dynamic?' *West European Politics* 24, no. 4 (2001): 22–39. https://doi.org/10.1080/01402380108425463.

Skenderovic, Damir. *The Radical Right in Switzerland: Continuity and Change, 1945–2000* (New York: Berghahn Books, 2009).

Smith, Anthony D. *Myths and Memories of the Nation* (New York: Oxford University Press, 1999).

Stanley, Ben. 'The Thin Ideology of Populism'. *Journal of Political Ideologies* 13, no. 1 (2008): 95–110. https://doi.org/10.1080/13569310701822289.

Startin, Nicholas. 'Where to for the Radical Right in the European Parliament? The Rise and Fall of Transnational Political Cooperation'. *Perspectives on European Politics and Society* 11, no. 4 (2010): 429–449. https://doi.org/10.1080/15705854.2010.524402.

Startin, Nicholas. '"Euromondialisme" and the Growth of the Radical Right'. In *Routledge Handbook of Euroscepticism*, edited by Benjamin Leruth, Nicholas Startin, and Simon Usherwood (London: Routledge, 2018): 75–85.

Szczerbiak, Aleks, and Paul A. Taggart. *Opposing Europe?: The Comparative Party Politics of Euroscepticism. Volumes 1 and 2* (Oxford: Oxford University Press, 2008).

Taggart, Paul. 'A Touchstone of Dissent: Euroscepticism in Contemporary Western European Party Systems'. *European Journal of Political Research* 33, no. 3 (1998): 363–388. https://doi.org/10.1023/A:1006853204101.

Vasilopoulou, Sofia. 'European Ingegration and the Radical Right. Three Patterns of Opposition'. *Government and Opposition* 46, no. 2 (2011): 223–244.

Vasilopoulou, Sofia. *Far Right Parties and Euroscepticism: Patterns of Opposition* (London; New York: Rowman & Littlefield, 2018).

White, Jonathan. *Political Allegiance after European Integration.* (Basingstoke; New York: Palgrave Macmillan, 2011).

Williams, Benedicte. 'Electoral Strategy Trumps Political Ideology'. In *Varieties of Right-Wing Extremism in Europe*, edited by Andrea Mammone, Emmanuel Godin, and Brian Jenkins (Abingdon: Routledge, 2013), 134–148.

Zúquete, José Pedro. 'The New Frontlines of Right-Wing Nationalism'. *Journal of Political Ideologies* 20, no. 1 (2015): 69–85. https://doi.org/10.1080/13569317.2015.991492.

1
Europe as ideological resource

Far-right parties have long suffered from a legitimacy deficit. Sullied by their association with the fascist regimes that wreaked havoc on the European continent, in the immediate aftermath of the Second World War they were relegated to a marginal position in most European countries.[1] While still present in some of them, these parties' prospects were gloomy: placed outside the realm of respectable politics and, for the most part, electorally irrelevant, they appeared as a nostalgic fringe destined to disappear in due course.

This picture changed in the 1980s. Whereas up until the 1970s, 'far right' was largely coterminous with 'neo-fascist',[2] the 1980s saw the emergence of a new brand of far-right parties that rejected any connection with the pre-war fascist movements. Unlike their predecessors, these parties were electorally successful, and became more or less permanent fixtures of European party systems. While in several countries they remained pariahs, albeit politically important ones,[3] in recent years, some of these parties have joined in coalition governments in countries such as Italy and Austria, and acted as external support to the centre-right in Denmark and in the Netherlands amongst others.[4] In 2022, a far-right-led coalition even won the elections in Italy, bringing Fratelli d'Italia—the political heirs of the MSI/AN—into government. Their positions have also progressively made their way into the mainstream, as right- and left-wing parties seeking to win back voters from the far right incorporated them in their platforms.[5] In short, since the 1980s,

---

[1] Paul Hainsworth, *The Extreme Right in Western Europe* (New York: Routledge, 2008), 1–2; Sofia Vasilopoulou and Daphne Halikiopoulou, *The Golden Dawn's 'Nationalist Solution': Explaining the Rise of the Far Right in Greece* (New York: Palgrave Pivot, 2015), 2, doi:10.1057/9781137535917.

[2] Piero Ignazi, *Extreme Right Parties in Western Europe* (Oxford: Oxford University Press, 2003), 1, doi:10.1093/0198293259.001.0001.

[3] Cas Mudde, *Populist Radical Right Parties in Europe* (Cambridge: Cambridge University Press, 2007), 6, doi:10.1111/j.1478-9302.2009.00194.x.

[4] Tjitske Akkerman and Sarah L. de Lange, 'Radical Right Parties in Office: Incumbency Records and the Electoral Cost of Governing', *Government and Opposition* 47, no. 4 (2012): 574–596, doi:10.1111/j.1477-7053.2012.01375.x; Sarah L. de Lange, 'New Alliances. Why Mainstream Parties Govern with Radical Right-Wing Populist Parties', *Political Studies* 60, no. 4 (2012): 899–918, doi:10.1111/j.1467-9248.2012.00947.x.

[5] Oliver Gruber and Tim Bale, 'And It's Good Night Vienna. How (Not) to Deal with the Populist Radical Right: The Conservatives, UKIP and Some Lessons from the Heartland', *British Politics* 9, no. 3 (2014): 237–254, doi:10.1057/bp.2014.7; Lise Esther Herman and James B. Muldoon, *Trumping the*

and, more markedly, since the year 2000,[6] far-right parties and ideas have been progressively legitimated.

The process of legitimation and incorporation of far-right parties and ideas into the mainstream has not gone unnoticed, or been uncontroversial. The inclusion of the Freiheitliche Partei Österreichs (Freedom Party of Austria, FPÖ) in government in 2000, for example, led other EU member states to introduce sanctions against Austria because, as the European Parliament resolution on the result of the legislative elections in Austria put it, 'the admission of the FPÖ into a coalition government legitimises the extreme right in Europe'.[7] More recently, far-right successes have been frequently described in catastrophizing language. They have been qualified as 'earthquakes'[8] or as sending 'shockwaves' through Europe.[9] As soon as these movements start making inroads, news outlets dedicate articles to the threat they pose to democracy.[10] Political opponents routinely mention the dangers posed by 'populism' to European societies (frequently stretching its meaning until it loses any substance).[11] Analyses of the effects of far-right success on European democracies also occupy the minds of academics reflecting on the dangers of mainstreaming the far right.[12] While one might wish to question the truthfulness of these accounts or warn about the risks of 'hyping' these movements,[13] what they do suggest is that the far right has been, and to some extent still is, largely depicted as an 'out of the ordinary' and threatening phenomenon.

Throughout the decades, far-right parties have sought to address this perception of them as lacking legitimacy in different ways and to varying degrees

---

Mainstream: The Conquest of Mainstream Democratic Politics by the Populist Radical Right (London; New York: Routledge, 2019).

[6] Anders Widfeldt, 'The Radical Right in the Nordic Countries', in *The Oxford Handbook of the Radical Right*, ed. Jens Rydgren, 2018, 557.

[7] European Parliament, 'European Parliament Resolution on the Result of the Legislative Elections in Austria and the Proposal to Form a Coalition Government between the ÖVP (Austrian People's Party) and the FPÖ (Austrian Freedom Party)' (OJ C 309, 27.10.2000, 2000), https://www.europarl.europa.eu/sides/getDoc.do?pubRef=-//EP//TEXT+TA+P5-TA-2000-0045+0+DOC+XML+V0//EN.

[8] Chris Morris, 'Eurosceptic "earthquake" Rocks EU Elections', *BBC News*, May 2014, https://www.bbc.com/news/av/world-europe-27572312.

[9] Michael Bruter and Sarah Harrison, *Mapping Extreme Right Ideology*, 2011, 7, doi:10.1057/9780230336834.

[10] Cas Mudde, 'Three Decades of Populist Radical Right Parties in Western Europe: So What?', *European Journal of Political Research* 52, no. 1 (2013): 1–19, doi:10.1111/j.1475-6765.2012.02065.x.

[11] Jakob Schwörer and Belén Fernández-García, 'Demonisation of Political Discourses? How Mainstream Parties Talk about the Populist Radical Right', *West European Politics* 44, no. 7 (2020): 1401–1424, doi:10.1080/01402382.2020.1812907.

[12] Aurelien Mondon and Aaron Winter, *Reactionary Democracy: How Racism and the Populist Far Right Became Mainstream* (London: Verso, 2020); Herman and Muldoon, *Trumping the Mainstream*.

[13] Jason Glynos and Aurelien Mondon, 'The Political Logic of Populist Hype: The Case of Right-Wing Populism's "Meteoric Rise" and Its Relation to the Status Quo' (Thessaloniki: POPULISMUS Working Papers, 2016).

of success. The MSI represents a first successful case of far-right legitimation. Emerging from the ruins of the Italian Fascist Party, the MSI remained a relatively electorally successful, but largely marginal, force in Italian politics between its foundation in 1946 and the early nineties. At that time, it started a slow (and by many accounts unambitious)[14] process of revising its ideological message, culminating in it joining government and transforming into the 'post-fascist' AN. More recently, Marine Le Pen's process of 'de-demonization' of the RN has received significant academic and media attention,[15] although it should be noted that the RN has been on a quest to legitimize its message since the 1980s.[16] Since taking the helm of the party, Marine Le Pen has sought to transform it into a more 'acceptable' party by amending its political message and even changing its name in 2018. Her work has had some success: the RN is now a much more electorally successful party than it was before, having secured 88 MPs in the 2022 legislative elections; however, this has yet to translate into significant direct political influence because other parties still largely refuse to accept it as a legitimate contender for power. While these two parties are the ones that this work focuses on, their attempts at gaining legitimacy are not unique, and can be observed in other members of the party family such as the Jobbik Magyarországért Mozgalom (Movement for a Better Hungary, Jobbik) in Hungary or the Vlaams Belang (Flemish Interest, VB) in Belgium.[17]

The objective of this chapter is to consider specifically how taking part in European integration provided far-right parties with additional resources to construct their path towards legitimation. Presenting Europe as an ideological resource, it suggests that engaging with EU politics gave them an opportunity to reconfigure their ideological message and shift their positions

---

[14] Piero Ignazi, *Postfascisti?: Dal Movimento Sociale Italiano Ad Alleanza Nazionale* (Bologna: Il Mulino, 1994); Marco Tarchi, 'The Political Culture of the Alleanza-Nazionale: An Analysis of the Party's Programmatic Documents (1995–2002)', *Journal of Modern Italian Studies* 8 (2003): 135–181.

[15] Nicolas Lebourg, 'Comment l'extrême Droite a Inventé La "Dédiabolisation"', *Le Journal Du Dimanche*, April 2017, https://www.lejdd.fr/Politique/comment-lextreme-droite-a-invente-la-dediabolisation-3296501; Julien Licourt, 'Dédiabolisation? "Parler de Nouveau FN Relève de La Fiction Politique"', *Le Figaro*, 2015, https://www.lefigaro.fr/politique/2015/05/01/01002-20150501ARTFIG00001-dediabolisation-parler-de-nouveau-fn-releve-de-la-fiction-politique.php; Gilles Ivaldi, 'A New Course for the French Radical Right? The Front National and "de-Demonisation"', in *Radical Right-Wing Populist Parties in Western Europe: Into the Mainstream?*, ed. Tjitske Akkerman, Sarah L. de Lange, and Matthijs Rooduijn (London: Routledge, 2016), 225–246; James Shields, 'Marine Le Pen and the "New" FN: A Change of Style or of Substance?', *Parliamentary Affairs* 66, no. 1 (2013): 179–196, doi:10.1093/pa/gss076.

[16] Alexandre Dézé, 'La "dédiabolisation". Une nouvelle stratégie?', in *Les faux-semblants du Front national*, Académique (Paris: Presses de Sciences Po, 2015), 25–50.

[17] András Bíró-Nagy and Tamás Boros, 'Jobbik Going Mainstream. Strategy Shift of the Far-Right in Hungary', in *L'extreme Droite En Europe*, ed. Jerome Jamin (Brussels: Bruylant, 2016); Jan Erk, 'From Vlaams Blok to Vlaams Belang. The Belgian Far-Right Renames Itself', *West European Politics* 28 (2005): 493–502.

in a more acceptable direction. The chapter opens with a discussion of the sources of illegitimacy for far-right parties, and then moves on to discuss how these actors have sought to address them. It then introduces the concept of Europe as an ideological resource and its role in the far right's attempts at constructing legitimacy. The concluding section of the chapter presents the book's empirical approach to this question.

The importance of being legitimate

The definition of a 'legitimate' political actor is one that is fraught with difficulty, largely because of the complexity of the concept of legitimacy itself. At the heart of the concept of legitimacy is a question about power and its rightful exercise. As David Beetham highlights:

> since the dawn of human history, those occupying positions of power, and especially political power, have sought to ground their authority in a principle of legitimacy, which shows why their access to, and exercise of, power is rightful, and why those subject to it have a corresponding duty to obey.[18]

A legitimate actor, or institution, in this sense, is one that is perceived as having a right to wield power and be obeyed.

While legitimacy is most often studied as an attribute of political systems and institutions,[19] one may also view it as a characteristic belonging to specific actors within a political system. These actors may be those who effectively wield power, such as governmental actors, but also those who compete to do so in the future, such as political parties.[20] In particular, Raphael Zariski suggested applying the concept to a counter-elite, as while they may not already

---

[18] David Beetham, 'Political Legitimacy', in *The Wiley-Blackwell Companion to Political Sociology*, ed. Edwin Amenta, Nash Kate, and Alan Scott. (Chichester: John Wiley & Sons, 2012), 120, doi:10.1002/9781444355093.ch11.

[19] David Easton, *A Systems Analysis of Political Life* (Chicago: University of Chicago Press, 1979); Bruce Gilley, *The Right to Rule: How States Win and Lose Legitimacy* (New York: Columbia University Press, 2009); Pippa Norris, *Critical Citizens: Global Support for Democratic Government* (New York: Oxford University Press, 1999).

[20] While one might be tempted here to equate legitimacy and electoral success, this book cautions against taking such a view, especially with controversial parties such as those of the far right. Legitimacy requires that one is acknowledged as someone who is allowed to wield power. In the context of political competition, this does not entail voting for that party, but merely accepting that that party be considered as a contender for, and potential holder of, power. What is particular about the far right is that even when it is electorally successful, its status as a legitimate holder of power is questioned. The RN offers a good example of why the two are better thought of as separate. While the RN is by many measures electorally successful, it is still kept out of power, to the point that when it makes it to run-offs, other candidates tend to form a so called 'republican front' against it. This reflects the idea that even though the party may be electorally successful, its legitimacy is still in question—although this seems to be changing (see Marta Lorimer and Lise Esther Herman, 'The French Elections of 2022: Macron's Half Victory in a Changing

be in power, they may raise a claim to power that would require them to appear legitimate in order for it to be successful.[21] In focusing on left-wing 'anti-system' parties, Zariski highlights how complicated this acquisition of legitimacy is for actors who have long been opponents to the system, or out of power—a category that far-right parties fall well into.

Analysing the far right from the perspective of a legitimacy deficit, it is possible to identify at least three reasons why their right to (potentially) wield power has been put into question: their legality, their credibility, and their acceptability. Though the relevance of each dimension may vary across time and across countries—depending, for example, on a country's experience with fascism or on the relationship between the far right and the mainstream—they present helpful analytical categories to think about where the far right's legitimacy deficit stems from.

At the heart of the legality argument against far-right legitimacy is the idea that far-right parties are illegitimate because they do not respect certain fundamental legal principles enshrined in constitutions and which are necessary for the functioning of the democratic order. The legal provisions may either be specific—such as those prohibiting the use of violence and formal bans on reforming parties similar to those that challenged the democratic order in the interwar period and during the Second World War—or be of a more general nature, assessing the legitimacy of parties based on their overall approach to the existing democratic system. The latter is best exemplified in Germany's Federal Office for the Protection of the Constitution, which bans 'extreme' parties on grounds that they do not accept the democratic constitutional state.

While questions of legality were particularly prominent in the first few decades following the Second World War and recently came back to the fore with the Chrysí Avgí (Golden Dawn, GD) Trial in Greece,[22] they do not appear as the strongest source of illegitimacy for far-right parties on either empirical or theoretical grounds. From an empirical perspective, the question of legality has broadly been solved for all but the small, radical fringes of the far right. Most far-right parties now operate within the confines of legality—or at least, attempt to do so.[23] In theoretical terms, one may also

---

Political Landscape', *Journal of Common Market Studies* (2023), https://doi-org.gate3.library.lse.ac.uk/10.1111/jcms.13528).

[21] Raphael Zariski, 'The Legitimacy of Opposition Parties in Democratic Political Systems: A New Use for an Old Concept', *Political Research Quarterly* 39, no. 1 (1986): 30, doi:10.1177/106591298603900104.

[22] In 2020, the Greek neo-fascist party's leadership was found guilty of operating a criminal organization.

[23] While this observation is mostly accurate as far as party leadership is concerned (although it does not always apply—see for example the case of the Alternative für Deutschland (Alternative for Germany, AfD), where a section of the party leadership was put under surveillance by the German intelligence

wish to question the link between legality and legitimacy. While the two concepts are undoubtedly close, they do not line up evenly. A revolution, for example, is rarely a legal action, but it may nonetheless be a legitimate one if it is against an order that is itself illegitimate on non-legal grounds. An authoritarian regime may, in this sense, be backed by a legal order, but still be illegitimate because it violates fundamental democratic principles.

Credibility and acceptability appear as more pertinent sources of (il)legitimacy worth addressing. As far as the former is concerned, a key source of illegitimacy for counter-elites is their inexperience with government. In this approach, they lack the credibility to be considered actors who are 'fit to govern' and able to wield power in a legitimate manner. This argument appears eminently plausible with far-right parties. In fact, although some far-right parties have exercised power for decades now,[24] most have limited experience in power, leaving them open to criticism that they are unprepared for it. This factor is further compounded by the fact that they often (although not always) lack suitable cadres or strong party organization and the financial resources to support themselves. Beyond the practical aspects of government, one may also wish to think of credibility in terms of trustworthiness and the extent to which parties may be expected to keep faith with their electoral promises when in government. In this case, the far right's limited experience of power provides observers and voters with few cues concerning whether, once in power, they would behave according to plan, thus creating further issues in terms of credibility. In sum, far-right parties' legitimacy deficit may stem not so much from them not being legally entitled to run for power, but from the fact that they lack the professional experience and resources needed to be considered credible holders of power.

Whereas legitimacy as credibility touches upon the far right's ability to govern effectively, legitimacy as acceptability taps into the content of its ideas and its fit with what is commonly considered acceptable. Based on this view,

---

services or the previously mentioned case of the Golden Dawn), it must be noted that at times the borders between far-right parties and fringe movements are blurred. The relationship between the Rassemblement National and the extremist Group Union Defense (GUD), for example, has been placed under scrutiny by a number of journalists, e.g. Maxime Vaudano et al., 'Qui Sont Les Trente Proches de Marine Le Pen Qui Comptent Au Sein Du FN?', *Le Monde*, 2017, https://www.lemonde.fr/les-decodeurs/article/2017/04/26/qui-sont-les-trente-proches-de-marine-le-pen-qui-comptent-au-sein-du-fn_5118119_4355770.html (last accessed 17 May 2023).

[24] Daniele Albertazzi and Duncan McDonnell, *Populists in Power* (London: Routledge, 2016); Franz Fallend, 'Populism in Government', in *Populism in Europe and the Americas: Threat or Corrective for Democracy?*, ed. Cas Mudde and Cristóbal Rovira Kaltwasser (Cambridge: Cambridge University Press, 2012), 113–135, doi:10.1017/CBO9781139152365.007; Andrej Zaslove, 'The Populist Radical Right in Government: The Structure and Agency of Success and Failure', *Comparative European Politics* 10, no. 4 (2012): 421–448, doi:10.1057/cep.2011.19.

one may concede that far-right parties are legal, and possibly even fit to govern, but they remain illegitimate because what they do, or what they say, is not socially or politically acceptable. To develop this point, it is helpful to return to David Easton's writings on the legitimacy of political systems. Easton defined legitimacy as the belief

> that it is right and proper [. . .] to accept and obey the authorities and to abide by the requirements of the regime. It reflects the fact that in some vague or explicit way [a person] sees these objects as conforming to his own moral principles, his own sense of what is right and proper in the political sphere.[25]

While here the question is not of obeying the authorities but of accepting the parties and what they say, it is still possible to observe that an underlying quality of legitimacy is that it is grounded in notions of 'what is right and proper'—and thus, acceptable.[26] In this sense, far-right parties' legitimacy deficit may be viewed as stemming from the notion that the ideas they hold violate the deeply held values of a society, or draw on arguments that are not acceptable because they go against a widely shared consensus. For example, they may be considered illegitimate because what they say about immigration goes against a normative commitment to equality and solidarity by a large part of the population or the political class, or because of their dubious commitment to liberal-democratic principles.[27]

Critiques of the far right on grounds of acceptability are not unheard of. Indeed, they are at the heart to the so-called normal pathology hypothesis concerning far-right parties: that they profess values that are alien to 'normal' politics.[28] Thus, the question moves from the actors themselves to their place in a given society, following a logic of appropriateness and seeking to ascertain whether their opinions and their behaviour as a whole are fit for a certain society, or can at least be respected as somehow conforming with what is broadly accepted as 'proper'.

Far-right parties have been aware of their legitimacy deficit on grounds of credibility and acceptability and have sought to address it to some extent. One way in which they have sought to do so has been through the alteration of their behaviour and beliefs to fit in with what is considered as legitimate

---

[25] Easton, *A Systems Analysis of Political Life*, 278.
[26] For a similar point, see also Michael Freeden, *Liberal Languages: Ideological Imaginations and Twentieth-Century Progressive Thought* (Princeton: Princeton University Press, 2005), 79.
[27] Rather than democratic tout court—e.g. Mudde, *Populist Radical Right Parties in Europe*; Cas Mudde and Cristóbal Rovira Kaltwasser, 'Exclusionary vs. Inclusionary Populism: Comparing Contemporary Europe and Latin America', *Government and Opposition* 48, no. 2 (2013): 147.
[28] Cas Mudde, 'The Populist Radical Right. A Pathological Normalcy', *West European Politics* 33, no. 6 (2010): 1170–1171.

in a given society. This process is commonly referred to as 'mainstreaming',[29] but we may wish to think of it more broadly, as the term appears to imply that the only way to look legitimate is to conform with the political mainstream (while this may not always be the case, especially in times of scarce trust in politics).[30] Tjitske Akkerman, Sarah de Lange, and Matthijs Rooduijn identify four strategies that radical-right parties can use to pursue mainstreaming. They can: moderate their positions on core issues; show more respect for the rules of the game; expand the issue agenda; and try to overcome their extremist reputation.[31] Several of these tendencies can be observed in the far right. At the level of behaviour, far-right parties have sought to respect the rules of the game and take part in democratic processes, presenting themselves as credible alternatives to the mainstream. However, their ability to stress credibility has remained somehow limited. Changes in behaviour require being given the opportunity to exercise power, raising a chicken-and-egg issue: the far right's limited legitimacy keeps it out of power, but it needs that power to construct credibility. At the level of ideas, this chapter's opening section highlighted how parties such as the RN, Jobbik, and the Vlaams Belang have sought to moderate their position on key issues and tweak their ideology as to project a more acceptable image, as Marine Le Pen did with her '*dédiabolisation*'. This tweaking has taken different forms. Rhetorically, it has involved the use of less inflammatory language, the eschewal of certain topics, the emphasis of less controversial ones, and a selective 'repackaging' of positions.[32] Substantively, it has entailed the abandonment of controversial policy commitments and ideas such as support for the death penalty. Compared with changing behaviour, this strategy has been easier to pursue, because it is less resource intensive, is reasonably visible for voters, and does not require one to already have power but merely to be competing for it.

While these adaptive practices may seem appealing, they are not without their own costs.[33] In fact, one issue with approaching the far right from the perspective of a legitimacy deficit is that it takes the view of outsiders who

---

[29] For a definition and processes of mainstreaming, see Tjitske Akkerman, Sarah L. de Lange, and Matthijs Rooduijn, *Radical Right-Wing Populist Parties in Western Europe: Into the Mainstream?* (London: Routledge, 2016), 14.

[30] Colin Hay, *Why We Hate Politics* (Cambridge; Malden: Polity Press, 2007); Peter Mair, *Ruling the Void: The Hollowing of Western Democracy* (London; New York: Verso, 2013).

[31] Akkerman, de Lange, and Rooduijn, *Radical Right-Wing Populist Parties in Western Europe: Into the Mainstream?*

[32] Pytlas, 'Hijacking Europe: Counter-European Strategies and Radical Right Mainstreaming during the Humanitarian Crisis Debate 2015–16.'

[33] Caterina Froio, 'Race, Religion, or Culture? Framing Islam between Racism and Neo-Racism in the Online Network of the French Far Right', *Perspectives on politics* 16, no 3(2018): 696–709

are not already sold on the parties' message, and neglects the internal view of party activists and voters who may support a far-right party for the very same reasons that lead others to reject it. For them, legitimacy may come from the party's ability to represent their grievances, and may be entirely reliant on expecting the party to do exactly the radical things that a broader public may find unacceptable. If the party is understood as a 'community of principle'[34] of this type, then changing core ideas creates a problem of internal credibility with supporters, because activists and voters may view the party as betraying its long-standing commitments. This has been particularly visible in the most recent French presidential election, when Marine Le Pen lost a number of party cadres and voters to Éric Zemmour, a more radical candidate frequently said to be a better embodiment Jean-Marie Le Pen's 'original' RN.

One obvious response to this state of affairs for far-right parties is to privilege their supporters, cease mainstreaming, and hope that society adjusts to their presence. Given mainstream parties' tendency to co-opt elements of the far-right agenda and mainstream their ideas,[35] the strategy appears as reasonably sound and might eventually pay off. However, it is also somewhat risky, insofar as it takes a long time, and is strongly reliant on others amplifying one's message. On the first count, time is a precious commodity for political parties, and not all may have the financial or human resources to sustain a long period on the margins of the political system. Having one's message amplified or even adopted by others also poses its own problems. As Stijn van Kessel noted about populist parties—a category of parties that includes several far-right parties and shares common characteristics with far-right parties in general—a populist party's appeal is reliant on its ability to 'dissociate itself from both the political establishment as well as political extremism' and 'seize the ownership of salient social issues' while convincing potential voters that it 'is able to "handle" the problems it identifies better than its opponents.'[36] While Jean-Marie Le Pen's assertion that 'people always prefer the original to the copy'[37] may be correct, seeing their message adopted by others may then reduce their ability to present themselves as a unique offering in the political

---

[34] Jonathan White and Lea Ypi, *The Meaning of Partisanship* (Oxford: Oxford University Press, 2016), 14.
[35] Herman and Muldoon, *Trumping the Mainstream*; Aurelien Mondon, 'The Front National in the Twenty-First Century: From Pariah to Republican Democratic Contender?', *Modern & Contemporary France* 22, no. 3 (2014): 301–320, doi:10.1080/09639489.2013.872093.
[36] Stijn Van Kessel, *Populist Parties in Europe: Agents of Discontent?* (Basingstoke: Palgrave Macmillan, 2015), 22.
[37] 'Les Gens Préfèrent l'Original à la Copie', *Le Monde*, April 1990, https://www.lemonde.fr/archives/article/1990/04/03/les-gens-preferent-l-original-a-la-copie_3964167_1819218.html.

system, and places them at risk of not being perceived as the best placed to resolve the issue.[38]

Far-right parties, then, are caught in a conundrum: on one hand, they need to maintain their core of supporters and demonstrate an attachment to the ideological commitments that keep them together, while on the other, if they are to reach power and enact their programme, they need to appeal to a larger constituency. In short, they need to find a way to 'serve two masters'[39] and balance the imperatives of external legitimization and validation with those of internal ideological consistency. While one way to address this conundrum is to 'mix and match' and adopt elements of both radicalization and mainstreaming, the following section shows how the introduction of the issue of European integration could help parties navigate between the Scylla of legitimization and the Charybdis of ideological consistency. Drawing on literature on Europeanization, it develops the contention that taking part in EU politics has provided far-right parties with certain ideological resources which they could leverage in their process of legitimization.

Europe as ideological resource

The study of Europeanization has emerged as a key theme in European studies in the last twenty years. 'Europeanization' refers to the 'responses by actors—institutional and otherwise—to the impact of European integration.'[40] It broadly consists of two different processes: a 'top-down' dimension, in which changes at the EU level shape developments at the national level; and a 'bottom-up' process through which domestic actors take advantage of the possibilities offered by European integration.[41]

A key insight from literature on Europeanization as a 'bottom-up' process is that European integration not only generates pressures for domestic bodies and institutions to adapt, but also creates new opportunities and

---

[38] Bonnie M. Meguid, 'Competition between Unequals: The Role of Mainstream Party Strategy in Niche Party Success', *The American Political Science Review* 99, no. 3 (December 2005): 347–359.

[39] Richard S. Katz, 'No Man Can Serve Two Masters: Party Politicians, Party Members, Citizens and Principal–Agent Models of Democracy', *Party Politics* 20, no. 2 (January 2014): 183–193, doi:10.1177/1354068813519967.

[40] Robert Ladrech, 'Europeanization and Political Parties: Towards a Framework for Analysis', *Party Politics* 8, no. 4 (2002): 389, doi:10.1177/1354068802008004002.

[41] Kenneth H. F. Dyson and Klaus H. Goetz, *Germany, Europe and the Politics of Constraint* (Oxford: Oxford University Press, 2003); Cornelia Woll and Sophie Jacquot, 'Using Europe: Strategic Action in Multi-Level Politics', *Comparative European Politics* 8, no. 1 (2010): 110–126, doi:10.1057/cep.2010.7; Vivien A. Schmidt, 'The EU and Its Member States: From Bottom Up to Top Down', in *Reflections on European Integration: 50 Years of the Treaty of Rome*, ed. David Phinnemore and Alex Warleigh-Lack (London: Palgrave Macmillan, 2009), 194–211, doi:10.1057/9780230232839_11.

resources that political actors can mobilize and benefit from. Political actors may deliberately take advantage of these resources, a point highlighted by Cornelia Woll and Sophie Jacquot.[42] As they argued, European integration makes it possible for political actors to 'use' Europe 'as a set of opportunities, be they institutional, ideological, political or organizational.'[43] Deliberate use, however, is not a condition *sine qua non* for EU integration to generate positive (or negative) outcomes for those involved in the process. The resources it generates are present whether or not they are deliberately 'used' by political actors, although deliberate usage may enhance their effects.

It is in this sense that European integration may have constituted an ideological resource for far-right parties. An ideological resource can be conceived of as a device that offers political parties an opportunity to revise and reframe their political message and belief system. Demanding programmatic adaptation from them,[44] because of its nature both as a new issue and as one with wide-ranging implications on domestic politics, it provides parties with the opportunity to adapt their message to a new issue and, in the specific case of far-right parties, potentially shift it in a more acceptable direction.

There are a few characteristics of European integration that suggest it could have functioned as a powerful ideological resource for far-right parties seeking legitimation. As a new issue, it has given these parties an opportunity to expand their issue agenda—one of the aspects of mainstreaming mentioned by Akkerman and her co-authors.[45] The expansion of their issue agenda matters because it shifts focus from existing controversial positions to new, and potentially less controversial ones. It also provided them with an opportunity to revise their existing political message in response to this new issue, and reframe it in a more acceptable fashion which could appeal to old and new voters alike. In this sense, rather than simply allowing them to 'mainstream' by looking like other actors, it made it possible for them to pursue various mainstreaming strategies at the same time.

Importantly, the European issue's 'wedge' character made it possible for far-right parties to follow this process without appearing to be inconsistent. Wedge issues are political issues that do not fit neatly into pre-existing dimensions of political contestation and are typically divisive and able to split or destabilize governing parties or coalitions.[46] Because of its character as a new

---

[42] Woll and Jacquot, 'Using Europe: Strategic Action in Multi-Level Politics'.
[43] Ibid.
[44] Ladrech, 'Europeanization and Political Parties: Towards a Framework for Analysis'.
[45] Akkerman, de Lange, and Rooduijn, *Radical Right-Wing Populist Parties in Western Europe: Into the Mainstream?*
[46] Marc van de Wardt, Catherine E. De Vries and Sara B. Hobolt, 'Exploiting the Cracks: Wedge Issues in Multiparty Competition', *The Journal of Politics* 76, no 4 (2014): 986–999.

issue with no straightforward ideological answer,[47] adopting a position on European integration originally came at a low ideological cost for the far right because its parties had some choice in terms of the position they adopted.[48] While these positions were plausibly informed by existing beliefs[49] or at least had to be presented as consistent with the parties' other commitments, they were left with more space for interpretation. As a result, discussing European issues offered them an opportunity to develop a more legitimate image without reneging on existing commitments.

The divisiveness of EU integration is likely to have further strengthened the far right's position. European integration has divided both political parties[50] and electorates.[51] Although there have been peaks and troughs in the salience of public contestation of the EU, and voters' attitudes have proven to be more complex than the simple dichotomy Eurosceptic/pro-EU captures,[52] they nonetheless illustrate that European integration has been an issue on which disagreements of various types have been widespread. This divisiveness strengthened Europe's nature as ideological resource for the far right for two reasons. First, and consistent with theories on 'wedge' issues, it helped them exploit to their advantage the divisions within other political parties on the issue.[53] Second, and more importantly for the purposes of this book, the EU issue's divisive nature also meant that it was a topic on which disagreement was not only acceptable, but also common. Because it was a divisive issue, and one on which a variety of different positions could exist, it was

---

[47] John Gaffney, *Political Parties and the European Union* (London; New York: Routledge, 1996), 16; Chris Flood, 'Euroscepticism: A Problematic Concept (Illustrated with Particular Reference to France)', *UACES 32nd Annual Conference* (Belfast, 2002), 7–11.

[48] Marta Lorimer, 'Europe as Ideological Resource: The Case of the Rassemblement National', *Journal of European Public Policy* 27, no. 9 (2020): 1388–1405, doi:10.1080/13501763.2020.1754885.

[49] Liesbet Hooghe, Gary Marks, and Carole J. Wilson, 'Does Left/Right Structure Party Positions on European Integration?', *Comparative Political Studies* 35, no. 8 (2002): 965–989, doi:10.1177/001041402236310; Aleks Szczerbiak and Paul A. Taggart, *Opposing Europe?: The Comparative Party Politics of Euroscepticism* (Oxford: Oxford University Press, 2008).

[50] Suffice it to think of the British Conservative Party's divisions over the question of European integration.

[51] Liesbet Hooghe and Gary Marks, 'A Postfunctionalist Theory of European Integration: From Permissive Consensus to Constraining Dissensus', *British Journal of Political Science* 39, no. 1 (2009): 1–23, doi:10.1017/S0007123408000409; Eurobarometer, 'Public Opinion in the European Union. Eurobarometer 92 Autumn 2019' (Brussels: European Commission, 2019). For works explaining the sources of public Euroscepticism, see for example Catherine E. De Vries, *Euroscepticism and the Future of European Integration* (Oxford: Oxford University Press, 2018), doi:10.1093/oso/9780198793380.001.0001; Simona Guerra, *Central and Eastern European Attitudes in the Face of Union* (London: Palgrave Macmillan, 2013), doi:10.1057/9781137319487.

[52] See Sara B. Hobolt and Catherine E. De Vries, 'Public Support for European Integration.' *Annual Review of Political Science* 19, no. 1 (2016): 413–432 for an overview.

[53] Marc van de Wardt, Catherine E. De Vries, and Sara B. Hobolt, 'Exploiting the Cracks: Wedge Issues in Multiparty Competition', *The Journal of Politics* 76, no. 4 (October 2014): 986–999, doi:10.1017/S0022381614000565.

more acceptable for the far right to express unorthodox or extreme positions on it rather than on issues such as migration or law and order, in which more homogeneous and (at least until recently) moderate positions tended to prevail.[54]

In sum, integrating European issues in their ideology offered far-right parties an opportunity to expand their issue agenda in a particularly beneficial way. It allowed them to reorient their message in a novel direction without abandoning their existing commitments, hence facilitating the task of speaking to their existing supporters while also attracting new ones and building an image of 'legitimate opposition'. In this sense, what was important was not just that it allowed them to discuss a new issue, but rather that it allowed them to do so while at the same time appearing to be consistent with previous messaging. As such, it facilitated their attempts to 'serve two masters'.[55]

Studying Europe as an ideological resource: an empirical approach

The remainder of this monograph takes an empirical and analytical turn to explore how Europe functioned as a powerful ideological resource for far-right parties seeking legitimation. To do so, it focuses on how two far-right parties (the MSI/AN in Italy and RN in France) integrated Europe in their political ideologies, and to what effects.

The cases: the Movimento Sociale Italiano/Alleanza Nazionale and the Rassemblement National

The Movimento Sociale Italiano was the 'grandfather' of post-war European far-right parties. Founded in 1946 from the ashes of the Italian Fascist party, it was for a long time the only successful far-right party in Europe. While the MSI never reached particularly high peaks in terms of vote share (its best electoral score was a little under 9% of the popular vote in the 1972 general election, but in general hovered around the 5–6% mark), it was a constant presence in the Italian and European parliaments.

[54] On this, see also Nicholas Startin, '"Euromondialisme" and the Growth of the Radical Right', in *Routledge Handbook of Euroscepticism*, ed. Benjamin Leruth, Nicholas Startin, and Simon Usherwood (London: Routledge, 2018), 76.
[55] Katz, 'No Man Can Serve Two Masters: Party Politicians, Party Members, Citizens and Principal–Agent Models of Democracy'.

In the context of Italy's 'polarized pluralism',⁵⁶ the MSI occupied the far-right pole of a political system dominated by the Democrazia Cristiana (Christian Democracy, DC) in the centre and the Partito Comunista Italiano (Italian Communist Party, PCI) on the far left. Originally opposed to Italy's post-war liberal-democratic settlement, especially in its early years the MSI oscillated between on one hand pursuing a policy of *inserimento* (insertion) and moderation, and on the other pushing for outright opposition to the political system as a whole.⁵⁷ The question of which strategy to pursue was a source of tension between the party's internal factions. The MSI's right-wing faction, whose positions aligned with the conservative and authoritarian stance of the pre-war fascist regime, pushed for mainstreaming. On the other side, the left-wing faction, which took inspiration from the 'social' and anti-bourgeois fascism of the short-lived Italian Social Republic, aimed for further radicalization.⁵⁸ Although the former initially imposed themselves, the MSI's early attempts at *inserimento* were unsuccessful because of other parties' refusal to collaborate with them, and by the 1970s, the party had settled more or less comfortably in a position of permanent opposition. Put simply, the MSI was, for a large part of its history, a pariah party. It was kept away from the circles of power and, having failed to insert itself into the political system in its early years, it embraced its anti-system role in later years.

The seeds for the transition of the MSI from anti-system party to mainstream party were planted in the 1980s. The process of historicization of fascism, along with the growing willingness of other political actors to include the MSI in politics, presented the MSI with an environment that was conducive to its legitimation—although the party leadership by and large failed to take advantage of the opportunities it was offered.⁵⁹ It was only in the 1990s that the party initiated its transition to the mainstream in earnest. The *Tangentopoli* ('Bribesville') scandal, evolving voter preferences and changes to the electoral law, radically altered the context of Italian politics.⁶⁰ *Tangentopoli* revealed the extent of corruption within the political system and, coupled with the decline of traditional party loyalties, led to a collapse of the Italian post-war party system. Furthermore, a change to the electoral law

---

[56] Giovanni Sartori, *Parties and Party Systems: A Framework for Analysis* (Colchester: European Consortium for Political Research, 2005), 116ff.

[57] James L. Newell, 'Italy: The Extreme Right Comes in from the Cold', *Parliamentary Affairs* 53 (2000): 469–470.

[58] On the MSI's factions, see Piero Ignazi, 'La Cultura Politica Del Movimento Sociale Italiano', *Italian Political Science Review/Rivista Italiana Di Scienza Politica* 19, no. 3 (1989): 431–465, doi:10.1017/S0048840200008650; Piero Ignazi, *Il Polo Escluso: Profilo Storico Del Movimento Sociale Italiano* (Bologna: Il Mulino, 1998); Marco Tarchi, *Dal MSI Ad AN: Organizzazione e Strategie* (Bologna: Il Mulino, 1997).

[59] Roberto Chiarini, 'Prifilo Storico-Critico Del MSI', *Il Politico* 54, no. 3 (151) (1989): 369–389; Ignazi, *Il Polo Escluso: Profilo Storico Del Movimento Sociale Italiano*.

[60] Newell, 'Italy: The Extreme Right Comes in from the Cold', 475.

pushed for the formation of coalitions and an overall restructuring of the political system on a Left/Right cleavage.[61]

These changes provided the MSI's reform-oriented party leader Gianfranco Fini with ammunition to advocate for a fundamental rebranding of the party, with the objective of bringing it into power. Largely untouched by the *Tangentopoli* scandal, between 1994 and 1995 the MSI underwent a transformation from a 'neo-fascist' party to the 'post-fascist' AN. Following the 1994 election, in which it won 13.5% of the vote, it entered government in a short-lived coalition with Forza Italia and the Lega Nord (Northern League, now simply 'La Lega'). In 1995, at the Fiuggi Congress, the MSI formally changed its name to Alleanza Nazionale. While most of the party's personnel remained the same (with a few exceptions, such as Pino Rauti's radical faction which converged into the MSI-Fiamma Tricolore, MSI-Tricolour Flame) and their core ideas were only moderately refashioned,[62] Fiuggi represented the first step in a march towards normalization. AN's mainstreaming continued in the following years as the party sought to develop a political culture independent of the MSI's heritage and an increasingly respectable face.[63] Between 2001 and 2005, it also developed its experience in government by holding prestigious ministries (most notably, Fini held the positions of Foreign Minister and Deputy Prime Minister). The process of mainstreaming culminated in 2009 with the merging of Alleanza Nazionale and Silvio Berlusconi's Forza Italia into a single party, the Popolo delle Libertà (People of Freedom, PDL).[64]

In the academic literature on the far right, the MSI is commonly considered as the 'archetype' of the 'old' neo-fascist far right,[65] and an early source of inspiration (especially in terms of organization) for several of the parties that came after it. AN, on the other hand, is regarded as an interesting experiment in ideological transformation.[66] It was the first far-right party to be included

---

[61] Alan Renwick, Chris Hanretty, and David Hine, 'Partisan Self-Interest and Electoral Reform: The New Italian Electoral Law of 2005', *Electoral Studies* 28, no. 3 (2009): 437–447, doi:10.1016/j.electstud.2009.04.003; Stefano Fella, 'From Fiuggi to the Farnesina: Gianfranco Fini's Remarkable Journey', *Journal of Contemporary European Studies* 14, no. 1 (April 2006): 13–14, doi:10.1080/14782800600617888; Piero Ignazi, 'Legitimation and Evolution on the Italian Right Wing: Social and Ideological Repositioning of Alleanza Nazionale and the Lega Nord', *South European Society and Politics* 10, no. 2 (2005): 334, doi:10.1080/13608740500135058.

[62] Ignazi, *Extreme Right Parties in Western Europe*; Tarchi, 'The Political Culture of the Alleanza-Nazionale'.

[63] Tarchi, 'The Political Culture of the Alleanza-Nazionale', 177–178.

[64] In 2012, a group of former MSI/AN politicians formed a new political party, Fratelli d'Italia. The party brought together several former members of the MSI/AN and continued using its symbols such as the tricolour flame party logo. As its nature as a successor party is somewhat contested and still the subject of critical scrutiny, this book does not include it in the analysis but will discuss points of continuity and break between the parties' positions on Europe in the Conclusion.

[65] Ignazi, *Extreme Right Parties in Western Europe*.

[66] Roger Griffin, 'The "Post-Fascism" of the Alleanza Nazionale: A Case Study in Ideological Morphology', *Journal of Political Ideologies* 1, no. 2 (1996): 123–145, doi:10.1080/13569319608420733.

in government (along with the Lega), even before the Fiuggi Congress that officially transformed it into a 'post-fascist' party. While the inclusion of AN may raise some scepticism, as the literature highlights its successful transition from 'post-fascist' to 'something else',[67] this book decides to follow it through its 'post-fascist' transition because transitions are usually long and tortuous, and often some elements from the past remain.[68]

The French Rassemblement National, on the other hand, once again according to Ignazi's classification, represents the archetype of the 'new' far-right party, or, as others have dubbed it, the 'populist radical-right' party. While not the most electorally successful far-right party in Europe, the RN's influence on others in Europe is well-documented, leading some to consider it as having provided the 'master-frame' for the parties of its type that followed.[69]

Born as Front National in 1972, the RN was founded with the objective of bringing together the various far-right groups operating in France. It started off as a hodgepodge of extremist groups, including neo-fascists, traditionalist Catholics, poujadistes, monarchists, and Algerian war veterans, kept together by the charismatic leadership of Jean-Marie Le Pen.[70] During its first years, referred to within the party as the 'crossing of the desert',[71] it struggled to have electoral relevance and remain cohesive.

The RN's electoral breakthrough only came about in the 1980s, following a series of transformations within the French system. Unhappiness with the Socialist government, increasing concerns about immigration, and an ongoing economic crisis helped the RN fashion itself as the anti-immigration and security champion.[72] This increased focus paid off and led the party to its first victories at the local level. Most notably, the 1982 cantonal elections in Dreux saw the party gain around 10% of the vote, and this was followed by a positive showing in the 1983 municipal elections. The RN finally emerged as

[67] Tarchi, 'The Political Culture of the Alleanza-Nazionale'.
[68] Griffin, 'The "Post-Fascism" of the Alleanza Nazionale: A Case Study in Ideological Morphology'; Sofia Vasilopoulou, 'European Integration and the Radical Right: Three Patterns of Opposition', *Government and Opposition* 46, no. 2 (2011): 223–244, doi:10.1111/j.1477-7053.2010.01337.x.
[69] Jens Rydgren, 'Is Extreme Right-Wing Populism Contagious? Explaining the Emergence of a New Party Family', *European Journal of Political Research* 44 (2005): 413–437; Steven M. Van Hauwaert, 'On Far Right Parties, Master Frames and Trans-National Diffusion: Understanding Far Right Party Development in Western Europe', *Comparative European Politics* 17, no. 1 (February 2019): 132–154, doi:10.1057/s41295-017-0112-z.
[70] Jean-Yves Camus, 'Origine et Formation Du Front National', in *Le Front National à Découvert*, ed. Nonna Mayer and Pascal Perrineau (Paris: Presses de la Fondation Nationale des Sciences Politiques, 1989), 17–36.
[71] Erwan Lecœur, *Un Néo-Populisme à La Française: Trente Ans de Front National* (Paris: Paris: Découverte, 2003), 29.
[72] Daniel Stockemer, *The Front National in France: Continuity and Change under Jean-Marie Le Pen and Marine Le Pen* (Cham, Switzerland: Springer, 2017); Michelle Hale Williams, *The Impact of Radical Right-Wing Parties in West European Democracies* (New York: Palgrave MacMillan, 2006).

a successful party on a national level when it gained over 10% of the national vote in the 1984 European elections, and in 1986 when it secured 35 MPs in national elections. In 1986 in particular, the RN benefitted from Mitterrand's choice to introduce a system of proportional representation.[73] While the President's main objective had been to limit the Parti Socialiste losses and split the right-wing vote between the RN and the Gaullist Rassemblement pour la République, he also helped the RN become a permanent fixture in the French political system.[74]

The 1980s were not only a period of electoral growth for the RN, but also one of organizational growth. Its electoral successes facilitated the establishment of a strong organizational structure, and it attracted new recruits at all levels.[75] Among the new recruits were a number of experienced politicians and intellectuals such as Bruno Mégret, Jean-Yves Le Gallou, and Yvan Blot, who sought to professionalize the party, consolidate its programme and grow its appeal.[76] These evolutions helped the party sustain its growth in the longer term and contributed to its firm establishment in the French political system.

Following a decade of growth, the 1990s and 2000s were marked by ebbs and flows in the party's successes. On one hand, the return to the two-round majoritarian system of voting and the continued ostracization of the party by other actors kept the RN out of power. Furthermore, in 1998, the party suffered the worst split in its history, when fundamental strategic disagreements and personal conflicts between Jean-Marie Le Pen and Bruno Mégret led to the expulsion of the latter from the RN.[77] Mégret did not leave alone but brought a sizeable chunk of the party's leadership (although not many of its voters) with him to his newly formed Mouvement National Républicain (MNR).[78] On the other hand, the RN's political programme remained appealing thanks to the dominance of issues such as globalization, corruption, and immigration.[79] In 2002, only a few years after the split, the RN achieved one of its most stunning feats when Jean-Marie Le Pen reached the second round of the French presidential election and secured around 18% of the vote in the final round.[80]

---

[73] Hans-Georg Betz and Stefan Immerfall, eds., *The New Politics of the Right. Neo-Populist Parties and Movements in Established Democracies* (New York: St Martin's Press, 1998), 21.
[74] Stockemer, *The Front National in France*, 17.
[75] Jens Rydgren, ed., *The Populist Challenge. Political Protest and Ethno-Nationalist Mobilization in France* (New York: Berghahn Books, 2004), 19.
[76] Jean-Paul Gautier, *Les extrêmes droites en France: de la traversée du désert à l'ascension du Front national: de 1945 à nos jours / Jean-Paul Gautier, Collection Mauvais temps* (Paris: Éditions Syllepse, 2009), 388, https://www.mediatheque.mc/Default/doc/SYRACUSE/653083/les-extremes-droites-en-france-de-la-traversee-du-desert-a-l-ascension-du-front-national-de-1945-a-n.
[77] Alexandre Dézé, *Le Front national: à la conquête du pouvoir?* (Paris: Armand Colin, 2012), 125.
[78] Stockemer, *The Front National in France*, 22.
[79] Ibid., 20.
[80] Gabriel Goodliffe, *The Resurgence of the Radical Right in France: From Boulangisme to the Front National* (New York: Cambridge University Press, 2012), 1.

In 2011, Marine Le Pen replaced her father as leader of the party and embarked on a process of 'de-demonization', aimed at making the RN a more respectable and 'coalitionable' political actor.[81] Following a series of negative electoral results in the late 2000s, and aware of the need for ideological renewal, she reoriented the party's political agenda while maintaining a strong continuity with the past.[82] The party has grown significantly in the 12 years since Marine Le Pen took over from her father. Most notably, Le Pen won almost 34% of the vote in the second round of the 2017 presidential election and secured 8 MPs in the legislative elections that followed. In 2018, in a bid to grow its electoral appeal, the party changed its name from 'Front National' to 'Rassemblement National', but the change was mostly cosmetic, with little evolution in terms of ideas. In 2022, Le Pen once again made it into the presidential election run-off, losing to Emmanuel Macron by a narrower margin than in 2017 (58% to 42%). Most strikingly, the RN secured an unprecedented 88 MPs in the legislative elections that followed, making it the largest opposition party in the French National Assembly.

In line with the exploratory and interpretive nature of this book, the MSI/AN and RN were purposively selected as methodologically and theoretically information-rich cases.[83] From a methodological standpoint, these parties' pioneering nature, along with their long political history (the MSI/AN was the first party of the family to emerge after the Second World War, while the RN remains one of the oldest far-right parties in Europe), provide the researcher with distinct advantages. Their pioneering character enabled them to have a significant influence on the parties that came after them. Although this does not mean that the findings derived from the study of these parties will be automatically generalizable to other parties, they are still likely to be transferrable,[84] making them potentially relevant to the analysis of other cases. Additionally, the MSI/AN and RN's long political history gave them the opportunity to construct a varied and accessible ideological corpus that could

---

[81] Gilles Ivaldi, 'A New Course for the French Radical-Right? The Front National and 'de-Demonization', in *Radical Right-Wing Populist Parties in Western Europe. Into the Mainstream?*, ed. Tjitske Akkerman, Sarah L. de Lange, and Matthijs Rooduijn (London: Routledge, 2016), 231–253, https://halshs.archives-ouvertes.fr/halshs-01385771; Shields, 'Marine Le Pen and the "New" FN'; Daniel Stockemer and Mauro Barisione, 'The "New" Discourse of the Front National under Marine Le Pen: A Slight Change with a Big Impact', *European Journal of Communication* 32, no. 2 (2016): 100–115, doi:10.1177/0267323116680132.

[82] Cecile Alduy and Stephane Wahnich, *Marine Le Pen Prise Aux Mots: Décryptage Du Nouveau Discours Frontiste* (Paris: Éditions du Seuil, 2015); Williams, *The Impact of Radical Right-Wing Parties in West European Democracies*.

[83] Michael Quinn Patton. 'Two Decades of Developments in Qualitative Inquiry: A Personal, Experiential Perspective', *Qualitative Social Work* 1, no. 3 (2002): 261–283

[84] Linda Dale Bloomberg and Marie Volpe, *Completing Your Qualitative Dissertation a Roadmap from Beginning to End* (Los Angeles: SAGE, 2008); Lisa M. Given, *The SAGE Encyclopedia of Qualitative Research Methods* (Thousand Oaks: SAGE, 2008).

be studied in some depth and over a long time span. Because thick description is an essential part of interpretive research, a rich corpus of this kind was considered essential to successfully unfolding the concept of an ideological resource.

These parties are also likely to be information-rich from a theoretical standpoint, because both the MSI/AN and the RN have suffered from legitimacy deficits that they have sought to address. As mentioned earlier, the MSI/AN was largely ostracized by fellow political parties, and deliberately sought legitimation especially in its early years and from the 1990s onwards (and was largely successful in its quest). In a similar vein, the RN was shunned by most of its competitors, and although most recent scholarship focuses on Marine Le Pen's attempts at 'de-demonizing' the party, the RN's quest for legitimacy pre-dates her arrival at the helm of the RN and can be traced back to the 1980s.[85] To this it is worth adding that, influenced by the ideas of the Nouvelle Droite, the RN has historically placed a strong focus on legitimation through language,[86] which makes it most likely to fully exploit the possibilities for ideological renewal offered by Europeanization. Both parties, in sum, were strongly likely to benefit from Europe as an ideological resource, and to use it deliberately with the aim of legitimizing their views.

These characteristics set the MSI/AN and RN apart from other likely contenders such as the Freiheitliche Partei Österreichs, Vlaams Belang, or even the Lega. While some of these parties would have allowed similarly long timeframes to be covered, they lack the pioneering character of the MSI/AN and RN and have a less extensive and well-documented history of seeking to acquire legitimacy. As such, they were considered less promising than the selected cases.

Analysing far-right ideology with morphological and discourse analysis

To study how these two parties integrated Europe in their ideology, and to what effects, the book combines two interpretive methods for the study of ideology: Michael Freeden's morphological analysis, and discourse analysis. While the former makes it possible to identify the key concepts the parties used to define Europe, the latter facilitates the analysis of the effects that

---

[85] Dézé, 'La "dédiabolisation". Une nouvelle stratégie?', 33–35.
[86] Jean-Yves Camus, 'Le Front National et La Nouvelle Droite', in *Les Faux-Semblants Du Front National*, ed. Sylvain Crépon, Alexandre Dézé, and Nonna Mayer (Paris: Presses de Sciences Po, 2015), 97–120.

integrating Europe in a certain way had. Taken together, the two methods provide a strong view of the 'character and effect'[87] of the far right's ideological approach to Europe.

At the heart of morphological analysis is an interest in the conceptual structure of political ideologies, intended as 'systems of political thinking, loose or rigid, deliberate or unintended, through which individuals and groups construct an understanding of the political world they, or those who preoccupy their thoughts, inhabit, and then act on that understanding.'[88] Developed by Michael Freeden in his seminal book *Ideologies and Political Theory*, morphological analysis approaches ideologies as specific configurations of political concepts. These concepts are defined as 'complex ideas that inject order and meaning into observed or anticipated sets of political phenomena and hold together an assortment of related notions.'[89] They are usually also 'essentially contested'—that is, concepts 'the proper use of which inevitably involves endless disputes about their proper uses on the part of their users.'[90] In Freeden's view, most ideologies employ similar concepts, but different traditions will attach different meanings to them depending on time- and space-dependent judgements about the description and assembly of the concepts' individual components,[91] as well as their relationship with other concepts in the ideology.

Different ideologies will also place political concepts in different positions. Concepts may be placed in a core, adjacent, or peripheral position depending on their centrality to the ideology in question and may shift from one position to the other over time. Core concepts are the long-term and shared features of all known cases of a given ideology.[92] One can think, for example, of 'liberty' as a core concept of all forms of liberalism, or of 'equality' as the core of any given instance of socialism. Core concepts are also those that hold the ideology together and thus shape its content most prominently.[93] Adjacent concepts are not as pervasive or ever-present as core concepts. However, they have the crucial role of 'finessing the core and anchoring it—at least temporarily—into a more determinate and decontested semantic field.'[94]

---

[87] Rochana Bajpai, *Debating Difference Group Rights and Liberal Democracy in India* (New Delhi: Oxford University Press, 2011), 72–73.
[88] Michael Freeden, *Ideologies and Political Theory: A Conceptual Approach* (Oxford: Oxford University Press, 1998), 3.
[89] Freeden, *Ideologies and Political Theory*, 52.
[90] Walter Bryce Gallie, 'Essentially Contested Concepts', *Proceedings of the Aristotelian Society* 56 (1955): 169.
[91] Freeden, *Ideologies and Political Theory*, 52.
[92] Michael Freeden, 'The Morphological Analysis of Ideology', in *The Oxford Handbook of Political Ideologies*, ed. Michael Freeden and Marc Stears (Oxford: Oxford University Press, 2013), 125.
[93] Ibid., 125.
[94] Ibid., 125–126.

Adjacent concepts can be culturally or logically adjacent, and flesh out the core concepts, leading to emphasizing one aspect of the conceptual core over the other. Finally, ideologies have peripheral concepts that 'add a vital gloss'[95] to core and adjacent concepts. These peripheral concepts are of two types: 'marginal' concepts and 'perimeter' concepts. Marginal concepts are those whose relevance to the ideology is insubstantial. Perimeter concepts, on the other hand, while being placed in a peripheral position with respect to the centre, are key to the operation of ideology in real-life contexts because they anchor it to reality. Unlike core and adjacent concepts, which allow the ideology to 'function on a long-term and wide-space basis',[96] perimeter concepts 'enable them [ideologies] to gain relevance for specific issues, to incorporate and identify significant facts and practices, to embrace external change, and to provide the greater degree of precision necessary to interpret the core and adjacent concepts'.[97] Ideas and concepts within an ideology will usually be identified following a trajectory that goes from the centre to the periphery via adjacent concepts or vice versa, bearing in mind, however, that the road followed is usually only one among many that are possible.[98]

European integration may be approached, at least initially, as a perimeter concept straddling 'the interface between the conceptualization of social realities and the external contexts and concrete manifestations in and through which these conceptualizations occur'.[99] Perimeter concepts' peculiarity is that they allow for ideologies to accommodate and influence current events, thus remaining relevant in the social world. Europe would appear to pertain to this area, on one hand due to the broad post-war reflections on the place of Europe in the world, and on the other because of the presence of the European Economic Community and then European Union as a real-life policy issue that needed to be addressed. Following this perspective, Europe embeds ideology in a given historical and political context, giving the far right's ideology as a whole a more grounded character.

While other works that use Freeden's morphological approach usually employ it to study full ideological frameworks,[100] its scope here is more limited. Because this book is primarily concerned with the far right's ideological approach to Europe, morphological analysis is mainly used to identify the

---

[95] Freeden, *Ideologies and Political Theory*, 78.
[96] Ibid., 79.
[97] Ibid., 79–80.
[98] Ibid., 81.
[99] Ibid., 79.
[100] See for example Bajpai, *Debating Difference Group Rights and Liberal Democracy in India*; Benjamin Franks, Nathan J. Jun, and Leonard A. Williams, *Anarchism: A Conceptual Approach* (New York: Routledge, 2018); Judi Atkins, *Justifying New Labour Policy* (New York: Palgrave Macmillan, 2011).

key concepts that the MSI/AN and RN use to understand Europe and place it within their ideological framework. Doing so makes it possible to identify links between the parties' ideological core and the new European issue, thereby helping understand how their approach to Europe fits in with their existing beliefs.

To further define the insights of morphological analysis, the content and features of each concept are studied by means of discourse analysis. The field of discourse studies is a varied and diverse one, brought together by an interest in analysing discursive practices in their various manifestations, be they written, spoken, pictorial, or artefactual.[101] Following the approach developed by scholars in the field of critical discourse studies, discourses are here defined as 'relatively stable uses of language serving the organization and structuring of social life'.[102] Viewing discourses as a form of 'social practice' implies a 'dialectical relationship between a particular discursive event and the situation(s), institution(s), and social structure(s) which frame it: the discursive event is shaped by them, but it also shapes them'.[103]

A key element of critical discourse studies which is of relevance to this study is the observation that 'language not only communicates, but also contributes to creating thoughts, ideas and, even at times, material realities'.[104] While this does not imply that 'creativity or "construction" can occur out of nothing, and regardless of the properties of the materials used in construction',[105] it is through language that thoughts and ideas are communicated, justified, and disseminated, providing the tools for interpretation of social phenomena.

As such, discourse analysis posits that the analysis of language can help us understand how discursive events have ideological effects—that is, how they can 'help produce and reproduce unequal power relations between (for instance) social classes, women and men, and ethnic/cultural majorities and minorities through the ways in which they represent things and position people'.[106] For many scholars this entails discovering hegemonic narratives or relations of power, frequently with emancipatory aims.[107] However, the aim of this study is less ambitious, in that it proposes analysing how the

---

[101] Ruth Wodak and Michael Meyer, *Methods of Critical Discourse Studies*. (Los Angeles: SAGE, 2016), 2; see also Teun A. van Dijk, *Discourse and Context: A Socio-Cognitive Approach* (Cambridge: Cambridge University Press, 2008) for an overview of the historical development of the field.
[102] Wodak and Meyer, *Methods of Critical Discourse Studies*, 6.
[103] Norman Fairclough and Ruth Wodak, 'Critical Discourse Analysis', in *Discourse Studies: A Multidisciplinary Introduction*, ed. Teun A. van Dijk (London: SAGE, 1997), 258.
[104] Kate Power, Tanweer Ali, and Eva Lebdušková, *Discourse Analysis and Austerity: Critical Studies from Economics and Linguistics* (Abingdon, Oxon: Routledge, 2019), 4.
[105] Andrew Sayer, cited in Power, Ali, and Lebdušková, 4.
[106] Fairclough and Wodak, 'Critical Discourse Analysis', 258.
[107] Wodak and Meyer, *Methods of Critical Discourse Studies*, 7.

discursive practices of the far right help normalize it. While it remains a critical approach, insofar as it alerts to the effects of the far right's discourse on its legitimacy, for the most part the explicit aim is not to address these effects or reverse them, but to understand how the legitimation of the far right may have proceeded through discourse.

The main strength of discourse analysis, then, is that it allows us to study how the far right's ideological positions, as expressed through discourse, contributed to its legitimation. This should provide an understanding of the ways in which Europe constituted an 'ideological resource' for the far right, allowing it to present itself as an actor whose place in the political system is not subject to question.

The source material for the empirical chapters is a variety of internally and externally directed party documents collected through online, library, and archival research. In order to gain a comprehensive view of how Europe became a part of the MSI/AN and RN's ideology, instead of focusing exclusively on party manifestoes as the 'official' expression of party ideology,[108] this monograph delves deeper into party literature, drawing in particular on party papers, newspapers, magazines, and books published by party elites.[109] The starting year for data collection was set as 1978, the year before the first European Parliament direct election. While the analysis could have credibly started earlier, at the time of the foundation of the parties (1946 for the MSI and 1972 for the RN), 1978 was considered as more suitable, since it is at this time that one would have expected European issues to start featuring more prominently in the parties' ideology. Where relevant, however, earlier documents are also referred to. The end point for the MSI/AN is 2009, when the party merged into the Popolo delle Libertà; for the RN, the analysis stops at the 2019 European election, the last major election to take place in the course of this project.

The full corpus of source materials consists of 410 documents, 175 for the MSI/AN (divided as follows: 93 MSI, 82 AN) and 235 documents for the RN (further information on the corpus and how it was created is presented in the Appendix). The documents for analysis were selected based on two criteria: they either had to be particularly significant to the life of the party (examples

---

[108] Olavi Borg, 'Basic Dimensions of Finnish Party Ideologies: A Factor Analytical Study', *Scandinavian Political Studies* 1, no. A1 (1966): 97, doi:10.1111/j.1467-9477.1966.tb00510.x; McDonnell Duncan, and Stefano Ondelli, 'The Language of Right-Wing Populist Leaders: Not So Simple'. *Perspectives on Politics* 20, no. 3 (2022): 828–841.

[109] For similar approaches, see also Ignazi, 'La Cultura Politica Del Movimento Sociale Italiano'; Cas Mudde, *The Ideology of the Extreme Right* (New York: Manchester University Press, 2000); Chris Flood and Rafal Soborski, 'Euroscepticism as Ideology', in *Routledge Handbook of Euroscepticism*, ed. Benjamin Leruth, Nicholas Startin, and Simon Usherwood (London: Routledge, 2018), 36–47.

include manifestoes and congress documents); and/or, they had to explicitly mention Europe (whether as the EU or as the continent and civilization associated with it), and not be of a purely factual nature (such as reports on votes in the European Parliament in which no evaluative judgement is expressed, accounts of laws passed by the EU, etc.). For the MSI/AN, documents include party programmes for European and national elections published between 1978 and 2009, internal congress documents, interview books, and a number of newspaper articles and interviews focusing on European issues. The RN source material includes party programmes for European and national elections presented between 1978 and 2019, books, magazine articles, interviews, speeches, and press releases dealing with European issues.

The analysis was carried out through a two-step procedure. At first, the corpus was manually analysed through a procedure referred to as 'concept coding'. In qualitative analysis, a code is 'a word or a short phrase that symbolically assigns a summative, salient, essence-capturing, and/or evocative attribute for a portion of language-based or visual data'.[110] Coding refers to the process of assigning codes to evidence collected by the researcher, with the aim of using such codes for purposes such as 'pattern detection, categorization, assertion or proposition development, theory building, and other analytical processes'.[111] Among the various coding techniques available to the researcher, concept coding appeared as a helpful method to abstract from specific utterances about Europe the more general conceptual categories of morphological analysis. In concept coding, in fact, the researcher focuses on the general ideas behind the data, rather than on behaviours or on specific objects.[112] Concept coding was used here to identify the main concepts discussed by parties in relation to Europe. While often in conceptual analysis there is a tendency to equate concepts with the words expressing them, in this case concepts were approached as 'realms of meaning' formed by associated notions which, while not having the same name as the general concept, are used as synonyms of it or express similar ideas.

In this round, all documents were read, summarized, and assigned keywords defining the individual concepts used by the parties to define Europe and its nature. This initial phase in the analysis proceeded in an inductive fashion and yielded four main concepts: identity, liberty, threat, and national interest. While occasionally other concepts such as prosperity, democracy, and spiritualism also appeared, these three concepts were retained because they were both dominant compared with other concepts (i.e. they appeared

---

[110] Johnny Saldaña, *The Coding Manual for Qualitative Researchers* (London: SAGE, 2016), 4.
[111] Ibid., 5.
[112] Ibid., 119–120.

more frequently and across longer time periods) and common to both cases rather than specific to either one. These concepts were set in conversation with the literature, with the objective of ensuring their credibility and potential transferability. Based on the view widely expressed in the literature and discussed in the previous chapter of far-right parties as primarily nationalist in nature, the concepts appeared as sufficiently plausible to be potentially applicable to a larger number of cases.

While the first round of analysis was aimed primarily at identifying the conceptual space of Europe, the second round was more concerned with analysing the meanings of the individual concepts and the key discursive features of the material. In this round, only a smaller purposive sample of 118 documents was recoded and analysed,[113] with the objective of identifying key passages of text that could be used to move from the skeletal reconstruction of the ideological space of Europe to the analysis of its meanings and effects. It was considered that, given the high ideological intensity observed in the studied parties (both by the author and by previous researchers),[114] a smaller sample would still guarantee saturation while avoiding 'informational redundancy'.[115]

The selected documents were those which articulated the parties' positions most clearly, thus providing the researcher and reader alike with a stronger analytical perspective and exemplary excerpts. The sample included at least one document per year, but for some years it was deemed necessary to include more than one document. This happened particularly around crucial events such as the first European Parliament election in 1979 (especially for the MSI), and the Maastricht and European Constitution referendum years for the RN. In order to facilitate the retrieval of key illustrative sentences, NVivo was employed as a tool to store and organize the data. It is mostly through the thick description and discourse analysis of the documents studied in this second round of analysis that the narrative of the empirical chapters is developed.

The following chapters present the results of the analysis and show how the concepts and discourses employed by the MSI/AN and RN in their decontestation of Europe provided them with ammunition to project a more

---

[113] Complete list available in the Appendix, Annexe 2.
[114] Alexandre Dézé, 'Idéologie et Stratégies Partisanes: Une Analyse Du Rapport Des Partis d'extrême Droite Au Système Politique Démocratique: Le Cas Du Front National, Du Movimento Sociale Italiano et Du Vlaams Blok' (Institut d'Etudes Politiques, 2008).
[115] Jill J. Francis et al., 'What Is an Adequate Sample Size? Operationalising Data Saturation for Theory-Based Interview Studies', *Psychology & Health* 25, no. 10 (2010): 1229–1245, doi:10.1080/08870440903194015; Greg Guest, Arwen Bunce, and Laura Johnson, 'How Many Interviews Are Enough?: An Experiment with Data Saturation and Variability', *Field Methods* 18, no. 1 (2006): 59–82, doi:10.1177/1525822X05279903.

legitimate image, while remaining consistent with their existing commitments. Chapters 2, 3, and 4 discuss primarily the external-facing aspects of the party's legitimation, whereas Chapter 5 refocuses on internal legitimacy by looking at how each of the concepts discussed earlier could be viewed as pertaining to the ideological core of the parties.

References

Akkerman, Tjitske, and Sarah L. de Lange. 'Radical Right Parties in Office: Incumbency Records and the Electoral Cost of Governing'. *Government and Opposition* 47, no. 4 (2012): 574–596. https://doi.org/10.1111/j.1477-7053.2012.01375.x.

Akkerman, Tjitske, Sarah L. de Lange, and Matthijs Rooduijn. *Radical Right-Wing Populist Parties in Western Europe: Into the Mainstream?* (London: Routledge, 2016).

Albertazzi, Daniele, and Duncan McDonnell. *Populists in Power* (London: Routledge, 2016).

Alduy, Cecile, and Stephane Wahnich. *Marine Le Pen Prise Aux Mots: Décryptage Du Nouveau Discours Frontiste* (Paris: Éditions du Seuil, 2015).

Atkins, Judi. *Justifying New Labour Policy* (New York: Palgrave Macmillan, 2011).

Bajpai, Rochana. *Debating Difference Group Rights and Liberal Democracy in India* (New Delhi: Oxford University Press, 2011).

Beetham, David. 'Political Legitimacy'. In *The Wiley-Blackwell Companion to Political Sociology*, edited by Edwin Amenta, Nash Kate, and Alan Scott. (Chichester: John Wiley & Sons, Ltd, 2012), 120–129. https://doi.org/10.1002/9781444355093.ch11.

Betz, Hans-Georg, and Stefan Immerfall, eds. *The New Politics of the Right. Neo-Populist Parties and Movements in Established Democracies* (New York: St Martin's Press, 1998).

Bíró-Nagy, András, and Tamás Boros. 'Jobbik Going Mainstream. Strategy Shift of the Far-Right in Hungary'. In *L'extrême Droite En Europe*, edited by Jerome Jamin (Brussels: Bruylant, 2016): 243–264.

Bloomberg, Linda Dale, and Marie Volpe. *Completing Your Qualitative Dissertation a Roadmap from Beginning to End* (Los Angeles: SAGE, 2008).

Borg, Olavi. 'Basic Dimensions of Finnish Party Ideologies: A Factor Analytical Study'. *Scandinavian Political Studies* 1, no. A1 (1966): 94–117. https://doi.org/10.1111/j.1467-9477.1966.tb00510.x.

Bruter, Michael, and Sarah Harrison. *Mapping Extreme Right Ideology* (London: Palgrave Macmillan, 2011). https://doi.org/10.1057/9780230336834.

Camus, Jean-Yves. 'Origine et Formation Du Front National'. In *Le Front National à Découvert*, edited by Nonna Mayer and Pascal Perrineau (Paris: Presses de la Fondation Nationale des Sciences Politiques, 1989), 17–36.

Camus, Jean-Yves. 'Le Front National et La Nouvelle Droite'. In *Les Faux-Semblants Du Front National*, edited by Sylvain Crépon, Alexandre Dézé, and Nonna Mayer (Paris: Presses de Sciences Po, 2015), 97–120.

Chiarini, Roberto. 'Prifilo Storico-Critico Del MSI'. *Il Politico* 54, no. 3 (151) (1989): 369–389.

De Lange, Sarah L. 'New Alliances. Why Mainstream Parties Govern with Radical Right-Wing Populist Parties'. *Political Studies* 60, no. 4 (2012): 899–918. https://doi.org/10.1111/j.1467-9248.2012.00947.x.

De Vries, Catherine E. *Euroscepticism and the Future of European Integration* (Oxford: Oxford University Press, 2018). https://doi.org/10.1093/oso/9780198793380.001.0001.

Dézé, Alexandre. 'Idéologie et Stratégies Partisanes: Une Analyse Du Rapport Des Partis d'extrême Droite Au Système Politique Démocratique: Le Cas Du Front National, Du Movimento Sociale Italiano et Du Vlaams Blok' (Institut d'Etudes Politiques, 2008).

Dézé, Alexandre. *Le Front national: à la conquête du pouvoir?* (Paris: Armand Colin, 2012).

Dézé, Alexandre. 'La "dédiabolisation". Une nouvelle stratégie?' In *Les faux-semblants du Front national Académique* edited by Sylvain Crépon, Alexandre Dézé, and Nonna Mayer (Paris: Presses de Sciences Po, 2015), 25–50.

Dijk, Teun A. van. *Discourse and Context: A Socio-Cognitive Approach* (Cambridge: Cambridge University Press, 2008).

Dyson, Kenneth H. F., and Klaus H. Goetz. *Germany, Europe and the Politics of Constraint* (Oxford: Oxford University Press, 2003).

Easton, David. *A Systems Analysis of Political Life* (Chicago: University of Chicago Press, 1979).

Erk, Jan. 'From Vlaams Blok to Vlaams Belang. The Belgian Far-Right Renames Itself'. *West European Politics* 28 (2005): 493–502.

Eurobarometer. 'Public Opinion in the European Union. Eurobarometer 92 Autumn 2019' (Brussels: European Commission, 2019).

European Parliament. 'European Parliament Resolution on the Result of the Legislative Elections in Austria and the Proposal to Form a Coalition Government between the ÖVP (Austrian People's Party) and the FPÖ (Austrian Freedom Party)' (OJ C 309, 27.10.2000, 2000). https://www.europarl.europa.eu/sides/getDoc.do?pubRef=-//EP//TEXT+TA+P5-TA-2000-0045+0+DOC+XML+V0//EN.

Fairclough, Norman, and Ruth Wodak. 'Critical Discourse Analysis'. In *Discourse Studies: A Multidisciplinary Introduction*, edited by Teun A. van Dijk (London: SAGE, 1997), 258–284.

Fallend, Franz. 'Populism in Government'. In *Populism in Europe and the Americas: Threat or Corrective for Democracy?*, edited by Cas Mudde and Cristóbal Rovira Kaltwasser (Cambridge: Cambridge University Press, 2012), 113–135. https://doi.org/10.1017/CBO9781139152365.007.

Fella, Stefano. 'From Fiuggi to the Farnesina: Gianfranco Fini's Remarkable Journey'. *Journal of Contemporary European Studies* 14, no. 1 (April 2006): 11–23. https://doi.org/10.1080/14782800600617888.

Flood, Chris. 'Euroscepticism: A Problematic Concept (Illustrated with Particular Reference to France)'. UACES 32nd Annual Conference (Belfast, 2002).

Flood, Chris, and Rafal Soborski. 'Euroscepticism as Ideology'. In *Routledge Handbook of Euroscepticism*, edited by Benjamin Leruth, Nicholas Startin, and Simon McDougall Usherwood (London: Routledge, 2018), 36–47.

Francis, Jill J., Marie Johnston, Clare Robertson, Liz Glidewell, Vikki Entwistle, Martin P. Eccles, and Jeremy M. Grimshaw. 'What Is an Adequate Sample Size? Operationalising Data Saturation for Theory-Based Interview Studies'. *Psychology & Health* 25, no. 10 (2010): 1229–1245. https://doi.org/10.1080/08870440903194015.

Franks, Benjamin, Nathan J. Jun, and Leonard A. Williams. *Anarchism: A Conceptual Approach* (New York: Routledge, 2018).

Freeden, Michael. *Ideologies and Political Theory: A Conceptual Approach* (Oxford: Oxford University Press, 1998).

Freeden, Michael. *Liberal Languages: Ideological Imaginations and Twentieth-Century Progressive Thought* (Princeton: Princeton University Press, 2005).

Freeden, Michael. 'The Morphological Analysis of Ideology'. In *The Oxford Handbook of Political Ideologies*, edited by Michael Freeden and Marc Stears (Oxford: Oxford University Press, 2013), 115–137.

Gaffney, John. *Political Parties and the European Union* (London; New York: Routledge, 1996).

Gallie, Walter Bryce. 'Essentially Contested Concepts'. *Proceedings of the Aristotelian Society* 56 (1955): 167–198.

Gautier, Jean-Paul. *Les extrêmes droites en France: de la traversée du désert à l'ascension du Front national: de 1945 à nos jours/Jean-Paul Gautier*. Collection Mauvais temps (Paris: Éditions Syllepse, 2009). https://www.mediatheque.mc/Default/doc/SYRACUSE/653083/les-extremes-droites-en-france-de-la-traversee-du-desert-a-l-ascension-du-front-national-de-1945-a-n.

Gilley, Bruce. *The Right to Rule: How States Win and Lose Legitimacy* (New York: Columbia University Press, 2009).

Given, Lisa M. *The SAGE Encyclopedia of Qualitative Research Methods* (Thousand Oaks: Thousand Oaks: SAGE, 2008).

Glynos, Jason, and Aurelien Mondon. 'The Political Logic of Populist Hype: The Case of Right-Wing Populism's "Meteoric Rise" and Its Relation to the Status Quo' (Thessaloniki: POPULISMUS Working Papers, 2016).

Goodliffe, Gabriel. *The Resurgence of the Radical Right in France: From Boulangisme to the Front National* (New York: Cambridge University Press, 2012).

Griffin, Roger. 'The "Post-Fascism" of the Alleanza Nazionale: A Case Study in Ideological Morphology'. *Journal of Political Ideologies* 1, no. 2 (1996): 123–145. https://doi.org/10.1080/13569319608420733.

Gruber, Oliver, and Tim Bale. 'And It's Good Night Vienna. How (Not) to Deal with the Populist Radical Right: The Conservatives, UKIP and Some Lessons from the Heartland'. *British Politics* 9, no. 3 (2014): 237–254. https://doi.org/10.1057/bp.2014.7.

Guerra, Simona. *Central and Eastern European Attitudes in the Face of Union* (London: Palgrave Macmillan, 2013). https://doi.org/10.1057/9781137319487.

Guest, Greg, Arwen Bunce, and Laura Johnson. 'How Many Interviews Are Enough?: An Experiment with Data Saturation and Variability'. *Field Methods* 18, no. 1 (2006): 59–82. https://doi.org/10.1177/1525822X05279903.

Hainsworth, Paul. *The Extreme Right in Western Europe* (New York: Routledge, 2008).

Hay, Colin. *Why We Hate Politics* (Cambridge; Malden: Polity Press, 2007).

Herman, Lise Esther, and James B. Muldoon. *Trumping the Mainstream: The Conquest of Mainstream Democratic Politics by the Populist Radical Right* (London; New York: Routledge, 2019).

Hooghe, Liesbet, and Gary Marks. 'A Postfunctionalist Theory of European Integration: From Permissive Consensus to Constraining Dissensus'. *British Journal of Political Science* 39, no. 1 (2009): 1–23. https://doi.org/10.1017/S0007123408000409.

Ignazi, Piero. 'La Cultura Politica Del Movimento Sociale Italiano'. *Italian Political Science Review/Rivista Italiana Di Scienza Politica* 19, no. 3 (1989): 431–465. https://doi.org/10.1017/S0048840200008650.

Ignazi, Piero. *Postfascisti?: Dal Movimento Sociale Italiano Ad Alleanza Nazionale* (Bologna: Il Mulino, 1994).

Ignazi, Piero. *Il Polo Escluso: Profilo Storico Del Movimento Sociale Italiano* (Bologna: Il Mulino, 1998).

Ignazi, Piero. *Extreme Right Parties in Western Europe* (Oxford: Oxford University Press Oxford, 2003). https://doi.org/10.1093/0198293259.001.0001.

Ignazi, Piero. 'Legitimation and Evolution on the Italian Right Wing: Social and Ideological Repositioning of Alleanza Nazionale and the Lega Nord'. *South European Society and Politics* 10, no. 2 (2005): 333–349. https://doi.org/10.1080/13608740500135058.

Ivaldi, Gilles. 'A New Course for the French Radical-Right? The Front National and 'de-Demonization'. In *Radical Right-Wing Populist Parties in Western Europe. Into the Mainstream?*, edited by Tjitske Akkerman, Sarah L. de Lange, and Matthijs Rooduijn (London: Routledge, 2016), 225–246.

Katz, Richard S. 'No Man Can Serve Two Masters: Party Politicians, Party Members, Citizens and Principal–Agent Models of Democracy'. *Party Politics* 20, no. 2 (January 2014): 183–193. https://doi.org/10.1177/1354068813519967.

Ladrech, Robert. 'Europeanization and Political Parties: Towards a Framework for Analysis'. *Party Politics* 8, no. 4 (2002): 389–403. https://doi.org/10.1177/1354068802008004002.

Le Monde. 'Les Gens Préfèrent l'Original à la Copie'. *Le Monde*, April 1990. https://www.lemonde.fr/archives/article/1990/04/03/les-gens-preferent-l-original-a-la-copie_3964167_1819218.html.

Lebourg, Nicolas. 'Comment l'extrême Droite a Inventé La "Dédiabolisation"'. *Le Journal Du Dimanche*, April 2017. https://www.lejdd.fr/Politique/comment-lextreme-droite-a-invente-la-dediabolisation-3296501.

Lecœur, Erwan. *Un Néo-Populisme à La Française: Trente Ans de Front National* (Paris: Découverte, 2003).

Licourt, Julien. 'Dédiabolisation? "Parler de Nouveau FN Relève de La Fiction Politique"'. *Le Figaro*, 2015. https://www.lefigaro.fr/politique/2015/05/01/01002-20150501ARTFIG00001-dediabolisation-parler-de-nouveau-fn-releve-de-la-fiction-politique.php.

Hooghe, Liesbet, Gary Marks, and Carole J. Wilson. 'Does Left/Right Structure Party Positions on European Integration?' *Comparative Political Studies* 35, no. 8 (2002): 965–989. https://doi.org/10.1177/001041402236310.

Lorimer, Marta. 'Europe as Ideological Resource: The Case of the Rassemblement National'. *Journal of European Public Policy* 27, no. 9 (2020): 1388–1405. https://doi.org/10.1080/13501763.2020.1754585.

Mair, Peter. *Ruling the Void: The Hollowing of Western Democracy* (London; New York: Verso, 2013).

McDonnell, Duncan, and Stefano Ondelli. 'The Language of Right-Wing Populist Leaders: Not So Simple'. *Perspectives on Politics*, 20, no. 3 (2022): 828–841.

Meguid, Bonnie M. 'Competition between Unequals: The Role of Mainstream Party Strategy in Niche Party Success'. *The American Political Science Review* 99, no. 3 (December 2005): 347–359.

Mondon, Aurelien. 'The Front National in the Twenty-First Century: From Pariah to Republican Democratic Contender?' *Modern & Contemporary France* 22, no. 3 (2014): 301–320. https://doi.org/10.1080/09639489.2013.872093.

Mondon, Aurelien, and Aaron Winter. *Reactionary Democracy: How Racism and the Populist Far Right Became Mainstream* (London: Verso, 2020).

Morris, Chris. 'Eurosceptic "earthquake" Rocks EU Elections'. BBC News, May 2014. https://www.bbc.com/news/av/world-europe-27572312.

Mudde, Cas. *The Ideology of the Extreme Right* (New York: Manchester University Press, 2000).

Mudde, Cas. *Populist Radical Right Parties in Europe* (Cambridge: Cambridge University Press, 2007). https://doi.org/10.1111/j.1478-9302.2009.00194.x.

Mudde, Cas. 'The Populist Radical Right. A Pathological Normalcy'. *West European Politics* 33, no. 6 (2010): 1167–1186.

Mudde, Cas. 'Three Decades of Populist Radical Right Parties in Western Europe: So What?' *European Journal of Political Research* 52, no. 1 (2013): 1–19. https://doi.org/10.1111/j.1475-6765.2012.02065.x.

Mudde, Cas, and Cristóbal Rovira Kaltwasser. 'Exclusionary vs. Inclusionary Populism: Comparing Contemporary Europe and Latin America'. *Government and Opposition* 48, no. 2 (2013): 147.

Newell, James L. 'Italy: The Extreme Right Comes in from the Cold'. *Parliamentary Affairs* 53 (2000): 469–485.

Norris, Pippa. *Critical Citizens: Global Support for Democratic Government* (New York: Oxford University Press, 1999).

Power, Kate, Tanweer Ali, and Eva Lebdušková. *Discourse Analysis and Austerity: Critical Studies from Economics and Linguistics* (Abingdon, Oxon: Routledge, 2019).

Renwick, Alan, Chris Hanretty, and David Hine. 'Partisan Self-Interest and Electoral Reform: The New Italian Electoral Law of 2005'. *Electoral Studies* 28, no. 3 (2009): 437–447. https://doi.org/10.1016/j.electstud.2009.04.003.

Rydgren, Jens. *The Populist Challenge. Political Protest and Ethno-Nationalist Mobilization in France* (New York: Berghahn Books, 2004).

Rydgren, Jens. 'Is Extreme Right-Wing Populism Contagious? Explaining the Emergence of a New Party Family'. *European Journal of Political Research* 44 (2005): 413–437.

Saldaña, Johnny. *The Coding Manual for Qualitative Researchers* (London: SAGE, 2016).

Sartori, Giovanni. *Parties and Party Systems: A Framework for Analysis* (Colchester: European Consortium for Political Research, 2005).

Schmidt, Vivien A. 'The EU and Its Member States: From Bottom Up to Top Down'. In *Reflections on European Integration: 50 Years of the Treaty of Rome*, edited by

David Phinnemore and Alex Warleigh-Lack (London: Palgrave Macmillan, 2009), 194–211. https://doi.org/10.1057/9780230232839_11.

Schwörer, Jakob, and Belén Fernández-García. 'Demonisation of Political Discourses? How Mainstream Parties Talk about the Populist Radical Right'. *West European Politics* 44, no. 7 (2020): 1401-1424. https://doi.org/10.1080/01402382.2020.1812907.

Shields, James. 'Marine Le Pen and the "New" FN: A Change of Style or of Substance?' *Parliamentary Affairs* 66, no. 1 (2013): 179–196. https://doi.org/10.1093/pa/gss076.

Startin, Nicholas. '"Euromondialisme" and the Growth of the Radical Right'. In *Routledge Handbook of Euroscepticism*, edited by Benjamin Leruth, Nicholas Startin, and Simon Usherwood (London: Routledge, 2018): 75–85.

Stockemer, Daniel. *The Front National in France: Continuity and Change under Jean-Marie Le Pen and Marine Le Pen* (Cham, Switzerland: Springer, 2017).

Stockemer, Daniel, and Mauro Barisione. 'The "New" Discourse of the Front National under Marine Le Pen: A Slight Change with a Big Impact'. *European Journal of Communication* 32, no. 2 (2016): 100–115. https://doi.org/10.1177/0267323116680132.

Szczerbiak, Aleks, and Paul A. Taggart. *Opposing Europe?: The Comparative Party Politics of Euroscepticism* (Oxford: Oxford University Press, 2008).

Tarchi, Marco. *Dal MSI Ad AN: Organizzazione e Strategie* (Bologna: Il Mulino, 1997).

Tarchi, Marco. 'The Political Culture of the Alleanza-Nazionale: An Analysis of the Party's Programmatic Documents (1995–2002)'. *Journal of Modern Italian Studies* 8 (2003): 135–181.

Van Hauwaert, Steven M. 'On Far Right Parties, Master Frames and Trans-National Diffusion: Understanding Far Right Party Development in Western Europe'. *Comparative European Politics* 17, no. 1 (February 2019): 132–154. https://doi.org/10.1057/s41295-017-0112-z.

Van Kessel, Stijn. *Populist Parties in Europe: Agents of Discontent?* (Basingstoke, Hants: Palgrave Macmillan, 2015).

Vasilopoulou, Sofia. 'European Integration and the Radical Right: Three Patterns of Opposition'. *Government and Opposition* 46, no. 2 (2011): 223–244. https://doi.org/10.1111/j.1477-7053.2010.01337.x.

Vasilopoulou, Sofia, and Daphne Halikiopoulou. *The Golden Dawn's 'Nationalist Solution': Explaining the Rise of the Far Right in Greece* (New York: Palgrave Pivot, 2015). https://doi.org/10.1057/9781137535917.

Vaudano, Maxime, Jérémie Baruch, Olivier Faye, and Agathe Dahyot. 'Qui Sont Les Trente Proches de Marine Le Pen Qui Comptent Au Sein Du FN?' Le Monde, 2017. https://www.lemonde.fr/les-decodeurs/article/2017/04/26/qui-sont-les-trente-proches-de-marine-le-pen-qui-comptent-au-sein-du-fn_5118119_4355770.html Last accessed 23 July 2019.

van de Wardt, Marc, Catherine E. De Vries, and Sara B Hobolt. 'Exploiting the Cracks: Wedge Issues in Multiparty Competition'. *The Journal of Politics* 76, no. 4 (October 2014): 986–999. https://doi.org/10.1017/S0022381614000565.

White, Jonathan, and Lea Ypi. *The Meaning of Partisanship* (Oxford: Oxford University Press, 2016).

Widfeldt, Anders. 'The Radical Right in the Nordic Countries'. In *The Oxford Handbook of the Radical Right*, edited by Jens Rydgren, (New York: Oxford University Press, 2018), 545–564.

Williams, Michelle Hale. *The Impact of Radical Right-Wing Parties in West European Democracies* (New York: Palgrave MacMillan, 2006).

Wodak, Ruth, and Michael Meyer. *Methods of Critical Discourse Studies.* (Los Angeles: SAGE, 2016).

Woll, Cornelia, and Sophie Jacquot. 'Using Europe: Strategic Action in Multi-Level Politics'. *Comparative European Politics* 8, no. 1 (2010): 110–126. https://doi.org/10.1057/cep.2010.7.

Zariski, Raphael. 'The Legitimacy of Opposition Parties in Democratic Political Systems: A New Use for an Old Concept'. *Political Research Quarterly* 39, no. 1 (1986): 29–47. https://doi.org/10.1177/106591298603900104.

Zaslove, Andrej. 'The Populist Radical Right in Government: The Structure and Agency of Success and Failure'. *Comparative European Politics* 10, no. 4 (2012): 421–448. https://doi.org/10.1057/cep.2011.19.

2
Europa patria nostra
Europe as identity

As will become clearer over the following chapters, the causes of the far right's legitimacy deficit are multiple. The acceptability of their nativist ideas, however, has been a major challenge. Recognized as a key part of their manifestoes,[1] and in several cases as influential ideas being picked up by other actors,[2] they are amongst the most recognizable policy issues addressed by these parties. However, they are also amongst the most criticized. In diverse societies, the need to integrate groups of people of different origins obviously clashes with the exclusionary implications of viewing the nation as inherently closed and 'others' as dangers. Nativism also comes into conflict with other values at the heart of European societies, such as the commitment to equality and the protection of human rights. While it is certainly not alien to European societies (and Chapter 3 will return to this claim), and in moderate forms seems to have become more common following a rightward shift from other parties,[3] it is nonetheless approached critically in its more extreme manifestations.

In a more historical perspective, the far right's nativism has been viewed with suspicion because of its association with the fascist parties of the interwar period responsible for the Second World War.[4] For those who have viewed post-war far-right parties as descendants or 'reincarnations' of the fascist parties of the past, the concern was that these parties' tendency to put

---

[1] See for example definitions of far-right parties and actors that focus on their xenophobic and racist nature, such as Reinhard Heinisch, 'Success in Opposition—Failure in Government: Explaining the Performance of Right-Wing Populist Parties in Public Office', *West European Politics* 26, no. 3 (2003): 91–130; Jens Rydgren, 'Is Extreme Right-Wing Populism Contagious? Explaining the Emergence of a New Party Family', *European Journal of Political Research* 44 (2005): 413–437; Ulrike M. Vieten and Scott Poynting, 'Contemporary Far-Right Racist Populism in Europe', *Journal of Intercultural Studies* 37, no. 6 (2016): 533–540, doi:10.1080/07256868.2016.1235099.

[2] Lise Esther Herman and James B. Muldoon, *Trumping the Mainstream: The Conquest of Mainstream Democratic Politics by the Populist Radical Right* (London; New York: Routledge, 2019).

[3] Markus Wagner and Thomas M. Meyer, 'The Radical Right as Niche Parties? The Ideological Landscape of Party Systems in Western Europe, 1980–2014', *Political Studies* 65, no. 1 suppl. (June 2016): 84–107, doi:10.1177/0032321716639065.

[4] Sofia Vasilopoulou and Daphne Halikiopoulou, *The Golden Dawn's 'Nationalist Solution': Explaining the Rise of the Far Right in Greece* (New York: Palgrave Pivot, 2015), doi:10.1057/9781137535917.

the nation above all else had the potential to lead to new conflicts or, at the very least, to a radical disruption of the existing European and global political order.⁵ While in recent years, far-right parties have not been guilty of seeking war with other countries, and whether they have much in common with the interwar groups that they are often compared to is a subject of debate,⁶ they have certainly challenged (or sought to challenge) the existing order. Most clearly, they have attacked the connected nature of European and global societies, leading to a concern that, if in power, they would pursue isolationist policies at odds with the existing economic and political order.

Both the MSI/AN and RN were clearly nativist and subject to the kind of criticisms mentioned above. Article 1 of the MSI's statute, for example, defined the party as a 'political organization inspired by a spiritual conception of life whose aim is to guarantee the dignity and interests of the Italian people'.⁷ AN's statute equally stressed how AN is a 'political movement whose aim is to guarantee the spiritual dignity and economic and social aspirations of the Italian people, in the full respect of its civilizational traditions and national unity'.⁸ The MSI (and, more indirectly and implicitly, AN) was not just nativist; it also drew a direct association between itself and one of the regimes of the Second World War. On its part, the RN's extreme opposition to immigration has long been its most recognizable feature, and one setting it apart from other political actors. Against this background, Europe functioned as an ideological resource by helping the MSI/AN and RN appear more open to other peoples and cultures. Taking part in the process of European integration demanded that they address and engage with a transnational project, providing them with opportunities to counter their image as nativists and build legitimacy through Europeanness. As this chapter will show, one of the ways in which they did so was by defining Europe through the lens of identity. Both the MSI/AN and RN defined Europe as a distinct civilization and

---

⁵ There is, of course, nothing inherently wrong with disruptive movements. However, they are frequently controversial because their ideas go against what is considered 'normal' or 'accepted'. It is this aspect that is of interest here.
⁶ The claim may hold for parties such as the MSI, but for parties such as the RN it is more open to contestation: for different positions see Nigel Copsey, 'Changing Course or Changing Clothes? Reflections on the Ideological Evolution of the British National Party 1999–2006', *Patterns of Prejudice* 41, no. 1 (2007): 61–82, doi:10.1080/00313220601118777; Paul Hainsworth, *The Extreme Right in Western Europe* (New York: Routledge, 2008); Andrea Mammone, 'The Eternal Return? Faux Populism and Contemporarization of Neo-Fascism across Britain, France and Italy', *Journal of Contemporary European Studies* 17, no. 2 (2009): 177, doi:10.1080/14782800903108635; Pierre-André Taguieff, *Du Diable En Politique: Réflexions Sur l'antilepénisme Ordinaire* (Paris: CNRS Éditions, 2014).
⁷ Mario Caciagli, 'The Movimento Sociale Italiano-Destra Nazionale and Neo-Fascism in Italy', in *Right-Wing Extremism in Western Europe*, ed. Klaus von Beyme (London: Frank Cass, 1988), 19–46.
⁸ Alleanza Nazionale, 'Statuto Alleanza Nazionale Approvato Dall'Assemblea Nazionale Il 21 Luglio 1995>', 1995, https://centri.unibo.it/osservatorio-sui-partiti-aldo-di-virgilio/en/statutes/statutes-a-d/alleanza-nazionale-1995.doc/@@download/file/Alleanza%20Nazionale%201995.doc.

displayed a European identity. Doing so, they were able to present a more open form of nationalism, all the while drawing on a 'mystique' of Europe.

Far-right European identities

The morphological analysis of the MSI/AN and RN's ideology shows that the parties drew upon the concept of identity to integrate Europe in their worldview. Identity, as Tajfel succinctly put it, is 'that part of the individual's self-concept which derives from his knowledge of his membership of a social group(s) together with the value and emotional significance attached to that membership'.[9] As such, it comprises two elements: first, the identification of a certain group, or community, carrying certain characteristics that differentiate it from other groups. Second, the existence of this community is not only acknowledged; the individual also expresses a sense of belonging to said group and assigns a certain emotional value to being part of it. The community, then, is not simply 'a community', but an 'us', frequently contrasted and compared with 'them'. These elements of the concept of identity formed a key part of the MSI/AN and RN's definition of Europe. The parties identified a series of characteristics that were distinctive of Europe and the Europeans, and explicitly drew the boundaries of that community. They also approached Europe as an 'us' of sorts and considered their European identity to be complementary to their national identity, thus crafting a position of 'pro-European nativism'.[10]

Italian and European: the Movimento Sociale Italiano/Alleanza Nazionale's European identity

The MSI's approach to Europe as a community has its roots in the writings of Filippo Anfuso. Anfuso was a diplomat in Mussolini's Italy and represented the Italian Social Republic in Berlin. Upon his return to Italy in 1950, he joined the recently founded MSI and was elected to the lower chamber. In 1951, he established a short-lived party magazine, titled *Europa Nazione* (Nation Europe), in which he sought to bring together the works and

---

[9] Henri Tajfel, *Differentiation between Social Groups: Studies in the Social Psychology of Intergroup Relations*, ed. Henri Tajfel (London: Academic Press for European Association of Experimental Social Psychology, 1978), 63.
[10] Manuela Caiani and Manès Weisskircher, 'Anti-Nationalist Europeans and Pro-European Nativists on the Streets: Visions of Europe from the Left to the Far Right', Social Movement Studies, 21, no 1–2 (2022): 216–233, doi: 10.1080/14742837.2021.2010527.

reflections of European authors on how to build a 'Nation Europe'.[11] In the foreword of the first issue, Anfuso presents his own view of Europe, claiming that to him 'Nation Europe' 'means a free and united Europe' and 'a bigger Nation' that the smaller individual nations will be a part of.[12] In this simple sentence, Anfuso expresses what will be the guiding principles of the MSI's vision of Europe: first of all, the idea of a community of smaller individual nations united under the banner of a larger, European nation. The idea of nation employed here to discuss Europe implies the presence of a shared heritage that guides its constituents towards unity. Second, he introduces the notion that Europe needs to be 'free'—a central part of the party's approach to Europe which will be discussed in depth in Chapter 3.

While Anfuso died in 1963, his ideas on 'Nation Europe' lingered on in the party, and the approach to Europe as a distinct community remains present in later MSI documents. The 1980s pamphlet *Il MSI dalla A alla Z* (The MSI, from A to Z) offers one of the clearest expressions of this view. The pamphlet discusses and comments on the principles of the MSI's doctrine most frequently 'used to interpret the various aspects of reality and inform its [the party's] praxis'.[13] Sitting between 'Equality' and 'Fascism', the entry on 'Europeanism' occupies a full page, and is defined as 'the ancient and always alive aspiration towards European unity, in the conscience of a community of interests and destinies, of history, of civilization, of tradition among Europeans'.[14] Thus, the MSI remained attached to the idea of a European community which should strive for unity in the name of its shared traditions.

The MSI not only defined Europe as a specific community, but also approached it as a clearly bound one. The boundaries of this European community, however, were defined primarily in opposition to its existing borders, and especially its Eastern border. The MSI problematized this border both at the Italian and at the European level. At the Italian level, it rejected the borders of Italy as defined in the Paris Peace Treaties of 1947, the London memorandum of 1954, and the subsequent Treaty of Osimo of 1975. Amongst other territorial adjustments, these treaties sealed the cession of Istria to Yugoslavia—by then in the hands of a Communist government. At the European level, the MSI objected to the territorial and 'spiritual' division of Europe between a Western sphere of influence and an Eastern sphere

---

[11] Andrea Mammone, *Transnational Neofascism in France and Italy* (Cambridge: Cambridge University Press, 2015), 84–85.
[12] Filippo Anfuso, 'Proemio', *Europa Nazione: Rivista Mensile*, no 1 (Rome: G. Volpe, 1951).
[13] Movimento Sociale Italiano, *Il Msi-Dn Dalla A Alla Zeta: Principii Programmatici, Politici e Dottrinari Esposti Da Cesare Mantovani, Con Presentazione Del Segretario Nazionale Giorgio Almirante* (Rome: Movimento sociale italiano-Destra nazionale, Ufficio propaganda, 1980), 9.
[14] Movimento Sociale Italiano, *Il Msi-Dn Dalla A Alla Zeta*, 25.

of influence. In both cases, the MSI's opposition to existing borders was entwined with its intense opposition to communism, as it considered the territories of both Italy and Europe had been unfairly placed under the control of Communist regimes following the Second World War, and with critiques to the political class, accused of having accepted these territorial losses.

As a result, and in line with its rabid anti-communism, the MSI frequently stressed that Europe's borders were not its true ones, insofar as parts of Europe (and Italy) were occupied by enemy states. A passage from a 1982 minority congress motion (which, however, reflects positions that were more widely held in the party) illustrates this well. Railing against the 'partition' between 'spheres of influence' agreed upon at Yalta, the motion holds that 'Europe [...] cannot and will not resign itself to consider closed [...] the unitary story of its life [...] its destiny cannot stop at 1945 or at the Oder-Neisse'.[15] By opposing the existing order, and calling upon a shared destiny, the motion reclaims a return to the 'natural' borders of Europe, borders which would include the captive nations of Central and Eastern Europe as an integral part of it. This form of irredentism remained a strong marker of the party, which, throughout the 1980s, kept stressing the need to review the European boundaries and ensure their congruence with the 'spiritual community' of Europe. Coherently with this position, when the revolutions of 1989 and the fall of the Berlin Wall came, the MSI expressed itself in favour of EU accession for the countries of Central and Eastern Europe as to ensure that Europe truly went from 'the Atlantic to the Urals', with a united Germany at its centre.[16]

Unlike the RN, which will be discussed later, the MSI did not identify countries that were to be kept out of Europe. For example, it supported the accession of both Portugal and Spain to the EU, considering them to be obvious members of the European family. It also did not have a strong opinion on Turkish accession to the European Union. Only in an article in the party newspaper *Secolo d'Italia* published a year before Turkey applied to join the EU is there a reflection on whether Turkey should or should not be allowed to join.[17] Interestingly, the author, journalist and politician Nazareno Mollicone, seems to take a rather neutral stance, highlighting both the arguments in favour of Turkish accession (such as its tight political and commercial relations with Europe, which, albeit often conflictual, 'bred reciprocal knowledge', and its place in NATO), and those standing against it

---

[15] Movimento Sociale Italiano, 'Destra '80. Mozione Congressuale, XIII Congresso Roma', *Secolo d'Italia*, January 1982.
[16] Movimento Sociale Italiano, 'Nuove Prospettive. Mozione Congressuale XVI Congresso Rimini'. (Rome: Archivio Fondazione Ugo Spirito, Fondo Movimento Sociale Italiano, serie 4, busta 22, fascicolo 64, 1990).
[17] Nazareno Mollicone, 'La Turchia e La Comunità Europea', *Secolo d'Italia*, 14 February 1986.

(namely the Common Agricultural Policy, the risk of Islamization, and the issue of immigration to Germany). While the article does not come to a solution on the question of Turkish membership, it does not exclude it a priori but considers it a political question, in need of a political answer.

Most importantly, the MSI expressed no doubts about its belonging and attachment to Europe. In spite of an ideology that placed the nation at its centre, the party considered European identity as a derivation of and complement to national identity. Their view on this issue is exposed most clearly in the aforementioned pamphlet *Il MSI dalla A alla Z*. Beyond providing the party's definition of Europe, the entry on Europeanism also discusses in more depth the party's feeling of belonging to European civilization and the relationship between European and national identities, asserting that 'individuality (in this case national) and community (in this case European) are not in opposition but in reciprocal integration and vivification'.[18] In sum, since European and national identities are not in conflict, the party can safely state its belonging to the wider community of Europeans.

The MSI's support for 'Europeanism' can by and large be read as a corollary of both its nationalism and its anti-communism. As a nationalist party, it rejected Italy's loss of power and territory in the aftermath of the Second World War. Its support for closer ties between European nations represented one way in which it thought Italy could retrieve some international clout, especially in the context of a bipolar world order. Its anti-communist stance only compounded this sentiment, as it pushed towards unity in front of a common enemy that one nation could not hope to defeat single-handedly.

However, while it is true that the MSI claimed a European identity compatible with the national one, its Europeanism was nuanced by the relationship it saw as existing between the two. For the MSI, national identity was prior to European identity insofar as only the conscience of a national identity could, in its view, lead to participation in a broader European nation. In this sense, the relationship was hierarchical, with the nation coming first. In no place is this as evident as it is in Pino Romualdi's *Intervista sull'Europa* (Interview on Europe), an interview book published shortly before the first European Parliament election of 1979. Romualdi was a central figure in the history of the MSI. Active in the Italian Social Republic, he spent the first years after the Second World War as a fugitive. In 1946, along with future leaders of the MSI Giorgio Almirante and Pino Rauti, he founded the Forze Armate Rivoluzionarie (FAR), a clandestine terrorist organization. Following the amnesty declared by Togliatti, Romualdi abandoned the FAR and became

---

[18] Movimento Sociale Italiano, *Il Msi-Dn Dalla a Alla Zeta*, 25.

a leader of the newly formed MSI, and remained an important party figure until his death in 1988.[19] Romualdi makes for interesting reading on European matters, as he was deeply interested in foreign and European policy. In the *Intervista*, he presents a clear definition of the relation between European and national identities that highlights the hierarchical relationship between the two, when he claims that 'to believe in Europe as a nation, one must have believed in England, in Germany, in France, in Italy as a Nation; one must have believed and believe in the values that the concept of Nation and Homeland bring with them.'[20] In line with this view, a later speech by Maurizio Gasparri, at the time president of the *Fronte Universitario d'Azione Nazionale* (University Front of National Action, FUAN, the MSI's university movement) and later leading AN political figure, highlighted that 'only he who preserves his historical memory, he who knows how to love his Homeland, he who knows how to defend his identity in front of the globalist homogenization desired by economic power, will be able to be a good European.'[21] The 'Good European', in this sense, is a 'Good Italian' (or equally a good citizen of France, the UK, Spain, etc.) first because only at the national level is one clearly aware of one's identity. Thus, as the congress motion *Impegno Unitario* (Unitary commitment) from 1990 put it, while there is an attachment to Europe, it is safe to say that one 'is European because one is Italian and not vice versa.'[22]

AN's approach to Europe was marked by both breaks and continuities with the MSI's view. Although the disappearance of the Iron Curtain and the fall of the Soviet Union brought about some important changes to AN's discourse, attachment to a European community remained a pillar of party policy. To study AN's definition of Europe as a community, it is necessary to turn to documents from the early 2000s. In fact, while virtually absent from its early documents, it features prominently in the party's 2002 Congress and 2004 Euromanifesto. The increased focus on European questions can be understood as the result of two parallel processes. First, from its first victories in the early and mid nineties, AN continued a process of ideological renewal aimed at attracting a larger number of voters and weakening its association

---

[19] Anna Cento Bull, 'Neo-Fascism', in *The Oxford Handbook of Fascism*, by R. J. B. Bosworth (Oxford: Oxford University Press, 2010).
[20] Pino Romualdi, *Intervista Sull'Europa* (Palermo: Edizioni Thule, 1979), 52.
[21] Maurizio Gasparri, 'Alla Logica Della Moneta Opporremo Storia e Cultura', *Secolo d'Italia*, 7 April 1988.
[22] Movimento Sociale Italiano, 'Impegno Unitario. Mozione Congressuale XVI Congresso Rimini' (Rome: Archivio Fondazione Ugo Spirito, Fondo Movimento Sociale Italiano, serie 4, busta 22, fascicolo 64, 1990).

Europa patria nostra: Europe as identity   65

with fascism.²³ This process was broadly successful, and in 2001 AN once again joined government in a coalition with Silvio Berlusconi's Forza Italia and Umberto Bossi's Lega Nord. Where doubts about AN's democratic credentials still existed, a renewed focus on European questions allowed AN to present itself as a 'trustworthy' partner attached to European values,²⁴ rather than as a party of fascist nostalgics. Second, the intensification of debates concerning the European Constitution also contributed to making the European question more central to the party, especially since AN leader Gianfranco Fini was a member of the EU Convention and minister for foreign affairs between 2004 and 2006. As we will see, the Convention affected the way the party discussed Europe in those years.

Like the MSI, AN recognized the existence of a distinct European 'spiritual' community and stressed the important place this occupied in its ideology. Unlike the MSI, however, AN was more explicit in its description of Europeanness, building its depiction of it in such a way as to echo the early 2000s debates on the European Constitution. The 2004 manifesto provides a particularly clear illustration of AN's view of Europe, showing both how the party defined it and the breaks and continuities with the past. The manifesto opens by defining Europe as 'one of the most qualifying ideals of the Italian right', before fleshing out what the party means by 'Europe':

> When we affirm 'Europe', in the political debate as well as in common speak, we mean to allude not only to a certain extension of lands, to a geographical conception of the continent [. . .]. We intend much more, something deeper, a certain form of civilization that has stratified in centuries of history, a 'way of being' of the human that marks the European, son of a long tradition. A history that has been articulated through two thousand years of common religious history, legal institutes founded on Roman law, reciprocal literary and artistic influences that have clearly selected a basis of common thought.²⁵

In the context of the discussion and ratification of the European Constitutional Treaty, AN also sought to draw a connection between this 'European civilization' and the European Union. For example, in a later passage in the document, it weighs in on the debate on the Judeo-Christian roots of

---

²³ Piero Ignazi, 'Fascists and Post-Fascists', in *The Oxford Handbook of Italian Politics*, by Erik Jones and Gianfranco Pasquino (Oxford: Oxford University Press, 2015).
²⁴ Marco Tarchi, 'The Political Culture of the Alleanza-Nazionale: An Analysis of the Party's Programmatic Documents (1995–2002)', *Journal of Modern Italian Studies* 8 (2003): 135–181.
²⁵ Alleanza Nazionale, 'Programma Elezioni Del Parlamento Europeo 12/13 Giugno 2004' (retrieved from European Manifesto Project, 2004).

Europe,²⁶ defining them as the 'shared foundation that has become the shared value of European identity'.²⁷ AN then advocates for the inclusion of a reference to these roots in the Constitutional Treaty so that a connection between this European civilization and the European Union could be reinforced. Failure to include a reference to the Judeo-Christian roots of Europe, the document argues, would 'tend to marginalise the spiritual aspect and thus reduce the Union to a simple market', while adding a reference to them would become 'the recognition of the secular unity that pre-existed a mere convenience deal. It means recognising the spirituality of Europe'.²⁸ More generally, the elements that AN mentions as defining European civilization are not randomly picked, but rather appear to resonate with the EU's own values as presented in the Treaty, such as the rule of law and the dignity of the person. Thus, the language of AN ends up dovetailing rather than clashing with that of the EU, anchoring its view of what Europe is to the specific project of European integration and the narratives underpinning it.

Because it developed its political existence at a time in which the need to define who belonged to Europe was less pressing, AN was less concerned about the borders of Europe than the MSI and dedicated little space to identifying who concretely belonged to it. Reflections of this type emerged exclusively in discussions of EU enlargement, where AN adopted a rather pragmatic stance. For example, unlike the MSI, it did not see the integration of Central and Eastern Europe as a 'spiritual' need for the divided continent. On the contrary, its 1994 manifesto cautioned against a 'rushed and premature accession' which might aggravate 'detrimental influences on Western Europe'.²⁹ The 1994 programme has an ambiguous status in the history of the party because it was published before the official transformation of the MSI into AN.³⁰ However, the positions expressed within it concerning the Europeanness of Central and Eastern Europe and the challenges posed by enlargement remained a marker of the party in subsequent years. This ambivalence is well illustrated in the 2004 Euromanifesto, which welcomed the 'reunification' with the East as the realization of 'an ideal which has long

---

²⁶ Marcin Frydrych, 'Fight Looms over Christianity in Constitution', *EU Observer*, October 2003, https://euobserver.com/institutional/12897.
²⁷ Alleanza Nazionale, 'Programma Elezioni Del Parlamento Europeo 12/13 Giugno 2004'.
²⁸ Alleanza Nazionale, 'Programma Elezioni Del Parlamento Europeo 12/13 Giugno 2004'.
²⁹ Alleanza Nazionale, 'Programma Per Le Elezioni Politiche', *Secolo d'Italia*, February 1994.
³⁰ In fact, while the MSI already ran under the new name of AN in the 1994 election, it did not complete its transition until the Fiuggi Congress of 1995. The 1994 programme can thus be seen as one seeking to present a new project while maintaining an attachment to the traditional themes of the old party.

been cultivated and that had been made possible by the fall of the Berlin Wall', but also, 'a challenge, not without difficulties, which has just started'.[31]

There is an interesting silence in AN's documents on the relationship between the European and the national dimensions, indicating possibly that it was a 'solved issue' or simply one that the party did not consider particularly important. The following passage from an interview with party leader Gianfranco Fini would appear to support the former interpretation, suggesting as it does that European identity was integral to European integration and accepted by the party:

> There is no antagonism but synergy between the supranational and intergovernmental aspects of the process of integration. No European institution [...] will really be able to affirm itself without a full European citizenship: the sense of a shared civil and social identity of the Union, a European 'demos' that will assert itself in time. The plurality of traditions, of cultures and of the constitutional assets is not a limit to integration but an irreplaceable resource.[32]

Unlike the more abstract discussions of the MSI, Fini here is speaking within a clear debate on the relationship between national and supranational decision-making. However, it does echo some of the MSI's language concerning the relationship between the national and European dimensions. In particular, it is possible to see the 'synergy between the supranational and intergovernmental aspects of the process of integration' as a modern adaptation in EU jargon of the 'integration and vivification' of the MSI. Whereas the MSI spoke more generally about the relationship between identities, AN here places itself more squarely within the discussion of EU decision-making; but it always suggests that the supranational (in this case, equivalent to community) and the intergovernmental (equivalent to the single nations) decision-making processes are in a synergic and, one might add, mutually reinforcing relationship, rather than an antagonistic one. The preceding quotation also display a highly positive view of European citizenship as a 'demos-building' exercise, which does not, however, seem to destroy identities but rather to build on them as 'irreplaceable resources'. Thus, this idea of creating a European demos based on Europe's 'plurality of traditions', 'cultures', 'constitutional assets', and 'diversities' appears to be reflective of

---

[31] Alleanza Nazionale, 'Programma Elezioni Del Parlamento Europeo 12/13 Giugno 2004'.
[32] Lucilla Parlato, 'Fini: "Vogliamo Un'Europa Dei Popoli"', *Secolo d'Italia*, 22 March 2002.

a view in which the national and the supranational have a complementary relationship.

Pro-European, anti-EU: the Rassemblement National's two Europes

Since its early years, the RN's definition of Europe as a community has been built around the identification of a distinct 'European civilization'. Following in the footsteps of the French intellectuals of the Nouvelle Droite,[33] its first explicit definition of Europe in these terms can be found in the 1984 programmatic book *Les Français d'Abord!* (French First!). In it, Jean-Marie Le Pen defines Europe as

> a historic, geographic, cultural, economic and social ensemble. It is an entity destined for action. Europe is currently divided, in decline [. . .] but it guards the possibilities for rebirth, should she rediscover a spiritual, intellectual, and political unity and all that has been its spirit: that is, a will to act for civilization, to refuse to be submerged and vanquished.[34]

The brief paragraph above already captures several elements of the RN's approach to Europe. First of all, Europe is clearly intended as a distinct 'social ensemble' with a claim to greatness. Second, as is often the case for far-right discourse concerning the nation, the narrative of a glorious past is contrasted with a narrative of decline and crisis. Equally, however, there is a promise that Europe can reacquire its prestige and recover its grandeur: it is, as the 1985 election programme defines it, 'a sleeping genie who can and must awake'.[35]

Importantly, in these early years at least, Le Pen suggested that the way to greatness for Europe was no longer an individual, national, path, but a collective path to be pursued through 'spiritual, intellectual and political unity' and the creation of a common 'European conscience' to support this unitary project. Thus, Le Pen advocated for Europeans to be 'proud of themselves and of their contribution to the world, proud of their past, their age-old culture and their uniquely rich historical experience'.[36] He also suggested that

---

[33] Pierre-André Taguieff, *Sur La Nouvelle Droite: Jalons d'une Analyse Critique* (Paris: Descartes & Cie, 1994); Tamir Bar-On, 'Transnationalism and the French Nouvelle Droite', *Patterns of Prejudice* 45, no. 3 (2011): 199–223, doi:10.1080/0031322X.2011.585013.

[34] Jean-Marie Le Pen, *Les Français d'abord* (Paris: Carrère—Michel Lafon, 1984), 154.

[35] Jean-Marie Le Pen, *Pour La France: Programme Du Front National* (Paris: Albatros, 1985), 190.

[36] Ibid., 190

in order to 'build Europe', it was necessary for Europeans to 'forget the conflicts that tore Europe apart in an extremely bloody way [...]. It is necessary to forget mutual faults, if one is to build or rebuild Europe in an effective and emotional way'.[37] Those who are familiar with Ernest Renan will recognize an echo of his *What is a Nation?* in Le Pen's writing. The notion of the forgetting of mutual faults is quite clearly a rephrasing of his idea that 'the essence of a nation is that all individuals have many things in common; and also that they have forgotten many things'.[38] In this sense, the parallel between Europe and the nation is easily drawn, and Europe defined as a nation in the making.

As with the MSI/AN, the early RN conceived this Europe as a clearly bound one, and, like the Italian party, it placed significant emphasis on the misplaced borders of Europe. Speaking from a heavily anti-Communist perspective, it criticized the division of Europe into Western and Eastern parts, viewing it as an unnatural split. For example, in *Les Français d'Abord*, Le Pen laments that people in the West, who have been 'taught history under the control of teachers who are favourable to the Soviet thesis' have accepted that countries such as Bulgaria, Czechoslovakia, and Romania 'no longer belong to Europe; that Eastern Europe is the traditional zone of influence of the Slavic world and that that is OK'.[39] As a result, he argues that these countries should, one day, access the common market. Le Pen also supported EU accession for Spain and Portugal, insisting on their role in writing 'some of the most unforgettable pages in European history', although, in order to protect key French interests, he thought accession should not happen immediately.[40] Interestingly, in those years the European country that the RN was most sceptical about was the United Kingdom. In the same passage in which he discusses Spain and Portugal's European credentials, Le Pen also questions 'the attitude of England in the concert of Europe' and 'its European will', suggesting that 'should London place itself in the position of blocking the regular functioning of Europe, I believe one would have reason to propose a referendum on the leaving or remaining of Great Britain'.[41]

While European unity appeared as necessary in the writings of the early RN and the party showed moderate approval of the EU as one way to unite

---

[37] Jean-Marie Le Pen, *Les Français d'abord* (Paris: Carrère—Michel Lafon, 1984), 156.
[38] Ernest Renan, *Qu'est-Ce Qu'une Nation?* (Paris: Presses-Pocket, 1992).
[39] Le Pen, *Les Français d'abord*, 155.
[40] Ibid., 161–162.
[41] Ibid.

European countries, in the second half of the 1980s the RN developed an increasingly sceptical view of the EU as a political project. The RN's shift was a response to the evolving nature of the EU and to a series of changes within the political party and its domestic context.[42] At the European level, the Single European Act of 1986 and the 1992 Maastricht Treaty constituted a decisive shift in the nature of the European project. The former marked the beginning of an increasingly close economic cooperation between European countries, a development at odds with the RN's view that European collaboration should be guided by the aim of transforming Europe into an international power with a strong common identity. The latter reinforced integration in 'core state powers'[43] which the RN considered an unacceptable relinquishing of national sovereignty. At the party level, the arrival of a group of more markedly Eurosceptic politicians such as Yvan Blot and Jean-Claude Martinez, as well as an increased knowledge (and scepticism) of European processes derived from having become part of the European Parliament, prompted a shift to more critical stances which crystalized into firm opposition during the campaign against the Maastricht Treaty. Finally, opposition to European integration also offered a strategic advantage to the RN in terms of domestic electoral competition. Faced with a primarily pro-EU political class, adopting strong anti-EU positions allowed the party to distinguish itself from other political actors, while appealing to sectors of public opinion who opposed European integration but could not find a party to represent these views.[44]

Even though the RN became more critical of European integration, it did not abandon its attachment to a broader European community; rather, it began to distinguish a 'true' European community from the 'fake' European Union. The opposition between 'Europe' and 'the EU' is a distinctive aspect of the RN's approach to Europe as a form of identification, and one that has remained part of its discourse throughout the last four decades. The opposition between these two conceptions of Europe was first discussed in some depth in the party magazine *Identité* (Identity). Founded at a time when the RN was working on developing a stronger political identity,[45] *Identité*

---

[42] Marta Lorimer, 'The Rassemblement National and European Integration', in *A Critique of Europe. Nationalist, Sovereignist and Right-Wing Populist Attitudes to the EU*, ed. Francesco Berti and Joanna Sondel-Cedarmas, (London: Routledge, 2022), 49–59.
[43] Ibid.
[44] Emmanuelle Reungoat, 'Mobilizing Europe in National Competition: The Case of the French Front National', *International Political Science Review* 36, no. 3 (2015): 296, doi:10.1177/0192512114568816.
[45] Jean-Paul Gautier, *Les Extremes Droites En France: De La Traverse Du Désert à l'ascension Du Front National (1945–2008)* (Paris: Editions Syllepse, 2009).

was a bimonthly publication aimed at discussing and developing key elements of the RN's political doctrine. In its first issue, published in May 1989 and dedicated entirely to 'Rethinking Europe', party intellectual Jean-Yves Le Gallou penned an article whose ideas would become entrenched in the party's approach to Europe. In his piece *Les deux conceptions de l'Europe* (The two conceptions of Europe), Le Gallou extensively develops the distinction between a 'cosmopolitan and technocratic' Europe being constructed in Brussels, and a 'true' Europe of the nations, 'rooted in its culture'.[46] While the former is viewed as a mere market, 'managed by a supranational State, a step towards world government', the latter is defined as an expression of Europe's shared history and a way for it to retrieve the influence it had lost following the Second World War.

The idea of a fundamental opposition between 'Europe' and 'the EU' finds its way into the party's political doctrine and remains present to this day. Thus, for example, a 1991 pamphlet presenting the RN to Anglophone audiences argues that

> The Europe which is being constructed in Brussels, with the complicity of the French political class, is a step on the road towards cosmopolitanism. The Front National considers that Europe is not only a great market of industrialised nations, but above all a community of civilisations. [Original in English.][47]

In the same year, an RN party guide presents the debate on Europe as 'completely distorted' because of the existence of two 'radically different conceptions of Europe': one based on the idea that 'the world is destined to homogenise and unite' and that Europe was but a step towards a 'world government', and the other 'founded on the idea that European nations are menaced in their survival and they have to unite to preserve their identity and retrieve their power'.[48] A few years later, the RN's 2002 programme makes similar points, acknowledging that 'European nations share the same civilization and face the same global threats', while holding that 'cooperation between European nations then rests on the sovereignty of all nations that geographically belong to Europe. But these are free nations who ally: they are not forced to suffer against their will the decisions taken by others'.[49] This

---

[46] Jean-Yves Le Gallou, 'Les Deux Conceptions de l'Europe', *Identité*, no 1 (Paris: Frazier, 1989).
[47] Groupe des Droites Europeennes, 'The Front National of France', *Numero Speciale d'Europe et Patries*, 1991.
[48] Front National, *Militer Au Front* (Paris: Editions Nationales, 1991), 115–116.
[49] Front National, 'Programme Du Front National' (retrieved from Comparative Manifesto Project, 2002).

discourse recently resurfaced in the party, likely in an attempt to assuage concerns that Marine Le Pen might be willing to push for 'Frexit', a fear sparked by her 2017 presidential bid. For example, in a 2018 speech in Kintzheim, Le Pen made a long list of the differences between 'Europe' and the EU, stating that

> The EU isn't just an economic, social, political, democratic and cultural failure; it is also, and more fundamentally, the negation of the European idea. Europe is a continent. The EU is a deracinated organization [. . .]. Europe is a variety of nations. The EU is the homogenization of the peoples and cultures of Europe, it is their programmed disappearance. Europe is a lively and joyful reality. The EU is an artificial, cold and exasperating ideological creation. [. . .] The partisans of the European Union are the gravediggers of the European idea.[50]

Similarly, the RN's 2019 EU election manifesto asserts the need to 'save Europe from the EU', positing once again the fundamental distinction between a European civilization formed of nation states, and a political union whose 'federalist ideology weakens nations'.[51] The citations above all share a common thread: while identifying a common European civilization shared by all European nations and expressing an attachment to it, they also point to the inadequacy of the European Union as a form to represent it, and even suggest that it is a kind of 'anti-Europe' because it destroys what is distinctive of Europe: its division into nations.

The notion of the EU as a violation of what Europe truly is also manifested itself in the RN's opposition to the EU's enlargement process, and specifically in its approach to Turkey's accession to the EU. Turkey first applied to become a member of the European Union in 1987 and was recognized as an official candidate in 1999. The RN has opposed the accession of Turkey to the EU since the early 1990s, tracing the border between Europe and 'others' to the country. The bulk of the RN's argumentation is nicely summarized in a 2000 article published in the party magazine *Français d'abord!* (French First!) and written by Olivier Martinelli, Jean-Marie Le Pen's chief of staff at the time:

> We are told that 'Turkey is a European nation'. This statement is false on four counts. Geographically, only one thirtieth of the total area of the territory, snatched from the Greeks in 1453, belongs to Europe (the region of Constantinople). Linguistically, Turkish does not belong to the group of European idioms, since it does

---

[50] Marine Le Pen, 'Discours de Marine Le Pen à Kintzheim', February 2018, https://rassemblementnational.fr/discours/discours-de-marine-le-pen-a-kintzheim.
[51] Rassemblement National, 'Pour Une Europe Des Nations. Manifeste Pour Une Nouvelle Coopération En Europe: "L'Alliance Européenne Des Nations"', 2019.

not stem from Sanskrit, the Indo-European mother-tongue. As far as the population criteria go, the ancestors of the Turks descend from nomadic tribes close to the Mongolians, with the exception of the inhabitants of Thrace, who mixed with the prisoners from the Balkans (Greek, Albanian, Serbo-Croatian and Bosnians). On the cultural plane, finally, the progressive conversion to Islam of this anciently shamanic people sealed its exclusion from the European sphere, which is fundamentally Christian.[52]

In a discussion on borders, Martinelli's passage has the advantage of highlighting a variety of ways in which one might think of the notion of boundaries. Starting from the most basic one of geography and ending on the stronger definition of a cultural boundary (which is a religious boundary in disguise), he proceeds to explain all the ways in which Turkey is not European. Here it is worth noting in particular the last two points, which appear to be the ones that truly motivate the RN and which are restated in several other places as well, for example when the party expresses fear for the 'pluri-ethnicization' of Europe[53] and its rampant 'Islamization'.[54] Against this background, the EU's attempts to integrate Turkey become yet another violation of Europe's true spirit, and an attempt to push its borders beyond what can be credibly considered 'European'.

The fundamental division between Europe and the EU also forms the basis of the RN's claims to Europeanness, with the party claiming to be 'pro-Europe, but anti-EU'. In this context, it claims to have a European identity, while rejecting the notion of an EU identity. The RN's view of European and national identity as complementary is explicitly discussed in the party guide *Militer au Front* (Being an activist in the Front). The guide, put together by the *Institut de Formation National* (the body charged with the training and development of FN members) with the objective of 'educating' new partisans on the values of the party, states that 'Europe and the Nation are complementary' because

> In the face of cosmopolitanism, we are the defenders of identity, and our identity is made up of the multiple communities we belong to. The family, the blood community, the land, community of roots, the nation, community of history, Europe, community of civilization, religion, spiritual community. We are attached to all

---

[52] Olivier Martinelli, 'La Turquie et l'Union Européenne Un Mariage Impossible', *Français D'Abord*, January 2000.
[53] Front National, 'Programme Pour Les Élections Européennes de 2004' (retrieved from European Manifesto Project, 2004).
[54] Front National, 'Programme "Europe" Du Front National: Leur Europe n'est Pas La Notre! Voila l'Europe Que Nous Voulons' (retrieved from European Manifesto Project, 2009).

these entities and there is no contradiction between them. One can be attached to Brittany, proud of being Breton, all the while being a French patriot. One can also be French and proud to be European, a descendant of the most formidable civilization to exist on the planet.[55]

Once again, in line with what was discussed earlier, Europe is defined as a distinct community 'of civilization, religion, spirituality'. Most importantly, the idea that national and European identities are complementary is stressed from the beginning, and is further developed in the rest of the passage when the idea of multiple identities is defended.

While the passage in *Militer* does not discuss the hierarchical relationship between identities, this point is addressed in an earlier document upon which the party guide appears to draw. The passage above, in fact, echoes Jean-Marie Le Pen's 1984 statement 'I find it very easy to reconcile the double idea of a strong homeland in a strong Europe. In the same way that I feel more Morbihanais than Breton, more Breton than French, more French than European, more European than Atlanticist, more Atlanticist than Globalist'.[56] What the passage suggests is that while the relationship between European and national identity is not mutually exclusive, the 'terminal community'[57] is the one closest to home. Belonging, in this sense, moves from centre to periphery, in a sequence of concentric circles in which the ones closer to the author are also the most important.

At the same time as claiming a European identity, the RN also questioned whether the EU respected this identity. Thus, for example, in 1988 the RN MEP Jean-Marie Le Chevallier published an article in the party magazine *La Lettre de Jean-Marie Le Pen* advocating that the EU, in the name of a 'European spirit', was seemingly imposing a new identity that might destroy the national one by undoing the nation.[58] The 'new identity' that the author refers to here, also criticized in other documents, is a cosmopolitan one that is neither national nor European; in which borders become secondary, both within the Union, through for example the introduction of voting rights for foreign citizens, and between the EU and the rest of the world through the pursuit of primarily economic integration. The line of criticism of the EU as harming national identities remains relevant through the years, with the

---

[55] Front National, *Militer Au Front*, 115–116.
[56] Le Pen, *Les Français d'abord*, 164.
[57] Karl W. Deutsch, *Nationalism and Social Communication: Inquiry into the Foundations of Nationality* (Cambridge, MA: MIT Press, 1966).
[58] Jean-Marie Le Chevallier, 'Un Nouveau Pas Vers l'Europe Du Tiers-Monde', *La Lettre de Jean-Marie Le Pen*, September, no 1, 1988.

EU accused at various times of wanting to 'destroy the identities of the peoples' through standardization, immigration, and European 'destruction',[59] the 'Balkanization' of nations,[60] or through the removal of sovereignty.[61] In contrast, the RN presents itself as the true representative of Europe, and holder of a genuine European identity. In a recent speech which will be analysed further in what follows, Marine Le Pen summarized this clearly when claiming that 'even though we are resolutely opposed to the European Union, we are resolutely European; [. . .] I'd go as far as saying that it is because we are European that we are opposed to the European Union'.[62] While one might want to read this statement as a means for Le Pen to backtrack on the positions on Europe that negatively affected her 2017 campaign, it also inserts itself well into the history of the party. Being European, then, is not in question for the RN: what is in question is the extent to which the EU has anything to do with Europe.

Europe and the 'opening' of far-right ideology: legitimacy through Europeanness

Reading Europe through the prism of identity, both the MSI/AN and the RN presented a 'Europeanized' face to the world. How can we see these claims of Europeanness as ideological resources? Two possibilities are analysed in this section, one concerning Europe's ability to 'open' the parties' ideologies to a transnational dimension, and the other touching upon the strength of 'Europe' as a legitimizing device.

The opening section of this chapter suggested that the far right's nativism has been a key source of its legitimacy deficit. The strength of Europe as an ideological resource in this case lies in its ability to refocus the far right's ideology on transnational issues that help them appear more 'open' to other peoples. Speaking of Europe in terms of an identity, as the MSI/AN and RN did, served this purpose: by claiming Europeanness, these parties 'opened' their ideology to a transnational form of belonging, stressing their open rather than their closed character. Thus, the nation, while remaining the fulcrum of their ideology, shifted from being an exclusive community of

---

[59] Carl Lang, 'L'Europe Des Collabos', *Français d'Abord*, February, no 1, 2002.
[60] Jean-Marie Le Pen, 'Discours Au Conseil National Du Front National' (retrieved from Archives de l'Internet, Bibliothèque nationale de France, 2003).
[61] Marine Le Pen, 'Discours de Fréjus' (2016, retrieved from https://www.youtube.com/watch?v=7SduAX4knp4), last accessed 25 October 2023.
[62] Marine Le Pen, 'Discours de Marine Le Pen à la journée des élus FN au Futuroscope de Poitiers', 2017, https://www.youtube.com/watch?v=fyty5HSaAx0/.

belonging to one amongst others.⁶³ To illustrate this dynamic more clearly, it is worth analysing two previously mentioned citations in more depth. The first is the MSI's 'Europeanism' entry in the party's A–Z booklet:

> Europeanism: it is the ancient and always alive aspiration towards European unity, in the conscience of a community of interests and destinies, of history, of civilization, of tradition among Europeans. [. . .]
>
> The national character which is specific to the MSI-DN does not consider the nation as a particularistic and static fact, but as a dynamic and spiritual fact, whose natural tendency is the universal.
>
> Individuality (in this case national) and community (in this case European) are not in opposition but in reciprocal integration and vivification. A community that ignores or steps on individualities would be an abstraction; the same way that an individuality that would deny itself a possible communitarian destiny would condemn itself to a suffocating atomism.
>
> As Italians, we are and we intend to remain European.⁶⁴

The second citation is from a speech Marine Le Pen gave in Poitiers in 2017:

> On Europe, the MEPs and their assistants will be charged with developing the European project because, even though we are resolutely opposed to the European Union, we are resolutely European [. . .] I'd go as far as saying that it is because we are European that we are opposed to the European Union. [. . .] For us, Europe is not an idea. Europe is a culture, it's a civilization with its values, its codes, its great men, its accomplishments, its masterpieces. For us Europe is not only a history but also a geography, where Turkey does not belong. Europe is a series of peoples whose respective identities exhale the fecund diversity of the continent [. . .]. I return to the definition brought forward by Paul Valéry in considering as European all peoples of each land that has been successively Romanized, Christianized and subject, in matters of the mind, to the rigour of the Greeks. I believe in a common destiny of the nations and peoples of Europe impregnated by the millenary civilization that they share.⁶⁵

The passages above are practical illustrations of how the parties have sought to accommodate a transnational element in their nationalist ideologies,

---

⁶³ For a similar point, see also José Pedro Zúquete, *The Identitarians: The Movement against Globalism and Islam in Europe* (Notre Dame: University of Notre Dame Press, 2018).
⁶⁴ Movimento Sociale Italiano, *Il Msi-Dn Dalla A Alla Zeta: Principii Programmatici, Politici e Dottrinari Esposti Da Cesare Mantovani, Con Presentazione Del Segretario Nazionale Giorgio Almirante*, 25.
⁶⁵ Le Pen, 'Discours de Marine Le Pen à la journée des élus FN au Futuroscope de Poitiers'.

'opening' them as a result. For the MSI, the way forward was to stress the commonalities of Europeans and insist on the relationship between 'individuality' and 'community'. Thus, it reassessed the importance of the individual nations, as well as the need for a communal destiny that allowed for their full realization. The result was a notion that a transnational belonging strengthens the national belonging, and should, therefore, be embraced and valued.

For the RN, reclaiming Europeanness proceeded in three steps. First, it reclaimed the meaning of Europe as opposed to the EU, an element which allowed for the identification of a certain view of Europe that the party could credibly profess to belong to. Second, by defining the nature of that Europe and arguing its heritage lives in all European nations, the party introduced an element of transnationalism into national identity. Third, by identifying Europe's 'fecund diversity' (and, by extension, national diversity) as its defining characteristic, it implied an idea expressed explicitly elsewhere[66] that the nation is the highest achievement of European civilization. This creates an equivalence between belonging to the nation and belonging to Europe by implying that 'all national identity is European identity', thereby opening the ideology while retaining a national attachment.

Importantly, speaking of a collective but bounded European identity rather than, for example, a cosmopolitan or individual one, made it possible for the MSI/AN and RN to maintain continuity with their existing discourse on the nation. In fact, while signalling a measure of transnational attachment, this definition of Europe mirrors closely that of the nation as a collective group of belonging, and maintains alive a clear boundary between 'us' and 'them'. While this border is brought to a higher level, it remains present, allowing parties both to dispel some doubts among those who think of them as closed nationalists, and also to ensure that the party remains internally credible with those who support it on those grounds.

This process of opening does, nonetheless, have its limits, and it is clear that the parties' allegiance to Europe is based on the fact that it is the civilization that created the nation, their primary community of belonging. The citations capture this caveat as well, when Le Pen stresses that no form of European unity should harm the nations that form it, or when the MSI notes that as Italians they wanted to remain European, suggesting that the former precedes the latter. The parties, in short, are European because they are Italian and

---

[66] For example, in Front National, 'Programme "Europe" Du Front National: Leur Europe n'est Pas La Notre! Voila l'Europe Que Nous Voulons'.

French first—a factor that nonetheless further reinforced the links between them and their existing supporters.

One might also wish to be critical of the extent to which being 'European' signals openness, or if it just a dubious ethnic or racist frame being recast at a higher level. As Gerard Delanty perceptively noted, Europeanism 'is not a fixed set of ideas and ideals which can be unilaterally aspired to as an alternative to national chauvinism and xenophobia. It is a strategy of discourse and is constituted by constantly shifting terms of reference';[67] this means that it lends itself to the defence of identity projects of various types, including nationalist ones.[68] This is a valid point, insofar as it highlights that while claiming to be 'European' opened the parties' ideology, this openness was still heavily qualified and limited to a specific group of peoples. While the RN, for example, has presented this in terms of cultural affinity—'civilizationism'[69] or 'civic' nationalism rather than race[70]—it is still not clear how this cultural affinity could be operationalized in practice, and whether this would be done by referring to for example skin colour, religion, or descent. In other words, while stressing Europeanness enabled the MSI/AN and RN to present a more 'open' face, this 'openness' remained limited.

Claiming a European identity, however, not only helped the parties stress openness: it also made it possible for them to claim a form of 'legitimacy by association' by positing a certain type of relationship between themselves and 'Europe'. While the MSI/AN, especially as AN, drew on direct association with the EU as a source of legitimation, the RN drew on the mystique of a 'Europe' beyond (and explicitly pitted against) the EU to achieve the same result.

AN's approach to European identity, as the previous section noted, was closely entwined with reflections on the state of the European Union. Its talk of a European identity mirrored debates about the roots of the EU and adopted a similar language to that used by the European institutions

---

[67] Gerard Delanty, *Inventing Europe: Idea, Identity, Reality*, ed. Jo Campling (Basingstoke, Hants: Macmillan, 1995), 130–131.

[68] On this, see also Ash Amin, 'Multi-Ethnicity and the Idea of Europe', *Theory, Culture & Society* 21, no. 2 (2004): 1–24, doi:10.1177/0263276404042132; Pim den Boer, *The History of the Idea of Europe*, ed. Ole Wæver et al. (Milton Keynes; New York: Open University; Routledge and Kegan Paul, 1995); Dieter Gosewinkel, 'Europe antilibérale ou Anti-Europe? Les conceptions européennes de l'extrême droite française entre 1940 et 1990', *Politique européenne* 62, no. 4 (2018): 152–179.

[69] Rogers Brubaker, 'Between Nationalism and Civilizationism: The European Populist Moment in Comparative Perspective', *Ethnic and Racial Studies* 40, no. 8 (2017): 1191–1226, doi:10.1080/01419870.2017.1294700.

[70] Daphne Halikiopoulou, 'Right-Wing Populism as a Nationalist Vision of Legitimating Collective Choice: A Supply-Side Perspective', *The International Spectator* 54, no. 2 (2019): 35–49, doi:10.1080/03932729.2019.1588544; Daphne Halikiopoulou, Steven J. Mock, and Sofia Vasilopoulou, 'The Civic Zeitgeist: Nationalism and Liberal Values in the European Radical Right', *Nations and Nationalism* 19, no. 1 (2013): 107–127, doi:10.1111/j.1469-8129.2012.00550.x.

themselves. The quest for legitimacy via Europeanness, in this sense, passed through association with the European Union, and through the construal of a European identity compatible with an EU identity. This process resembles closely that described by Sofia Vasilopoulou in *Far Right Parties and Euroscepticism*.[71] Her key argument is that AN moderated its positions on Europe to strategically place itself in the domestic political arena and signal its 'coalitionability' to other political parties. Thus, it sought to construct legitimacy by avoiding the strong Euroscepticism that characterizes fringe parties and by adopting a 'compromising' position vis-à-vis the EU. Stressing the compatibility between its definition of a European identity and that of the EU served a similar purpose: it indicated a certain level of moderation, and a sense of allegiance to the EU project commonly found in the political mainstream rather than on the fringes. It is also worth noting that AN had few incentives to adopt a more anti-EU position, since it worked in the context of a broadly EU-positive public opinion.[72] Associating itself with the EU did not risk losing it too many votes, all the while bringing distinctive advantages in terms of signalling legitimacy.

The situation was quite different for the RN. Unlike the AN, the RN's coalition opportunities remained null. Ostracized by most of the political class and internally divided on the question of alliances with the mainstream right, the RN had little interest in signalling 'coalitionability'. Moreover, in a domestic context in which Euroscepticism was more marked than in Italy, it would not have necessarily benefitted from direct association with the EU. Instead, the RN built legitimacy by association with the wider civilizational notion of Europe and in opposition to the EU. Whereas the AN's position on European identity was situated within the specific context of the EU project, the RN's position was constructed in opposition to it, and in a much vaguer civilizational space. This claim fed into the construction of legitimacy in two ways: first, by drawing on the 'mystique' of Europe to justify the party's positions, it created a connection between the RN and an 'unquestionably good' concept such as Europe. In addition, using these 'counter-European' claims[73] delegitimized the EU by breaking the symbolic bond between Europe and the EU. It is worth analysing this strategy in some depth, as separating between Europe and the EU is a shared feature of a number of members of the far-right

---

[71] Sofia Vasilopoulou, *Far Right Parties and Euroscepticism: Patterns of Opposition* (London; New York: Rowman & Littlefield, 2018).
[72] Lucia Quaglia, 'Euroscepticism in Italy', in *Opposing Europe?: The Comparative Party Politics of Euroscepticism*, ed. Aleks Szczerbiak and Paul A Taggart (Oxford: Oxford University Press, 2008), 58–74.
[73] Bartek Pytlas, 'Hijacking Europe: Counter-European Strategies and Radical Right Mainstreaming during the Humanitarian Crisis Debate 2015–16', *Journal of Common Market Studies* 59 (2021): 335–353, doi:10.1111/jcms.13092.

party family, such as the Vlaams Belang, the Alternative für Deutschland, the Freiheitliche Partei Österreichs, and the Partij voor de Vrijheid (Party for Freedom, PVV)[74]—but also beyond it.[75]

Europe, some have argued, is a useful idea for those seeking to justify new political projects or actions because 'the rhetoric of Europe provides a legitimation, which otherwise would be lacking, for political strategies that seek to mobilise new kinds of power'.[76] Richard von Coudenhove-Kalergi sought to justify his project for a 'pan-Europa' by providing it with a pedigree grounded in history.[77] Similarly, the early European Community justified its existence by referring to an ideology of Europeanness which held that the common culture of the European nations was more important than individual national cultures.[78] More recently, Europe as the EU has been invoked as a form of justification for everything from controversial liberalization measures, as the concept of the '*vincolo esterno*' (external constraint) would have it,[79] to the imposition of technocratic governments and austerity measures on crisis-stricken countries. While this can be read as a form of blame-shifting, or as leaders asking for Europe a 'power which they would never venture to ask for in their own name',[80] it also suggests that there is something particularly powerful about Europe as a legitimizing device which encourages actors to appeal to it.

Although it is not immediately clear what the 'something powerful' about Europe is, John Pocock puts its power down to its 'mystique', which makes it possible 'to use the word as an incantation with which there can be no argument'.[81] Its power, in this sense, lies in the fact that it is unquestionable and, most of the time, positive. In a similar vein, Delanty argues that the power of

---

[74] Vlaams Belang, 'Uw Stock Achter de Deur, Verkiezingsprogramma' (2014); Freiheitliche Partei Österreichs, 'Party Programme of the Freedom Party of Austria' (2011, retrieved from https://www.fpoe.at/themen/parteiprogramm/parteiprogramm-englisch/), last Accessed 23 July 2019; Geert Wilders, 'The Europe We Want. Speech, Ambrosetti Conference, Italy, Villa d'Este, September 2, 2017' 2018, no. 6 November (2014), https://www.geertwilders.nl/in-de-media-mainmenu-74/nieuws-mainmenu-114/94-english/2066-speech-geert-wilders-the-europe-we-want, last accessed 23 July 2019.
[75] Boris Johnson, 'Boris Johnson: "We Are Leaving the EU, Not Europe"', *BBC News*, 2016, https://www.bbc.co.uk/news/av/uk-politics-37641405/boris-johnson-we-are-leaving-the-eu-not-europe, last accessed 23 July 2019; Andrew Glencross, '"Love Europe, Hate the EU": A Genealogical Inquiry into Populists' Spatio-Cultural Critique of the European Union and Its Consequences', *European Journal of International Relations* 26, no. 1 (2020): 116–136, doi:10.1177/1354066119850242.
[76] Delanty, *Inventing Europe: Idea, Identity, Reality*, 143.
[77] Lionel Gossman, 'The Idea of Europe', *Common Knowledge* 16, no. 2 (2010): 198, doi:10.1215/0961754X-2009-087.
[78] J G A Pocock, 'Deconstructing Europe', *History of European Ideas* 18, no. 3 (1994): 329–345, doi:10.1016/0191-6599(94)90499-5.
[79] Kenneth Dyson and Kevin Featherstone, 'Italy and EMU as a "Vincolo Esterno": Empowering the Technocrats, Transforming the State', *South European Society and Politics* 1, no. 2 (1996): 272–299, doi:10.1080/13608749608539475.
[80] Cited in Edward Crankshaw, *Bismarck* (London: Macmillan, 1981).
[81] Pocock, 'Deconstructing Europe', 134.

Europe is rooted in its ability to 'evoke a transcendent point of unity beyond the nation state' and as such foster 'social integration'.[82] Thus, it would appear to be a powerful notion because it invokes ideas of a 'broader collective interest' which suggest that one is not self-interested but acting in the name of some higher good.

By asserting attachment to a true Europe and by presenting itself as its defender, the RN appeals to the legitimizing power of Europe to appear more acceptable. It calls upon a concept that is generally considered to be 'unquestionably good' to justify its own position; at the same time, it presents those positions as aligned with a 'European spirit' or 'European interest', which serves to justify its actions as ones which are being pursued in the name of some collective (and desirable, because 'European') interest. In this way, it strengthens its connection with Europe, building legitimacy by association. It also questions the EU's legitimacy by contesting the equation Europe = EU which constitutes one of the justifying narratives for the construction. As a result, it questions the extent of control that the EU has of the concept of Europe, an element which may destabilize it in the long term because it removes, or at least reopens to contestation, a powerful justification for its existence.

In sum, the two parties constructed the same type of legitimacy by association, although they associated themselves with different ideas of 'Europe'. This source of legitimacy has its own disadvantages. Most obviously, it requires one to believe that Europe is indeed unquestionably good, and that it is possible to gain in legitimacy by mere association with it. Furthermore, one may doubt the extent to which what is being sold as in the interest of Europe is really about a genuine collective interest—or whether it is instead about national interests being repackaged as European. However, in cases where the former condition is met, and the European and national interest converge, it can prove to be a powerful narrative.

Conclusion

This chapter has analysed how the MSI/AN and the RN's approach to Europe through the prism of identity enabled them to address critiques of their nativist ideology. It showed how the MSI/AN and the RN conceived of

---

[82] Delanty, *Inventing Europe: Idea, Identity, Reality*, 143.

Europe as a form of identity and argued that presenting Europe as a distinct civilization which they claimed to belong to served them in two ways. First, it made it possible for them to display a more open nationalism, hence clearing a path to acceptability through (moderate) transnationalism. Second, claiming Europeanness made it possible for the parties to draw on the mystique of Europe, thus facilitating a form of 'legitimacy by association'. While questions remain concerning the limits of their openness, and the extent to which mere association with something positive may increase acceptability, these claims to Europeanness helped the parties project an image of themselves that addressed one of the sources of their legitimacy deficit.

References

Alleanza Nazionale. 'Programma Per Le Elezioni Politiche'. *Secolo d'Italia*, February 1994.

Alleanza Nazionale. 'Statuto Alleanza Nazionale Approvato Dall'Assemblea Nazionale Il 21 Luglio 1995', 1995. https://centri.unibo.it/osservatorio-sui-partiti-aldo-di-virgilio/en/statutes/statutes-a-d/alleanza-nazionale-1995.doc/@@download/file/Alleanza%20Nazionale%201995.doc.

Alleanza Nazionale. 'Programma Elezioni Del Parlamento Europeo 12/13 Giugno 2004' (retrieved from European Manifesto Project, 2004).

Amin, Ash. 'Multi-Ethnicity and the Idea of Europe'. *Theory, Culture & Society* 21, no. 2 (2004): 1–24. https://doi.org/10.1177/0263276404042132.

Anfuso, Filippo. 'Proemio'. *Europa Nazione: Rivista Mensile*, no 1 (Rome: G. Volpe, 1951).

Bar-On, Tamir. 'Transnationalism and the French Nouvelle Droite'. *Patterns of Prejudice* 45, no. 3 (2011): 199–223. https://doi.org/10.1080/0031322X.2011.585013.

Boer, Pim den. *The History of the Idea of Europe*. With Ole Wæver, and Peter Bugge. Edited by Kevin Wilson and W. J. van der Dussen. MyiLibrary (Milton Keynes; New York: Open University; Routledge and Kegan Paul, 1995).

Brubaker, Rogers. 'Between Nationalism and Civilizationism: The European Populist Moment in Comparative Perspective'. *Ethnic and Racial Studies* 40, no. 8 (2017): 1191–1226. https://doi.org/10.1080/01419870.2017.1294700.

Caciagli, Mario. 'The Movimento Sociale Italiano-Destra Nazionale and Neo-Fascism in Italy'. In *Right-Wing Extremism in Western Europe*, edited by Klaus Beyme (London: Frank Cass, 1988), 19–46.

Caiani, Manuela, and Manès Weisskircher. 'Anti-nationalist Europeans and pro-European nativists on the streets: visions of Europe from the left to the far right', *Social Movement Studies* 21, no. 1–2 (2022): 216–233. https://doi.org/10.1080/14742837.2021.2010527.

Cento Bull, Anna. 'Neo-Fascism'. In *The Oxford Handbook of Fascism*, by R. J. B. Bosworth (Oxford: Oxford University Press, 2010): 586–605.

Copsey, Nigel. 'Changing Course or Changing Clothes? Reflections on the Ideological Evolution of the British National Party 1999–2006'. *Patterns of Prejudice* 41, no. 1 (2007): 61–82. https://doi.org/10.1080/00313220601118777.

Crankshaw, Edward. *Bismarck* (London: Macmillan, 1981).

Delanty, Gerard. *Inventing Europe: Idea, Identity, Reality* (Basingstoke, Hants: Macmillan, 1995).

Deutsch, Karl W. *Nationalism and Social Communication: Inquiry into the Foundations of Nationality* (Cambridge, MA: MIT Press, 1966).

Dyson, Kenneth, and Kevin Featherstone. 'Italy and EMU as a "Vincolo Esterno": Empowering the Technocrats, Transforming the State'. *South European Society and Politics* 1, no. 2 (1996): 272–299. https://doi.org/10.1080/13608749608539475.

Freiheitliche Partei Österreichs. 'Party Programme of the Freedom Party of Austria' (retrieved from https://www.fpoe.at/themen/parteiprogramm/parteiprogramm-englisch/, 2011, last accessed 23 July 2019).

Front National. *Militer Au Front* (Paris: Editions Nationales, 1991).

Front National. 'Programme Du Front National' (retrieved from Comparative Manifesto Project, 2002).

Front National. 'Programme Pour Les Élections Européennes de 2004' (retrieved from European Manifesto Project, 2004).

Front National. 'Programme "Europe" Du Front National: Leur Europe n'est Pas La Notre! Voila l'Europe Que Nous Voulons' (retrieved from European Manifesto Project, 2009).

Frydrych, Marcin. 'Fight Looms over Christianity in Constitution'. *EU Observer*, October 2003. https://euobserver.com/institutional/12897.

Gasparri, Maurizio. 'Alla Logica Della Moneta Opporremo Storia e Cultura'. *Secolo d'Italia*, 7 April 1988.

Gautier, Jean-Paul. *Les Extremes Droites En France: De La Traverse Du Désert à l'ascension Du Front National (1945–2008)* (Paris: Editions Syllepse, 2009).

Glencross, Andrew. '"Love Europe, Hate the EU": A Genealogical Inquiry into Populists' Spatio-Cultural Critique of the European Union and Its Consequences'. *European Journal of International Relations* 26, no. 1 (2020): 116–136. https://doi.org/10.1177/1354066119850242.

Gosewinkel, Dieter. 'Europe antilibérale ou Anti-Europe? Les conceptions européennes de l'extrême droite française entre 1940 et 1990'. *Politique européenne* 62, no. 4 (2018): 152–179.

Gossman, Lionel. 'The Idea of Europe'. *Common Knowledge* 16, no. 2 (2010): 198. https://doi.org/10.1215/0961754X-2009-087.

Groupe des Droites Europeennes. 'The Front National of France'. *Numero Speciale d'Europe et Patries*, 1991.

Hainsworth, Paul. *The Extreme Right in Western Europe* (New York: Routledge, 2008).

Halikiopoulou, Daphne. 'Right-Wing Populism as a Nationalist Vision of Legitimating Collective Choice: A Supply-Side Perspective'. *The International Spectator* 54, no. 2 (2019): 35–49. https://doi.org/10.1080/03932729.2019.1588544.

Halikiopoulou, Daphne, Steven J. Mock, and Sofia Vasilopoulou. 'The Civic Zeitgeist: Nationalism and Liberal Values in the European Radical Right'. *Nations and Nationalism* 19, no. 1 (2013): 107–127. https://doi.org/10.1111/j.1469-8129.2012.00550.x.

Heinisch, Reinhard. 'Success in Opposition—Failure in Government: Explaining the Performance of Right-Wing Populist Parties in Public Office'. *West European Politics* 26, no. 3 (2003): 91–130.

Herman, Lise Esther, and James B. Muldoon. *Trumping the Mainstream: The Conquest of Mainstream Democratic Politics by the Populist Radical Right* (London; New York: Routledge, 2019).

Ignazi, Piero. 'Fascists and Post-Fascists'. In *The Oxford Handbook of Italian Politics*, by Erik Jones and Gianfranco Pasquino (Oxford: Oxford University Press, 2015): 211–223.

Johnson, Boris. 'Boris Johnson: "We Are Leaving the EU, Not Europe"'. *BBC News*, 2016. https://www.bbc.co.uk/news/av/uk-politics-37641405/boris-johnson-we-are-leaving-the-eu-not-europe.

Lang, Carl. 'L'Europe Des Collabos'. *Français d'Abord*, February, no 1, 2002.

Le Chevallier, Jean-Marie. 'Un Nouveau Pas Vers l'Europe Du Tiers-Monde'. *La Lettre de Jean-Marie Le Pen*, September, no 1, 1988.

Le Gallou, Jean-Yves. 'Les Deux Conceptions de l'Europe'. In *Identité*, no 1 (Paris: Frazier, 1989).

Le Pen, Jean-Marie. *Les Français d'abord* (Paris: Carrère—Michel Lafon, 1984).

Le Pen, Jean-Marie. *Pour La France: Programme Du Front National* (Paris: Albatros, 1985).

Le Pen, Jean-Marie. 'Discours Au Conseil National Du Front National' (retrieved from Archives de l'Internet, Bibliothèque nationale de France, 2003).

Le Pen, Marine. 'Discours de Marine Le Pen à la journée des élus FN au Futuroscope de Poitiers', 2017. https://www.youtube.com/watch?v=fyty5HSaAx0/.

Le Pen, Marine. 'Discours de Marine Le Pen à Kintzheim', February 2018. https://rassemblementnational.fr/discours/discours-de-marine-le-pen-a-kintzheim.

Lorimer, Marta. 'The Rassemblement National and European Integration'. In *A Critique of Europe. Nationalist, Sovereignist and Right-Wing Populist Attitudes to the EU*, edited by Francesco Berti and Joanna Sondel-Cedarmas (London: Routledge, 2022): 49–59.

Mammone, Andrea. 'The Eternal Return? Faux Populism and Contemporarization of Neo-Fascism across Britain, France and Italy'. *Journal of Contemporary European Studies* 17, no. 2 (2009): 171–192. https://doi.org/10.1080/14782800903108635.

Mammone, Andrea. *Transnational Neofascism in France and Italy* (Cambridge: Cambridge University Press, 2015).

Martinelli, Olivier. 'La Turquie et l'Union Européenne Un Mariage Impossible'. *Français D'Abord*, January 2000.

Mollicone, Nazareno. 'La Turchia e La Comunità Europea'. *Secolo d'Italia*, 14 February (1986).

Movimento Sociale Italiano. *Il Msi-Dn Dalla A Alla Zeta: Principii Programmatici, Politici e Dottrinari Esposti Da Cesare Mantovani, Con Presentazione Del Segretario Nazionale Giorgio Almirante* (Rome: Movimento sociale italiano-Destra nazionale, Ufficio propaganda, 1980).

Movimento Sociale Italiano. 'Destra '80. Mozione Congressuale, XIII Congresso Roma'. *Secolo d'Italia*, January 1982.

Movimento Sociale Italiano. 'Impegno Unitario. Mozione Congressuale XVI Congresso Rimini' (Roma: Archivio Fondazione Ugo Spirito, Fondo Movimento Sociale Italiano, serie 4, busta 22, fascicolo 64, 1990).

Movimento Sociale Italiano. 'Nuove Prospettive. Mozione Congressuale XVI Congresso Rimini'. (Roma: Archivio Fondazione Ugo Spirito, Fondo Movimento Sociale Italiano, serie 4, busta 22, fascicolo 64, 1990).

Parlato, Lucilla. 'Fini: "Vogliamo Un'Europa Dei Popoli"'. *Secolo d'Italia*, 22 March 2002.

Pocock, J. G. A. 'Deconstructing Europe'. *History of European Ideas* 18, no. 3 (1994): 329–345. https://doi.org/10.1016/0191-6599(94)90499-5.

Pytlas, Bartek. 'Hijacking Europe: Counter-European Strategies and Radical Right Mainstreaming during the Humanitarian Crisis Debate 2015–16'. *Journal of Common Market Studies* 59 (2021): 335–353. https://doi.org/10.1111/jcms.13092.

Quaglia, Lucia. 'Euroscepticism in Italy'. In *Opposing Europe?: The Comparative Party Politics of Euroscepticism*, edited by Aleks Szczerbiak and Paul A. Taggart (Oxford: Oxford University Press, 2008), 58–74.

Rassemblement National. 'Pour Une Europe Des Nations. Manifeste Pour Une Nouvelle Coopération En Europe: "L'Alliance Européenne Des Nations"', 2019.

Renan, Ernest. *Qu'est-Ce Qu'une Nation?* (Paris: Presses-Pocket, 1992).

Reungoat, Emmanuelle. 'Mobilizing Europe in National Competition: The Case of the French Front National'. *International Political Science Review* 36, no. 3 (2015): 296–310. https://doi.org/10.1177/0192512114568816.

Romualdi, Pino. *Intervista Sull'Europa* (Palermo: Edizioni Thule, 1979).

Rydgren, Jens. 'Is Extreme Right-Wing Populism Contagious? Explaining the Emergence of a New Party Family'. *European Journal of Political Research* 44 (2005): 413–437.

Taguieff, Pierre-André. *Sur La Nouvelle Droite: Jalons d'une Analyse Critique* (Paris: Descartes & Cie, 1994).

Taguieff, Pierre-André. *Du Diable En Politique: Réflexions Sur l'antilepénisme Ordinaire* (Paris: CNRS Éditions, 2014).

Tajfel, Henri. *Differentiation between Social Groups: Studies in the Social Psychology of Intergroup Relations*. Edited by Henri Tajfel (London: Academic Press for European Association of Experimental Social Psychology, 1978).

Tarchi, Marco. 'The Political Culture of the Alleanza-Nazionale: An Analysis of the Party's Programmatic Documents (1995–2002)'. *Journal of Modern Italian Studies* 8 (2003): 135–181.

Vasilopoulou, Sofia. *Far Right Parties and Euroscepticism: Patterns of Opposition* (London; New York: Rowman & Littlefield, 2018).

Vasilopoulou, Sofia, and Daphne Halikiopoulou. *The Golden Dawn's 'Nationalist Solution': Explaining the Rise of the Far Right in Greece* (New York: Palgrave Pivot, 2015). https://doi.org/10.1057/9781137535917.

Vieten, Ulrike M., and Scott Poynting. 'Contemporary Far-Right Racist Populism in Europe'. *Journal of Intercultural Studies* 37, no. 6 (2016): 533–540. https://doi.org/10.1080/07256868.2016.1235099.

Vlaams Belang. 'Uw Stock Achter de Deur, Verkiezingsprogramma' (2014).

Wagner, Markus, and Thomas M. Meyer. 'The Radical Right as Niche Parties? The Ideological Landscape of Party Systems in Western Europe, 1980–2014'. *Political Studies* 65, no. 1 suppl (June 2016): 84–107. https://doi.org/10.1177/0032321716639065.

Wilders, Geert. 'The Europe We Want. Speech, Ambrosetti Conference, Italy, Villa d'Este, September 2, 2017' 2018, no. 6, November (2014). https://www.geertwilders.nl/in-de-media-mainmenu-74/nieuws-mainmenu-114/94-english/2066-speech-geert-wilders-the-europe-we-want, last accessed 23 July 2019.

Zúquete, José Pedro. *The Identitarians: The Movement against Globalism and Islam in Europe* (Notre Dame: University of Notre Dame Press, 2018).

3
The battle for Europe's freedom
Europe and liberty

If the nativism discussed in the previous chapter has been one source of the far right's legitimacy deficit, it is far from being the only one. Rather, it is just part of a broader set of claims concerning the far right's 'outsiderness'—the idea that far-right parties situate themselves outside the realm of normal politics. This image is partially self-cultivated, insofar as far-right parties actively seek to present themselves as different from the 'regular' parties they describe as 'all the same' and uninterested in defending the nation. However, it is also the result of a tendency to approach the far right as a 'normal pathology' of politics rather than as a 'pathological normalcy'.[1] In this view, the far right is a glitch in the system, the result of some kind of crisis that will eventually disappear once the crisis that made it emerge is resolved. Rather than being legitimate actors competing for power, far-right parties are presented as holding values alien to their political systems and standing outside the realm of acceptability.

The normal pathology thesis is not universally accepted (and is losing purchase as far-right parties increasingly entrench themselves in their political systems),[2] but it is certainly revelatory of how far-right parties have been perceived for several of the decades under study in this book. The MSI/AN and RN specifically have been political outsiders in the sense described above for the largest part of their political lives. The MSI was long known as the 'excluded pole' of Italian politics because of its attachment to fascism and its positioning outside the 'constitutional arc'.[3] Its early attempts at becoming a relevant player in Italian politics, such as its support for the

---

[1] Cas Mudde, 'The Populist Radical Right. A Pathological Normalcy', *West European Politics* 33, no. 6 (2010): 1167–1186.
[2] Christos Vrakopoulos, 'Political and Ideological Normalization: Quality of Government, Mainstream-Right Ideological Positions and Extreme-Right Support', *European Political Science Review* 14, no. 1 (2022): 56–73, doi:10.1017/S1755773921000308.
[3] Piero Ignazi, *Il Polo Escluso: Profilo Storico Del Movimento Sociale Italiano* (Bologna: Il Mulino, 1998); Roberto. Roberto Chiarini and Marco Maraffi. *La Destra Allo Specchio: La Cultura Politica Di Alleanza Nazionale* (Venezia: Marsilio, 2001).

Tambroni government in 1960, generated unprecedented backlash,[4] and the party ended up spending the rest of its political life being ostracized by other parties. It was not until its transformation into AN that it could fully become part of Italian politics and play a part in the democratic game. The RN has also long been considered as a potential threat to democracy and subject to a '*cordon sanitaire*' meant to keep it away from power.[5] The cordon sanitaire has weakened in recent years and perceptions of the RN as a threat to democracy have become significantly less widespread, but the RN is still far from being considered a party like all others. For example, the 2022 Kantar Public poll on the image of the RN shows that Marine Le Pen is still considered as a danger to democracy by 54% of voters, behind only Éric Zemmour (68%) and considerably ahead of Jean-Luc Mélenchon (39%), Emmanuel Macron (36%), and Éric Ciotti (27%).[6]

How did Europe function as an ideological resource for these parties to employ to counter their image as 'aliens' in their respective political systems? Similar to what was discussed in the previous chapter, Europe offered the MSI/AN and RN an opportunity to revise their ideology in a more acceptable direction, but also to recentre it around potentially less divisive themes and discourses, including ones shared by other political and societal actors. The remainder of this chapter develops this argument by considering the role played by the MSI/AN and RN's renewed focus on Europe as a source of, and limit to, liberty. The chapter shows how the MSI/AN and RN mobilized the concept of liberty to define Europe. For the MSI/AN, Europe was a space that needed to retrieve autonomy and power, and similarly, in the 1980s the RN claimed the need for European power and autonomy. However, from the 1990s onwards the RN began to reclaim self-rule for the nation. The use of the concept of liberty to define Europe, the chapter argues, enabled the two parties to present themselves as aligned with mainstream values and ideas, thereby constructing acceptability through shared narratives. In this approach, mainstreaming did not entail looking like all other *parties* in a country. Rather, it entailed showing allegiance to principles that most would consider foundational to political life.

---

[4] Mario Caciagli, 'The Movimento Sociale Italiano-Destra Nazionale and Neo-Fascism in Italy', in *Right-Wing Extremism in Western Europe*, ed. Klaus von Beyme (London: Frank Cass, 1988), 19–46; James L. Newell, 'Italy: The Extreme Right Comes in from the Cold', *Parliamentary Affairs* 53 (2000): 469–485.

[5] Meindert Fennema and Marcel Maussen, 'Dealing with Extremists in Public Discussion: Front National and "Republican Front" in France', *Journal of Political Philosophy* 8, no. 3 (2000): 379–400, doi:10.1111/1467-9760.00108.

[6] Kantar Public—EPOKA, 'Baromètre d'image Du Rassemblement National (Édition Décembre 2022)', 2022, https://www.kantarpublic.com/fr/barometres/barometre-d-image-du-rassemblement-national/barometre-d-image-du-rassemblement-national-2023.

Mobilizing the core: from liberty to Europe

Joining the concept of identity in the MSI/AN and RN's definition of Europe is the concept of liberty. Unlike identity, which is more distinctive of the far right, the concept of liberty is shared by different party families. However, the MSI/AN and RN use the term in quite a specific fashion: they mainly approach it as a collective concept, where the unit of analysis is Europe as a holistic community,[7] rather than the individual citizen (as one might have expected from a more 'liberal' conception).[8] When the parties use liberty in conjunction with Europe, they adopt two different meanings of liberty. First, they equate it with concepts of autonomy and self-rule to restate the importance of those principles for Europe and, in the case of the RN, for the nation. Second, in the realm of external relations between Europe and the world, they discuss liberty as a form of power and projection to present Europe as a community endowed with (or in need to regain) power outside its borders and the ability to shape world politics.

Autonomy, power, and Europe's 'secular mission': the Movimento Sociale Italiano/Alleanza Nazionale's foreign power Europe

The concept of liberty occupies a central place in the MSI/AN's definition of Europe, although the usage of the term has evolved and changed along with the party. In its early years, the MSI used the notion of liberty to stress the need for Europe to become free from foreign interference and project power in the external realm. Following its transformation into AN, it increasingly employed the language of liberty to redefine European nations' relationship with the EU and present its vision for Europe's role in the world.

In the language of the MSI, liberty appeared primarily as something that Europe had lost following the Second World War. Divided, powerless, and subject to the 'twin imperialisms' of the USA and the USSR, Europe was, for the MSI, devoid of autonomy and unable to assert itself and make its own decisions. This view of a powerless Europe is well captured by MSI

---

[7] While one may note significant overlap between this understanding of liberty and the more familiar notion of 'national sovereignty', this book opts for the former in an attempt to reflect the language of the parties and provide a more fine-grained analysis of what liberty has meant through time.
[8] Alisa L. Carse, 'The Liberal Individual: A Metaphysical or Moral Embarrassment?', *Noûs* 28, no. 2 (1994): 184–209, doi:10.2307/2216048; Michael Freeden, *Ideologies and Political Theory: A Conceptual Approach* (Oxford: Oxford University Press, 1998).

member and book editor Michele Rallo. In 1978, Rallo edited a programmatic book called *Intervista sull'Eurodestra* (Interview on the Euroright). The book was published on the occasion of the first open elections to the European Parliament. It contains a lengthy interview with party secretary Giorgio Almirante and details the programme of the *Eurodestra*, a coalition of three far-right parties (the MSI, the French *Parti des Forces Nouvelles*, and the Spanish *Fuerza Nueva*) aiming to create a united group in the European Parliament. In the preface of the *Intervista*, Rallo commented on the current situation of Europe, noting how 'Europe, after the two world conflicts, has lost its role as protagonist of History' because 'the Yalta agreements have subjected its oriental regions to Soviet imperialism, while its western regions are today exposed to a double military (reinforcement of the Warsaw Pact) and political (Eurocommunism) pressure from that same imperialism'.[9] The tight link between the Yalta agreements, European decline, and the lack of European autonomy is addressed more explicitly by Pino Romualdi, another of the MSI's historical leaders, in his interview-book *Intervista sull'Europa* (Interview on Europe). Romualdi argues that 'In Yalta, in the name of anti-fascism, the United States and Russia [. . .] carved up the world and Europe as well. In that moment [. . .] Europe was deprived [. . .] of its freedom and its political independence; and destined to become—from centre of the world as it still was at the time [. . .]—a huge territory divided in two'.[10]

Liberty to the MSI was not only something Europe had lost; it was also an attribute it should retrieve in order to recover from its decline in international politics, start making its own decisions, and project power beyond its borders. Although there were divisions within the party concerning whether Europe should retrieve power as part of NATO or against it,[11] there was general agreement that Europe should become more powerful. For example, in the 1979 majority congress motion *Continuare per Rinnovare* (Continue to Renew), party leader Giorgio Almirante and his faction discussed the tense international situation between the USA and the USSR, suggesting that the great powers' inability to compromise could be an opportunity for Europe to retrieve power. This, the motion argued, would only be possible if 'Europe realises that it is a continent, that it does not have to accept to be tied by the shackles of Yalta, to have within its hands the instruments to affirm its autonomy, to have the obligation and even the interest to look globally to its

---

[9] Giorgio Almirante, *Intervista Sull'Eurodestra*, ed. Michele Rallo (Palermo: Edizioni Thule, 1978), 7.
[10] Pino Romualdi, *Intervista Sull'Europa* (Palermo: Edizioni Thule, 1979), 47.
[11] Piero Ignazi, *Postfascisti?: Dal Movimento Sociale Italiano Ad Alleanza Nazionale* (Bologna: Il Mulino, 1994). See also Chapter 4.

people, [. . .] and to be able to influence the fortunes of the world'.[12] Similar points were also iterated in the minority congress motion brought forward by Pino Rauti, the leader of the MSI's spiritual, anti-modern, anti-capitalist (and anti-NATO) current,[13] in which his faction highlighted the need to make Europe a 'Third Way' that could mediate between the 'twin imperialisms' so as to 're-establish equilibrium' and 'lead world politics out of the duopolistic logic in which it has been closed for 35 years'.[14]

In the MSI's view, retrieving power was essential to the fulfilment of Europe's 'secular mission'.[15] While viewing Europe as currently in decline and having lost its leading place in the world as a force acting for civilization, the party claimed the need for Europe to retrieve the glorious influence of its past. The results of the European mission, as well as its future, were well captured by Pino Romualdi in the *Intervista* when he speaks of Europe's aim as

> a secular mission, certainly not free from mistakes and cruelty, but that cannot keep being considered as a crime, a disgusting sin [. . .] which one must make amends for through inconceivable concessions in all fields to countries and people still or in good part incapable of the great cultural, moral and political commitments and of those of the development of the human conditions of their peoples, in the respect and defence of the fundamental values of civilization. A civilizing endeavour which Europeans and the whole Western world need to be proud of in terms of what it represented concretely for the growth of the idea of liberty and feeling of national independence [. . .] in territories and between populations otherwise destined to remain for centuries or millennia in a backward state.[16]

Romualdi's vision here expresses a few familiar ideas. First, underlying the entire paragraph is the view of European civilization as superior to other civilizations, as highlighted by the view that countries colonized by Europeans would have otherwise remained for 'centuries or millennia in a backward state'. Second, however, and more importantly for this idea of external power, is the will to reclaim that heritage which, while not 'free from mistakes',

---

[12] Movimento Sociale Italiano, 'Continuare per Rinnovare. Mozione Congressuale XII Congresso Napoli' (Fondo Movimento Sociale Italiano (serie 1, busta 6, fascicolo 21). Archivio Fondazione Ugo Spirito, Roma, Italia, 1979).
[13] Salvatore Vassallo and Rinaldo Vignati, *Fratelli Di Giorgia: Il Partito Della Destra Nazional-Conservatrice* (Bologna: Il Mulino, 2023).
[14] Movimento Sociale Italiano, 'Spazio Nuovo. Mozione Congressuale XII Congresso Napoli' (Fondo Movimento Sociale Italiano (serie 1, busta 6, fascicolo 21). Archivio Fondazione Ugo Spirito, Roma, Italia, 1979).
[15] Romualdi, *Intervista Sull'Europa*, 17.
[16] Ibid.

should not stop Europe from fulfilling its role in educating and developing those parts of the world in which the fundamental values of civilization have not been fully acquired. The recognition of a European mission thus led the MSI to view Europe's natural role as that of a great power which should 'express its will in the international scene'[17] and 'return to be a protagonist in the world'.[18] Liberty as power, in this sense, served to both characterize Europe's nature and define its future role in opposition to the hegemonic powers of the time.

The MSI's focus on a great power Europe was by and large in opposition to what the EU looked like at the time. Much of the EU's early integration focused on economic aspects, with little to no engagement on matters of foreign policy.[19] The EU's primarily economic nature was problematized by the party, as it asserted that the EU's focus on economic integration meant it remained insufficiently 'political'—that is, insufficiently strong on foreign policy matters (see also Chapter 5). In the *Intervista*, for example, Romualdi lamented that part of the problem with Europe's lack of external power lay in the fact that the EU had not been built with the idea of becoming a great power at its heart.[20] Similar points were raised a decade later by the then leader of the youth branch of the MSI (Fronte Universitario d'Azione Nazionale, FUAN) and future MP, Maurizio Gasparri. In an article in party newspaper *Secolo d'Italia*, Gasparri both expressed the need for 'a united Europe' as 'the right way, the only one that Europe can follow if it wants to return to thinking big, if it wants to build a future of political, military and cultural autonomy, if it wants to measure up with its great past', and criticized the EU's limited ambitions in this area. Thus, he continued,

> it is a 'long march' that awaits us. We must face it because we are the only ones [. . .] that do not mistake a deal on legal tenders or on passports for a historical change. We need more! Our Nations alone cannot compare with the great empires. A common policy and a common defence are a binding necessity. [. . .] To return to making history, not being subject to it![21]

---

[17] Movimento Sociale Italiano, *Il Msi-Dn Dalla a Alla Zeta: Principii Programmatici, Politici e Dottrinari Esposti Da Cesare Mantovani, Con Presentazione Del Segretario Nazionale Giorgio Almirante* (Rome: Movimento sociale italiano-Destra nazionale, Ufficio propaganda, 1980), 25.

[18] Movimento Sociale Italiano, 'Destra '80. Mozione Congressuale, XIII Congresso Roma', *Il Secolo d'Italia*, 17 January 1982.

[19] Federiga M. Bindi, *The Foreign Policy of the European Union: Assessing Europe's Role in the World* (Washington, DC: Brookings Institution Press, 2010).

[20] Romualdi, *Intervista Sull'Europa*, 23.

[21] Maurizio Gasparri, 'Alla Logica Della Moneta Opporremo Storia e Cultura', *Secolo d'Italia*, 7 April 1988.

The MSI was not, however, simply a disinterested supporter of European power, but rather a supporter of European power with a strong Italian component to it. This is most clear in the MSI's statements concerning which areas of the world a powerful Europe should build stronger links with. Specifically, the party identified Latin America and the Mediterranean as strategic areas for European involvement.[22] In the case of Latin America, the MSI hoped that Italy would be able to play a role thanks to its numerous immigrant communities (a recurrent theme in party documents). The Mediterranean focus, on the other hand, was intimately related to another core issue for the party: the Italian South (the MSI's main electoral constituency), and the hope to contribute to its development by shifting the focus of politics and Europe from a Northern to a Southern perspective. European power, then, was a vehicle to pursue the European mission, but also a way to pursue national goals and restore Italy's influence in Europe.

References to a 'free' and 'political' Europe did not disappear following the MSI's transformation into AN, but the party's approach to Europe through the prism of liberty was significantly recast. As part of a broader transformation in which the party moved on from its neo-fascist heritage to embrace several elements of the liberal-democratic tradition,[23] AN also changed its approach to the notion of European autonomy. Reflecting a changed historical context in which Europe was no longer divided but the European Union had acquired new powers, as well as a renewed interest on the part of AN to become a party of government and stress its commitment to democracy and its institutions,[24] AN started tackling questions about the balance between a nation's ability to pass its own laws and the need for shared European commitments. Unlike the MSI, which focused primarily on the notion of Europe as a continent needing to become free from external control, AN's post-Fiuggi documents recentred on concerns about national collective self-rule and democracy within the European Union.

A first instance of AN's new focus on democracy is visible in the *Tesi di Fiuggi* (Fiuggi Theses). The *Tesi* were prepared on the occasion of AN's founding congress in 1995. The congress marked the party's transition from 'neo-fascism' to 'post-fascism' (although in its early phases, the difference between the two was moderate at best)[25] and the *Tesi* outlined the party's

---

[22] Movimento Sociale Italiano, 'Programma Elezioni 1987', *Secolo d'Italia*, 12 May 1987.
[23] Chiarini and Maraffi, *La Destra Allo Specchio*.
[24] Sofia Vasilopoulou, *Far Right Parties and Euroscepticism: Patterns of Opposition* (London; New York: Rowman & Littlefield, 2018); Chiarini and Maraffi, *La Destra Allo Specchio*.
[25] Roger Griffin, 'The "Post-Fascism" of the Alleanza Nazionale: A Case Study in Ideological Morphology', *Journal of Political Ideologies* 1, no. 2 (1996): 123–145, doi:10.1080/13569319608420733; Marco Tarchi, *Dal MSI Ad AN: Organizzazione e Strategie* (Bologna: Il Mulino, 1997); Ignazi, *Postfascisti?*.

new approach to politics. On European matters, the *Tesi* stressed how Italy should support those who were trying to give the EU a set of institutions 'able to democratically manage policies' falling under its competences 'in respect of the subsidiarity principle'.[26] This commitment to finding an appropriate balance between the national and the supranational, as well as to fostering democratic governance, is also discussed in a later document prepared for the 2002 programmatic conference tellingly called *Vince la Patria, Nasce l'Europa* (The Homeland wins, Europe is born). The document stresses the need to 'guarantee the maximum involvement of citizens and their respective representative bodies' in the European integration process and ensure that 'there is an actual recognition of the principle of subsidiarity'.[27]

If AN drew on the notion of democracy in its attempts to define the correct balance between the national and the supranational in the EU, it also employed it to critique certain features of the latter. In particular, its commitment to subsidiarity and national democratic involvement came with a strong opposition to bureaucratic and technocratic bodies in Brussels, perhaps the main point of convergence with the RN (albeit with some important differences). In fact, if AN considered the 'technocratic structures' of the EU as reflective of a 'Jacobin, technocratic, dirigiste and elitist Europe',[28] or as contributing to endangering the European project by taking ill-judged decisions,[29] it did not take this as a reason to reject the EU *in toto*. Democracy served to define the appropriate contours of the EU, not as a concept to be used against it. While the familiar debate on the EU's democratic deficit and its remoteness from its citizens made itself heard, this was mostly done in a pragmatic way in which the focus was on correcting perceptions and structures that gave rise to the issue, rather than merely pointing towards them as a source of illegitimacy for the EU as an actor.

The AN's new focus on matters of democracy and subsidiarity can be interpreted as reflecting an evolution in the notion of autonomy: if for the MSI autonomy was about Europe being free from external interference, for AN the real concern was to ensure that there was an appropriate balance between a nation's ability to decide its own measures (its ability to be autonomous from interference from the EU) and the need to pursue common policies that

---

[26] Alleanza Nazionale, 'Pensiamo l'Italia: Il Domani C'è Già. Valori, Idee e Progetti per l'Alleanza Nazionale' (retrieved from https://webcache.googleusercontent.com/search?q=cache:ws3qnPVyqTwJ:web.tiscali.it/riformistiandreolesi/Tesi%2520AN.doc+&cd=10&hl=it&ct=clnk&gl=it, 1995).
[27] Alleanza Nazionale, 'Vince La Patria, Nasce l'Europa. Bologna. 4–7 Aprile 2002', *Secolo d'Italia*, 4 April 2002.
[28] Alleanza Nazionale, 'Programma Elezioni Del Parlamento Europeo 12/13 Giugno 2004' (retrieved from European Manifesto Project, 2004).
[29] Agostino Carrino, 'Questa Europa Poco Amata Dagli Europei', *Secolo d'Italia*, 13 June 2008.

could enhance a nation's autonomy because they would be better tackled at the supranational level.

Where AN retained a stronger level of continuity with the MSI is in the definition of Europe through the notion of power, although it ceased to refer to an 'expansionist' project based on the superiority of European culture and shifted to a commitment more in line with mainstream discourses on the European Union's 'soft power'—that is, its ability to influence the behaviour of others through persuasion, attraction, and values.[30] AN thus moderated its view of power, removing its hierarchical characteristics, while remaining committed to the idea that Europe (in the shape of the EU) had some mission to fulfil in the world. Evidence of AN's moderation in terms of its understanding of power was present from its foundation. In the Fiuggi Theses, the newly created AN insisted on some traditional themes of the MSI, such as pursuing the objective of giving weight to the 'Great Europe' by strengthening the European pillar of NATO and ensuring that the fall of communist regimes in Central and Eastern Europe did not distract from the need for a Mediterranean policy and a stronger focus on the Middle East. However, it also predicated a role for Europe in international development, 'encouraging cooperation aimed at self-centred development of the beneficiary countries, the selection of credible political classes in the developing world, the education of the technical and managerial personnel that can manage long-term projects in developing countries, [and] renegotiating the debt accumulated by poor countries.'[31]

This gradual shift to a 'soft power' project continued in subsequent years, at first remaining fairly faithful to old lines, but then integrating them with new commitments. Thus, if the 1999 European election manifesto highlighted the need for political union and a common foreign policy to restore Europe's power in the external realm,[32] later documents coupled this with concerns such as human rights, human dignity, stability, and prosperity, including a call in 2000 for different relationships with totalitarian countries that violate these values.[33] This brought AN's notion of power broadly in line with that of the EU, all the while reassessing the notion that Europe had a mission to fulfil in the world.

---

[30] Kristian L Nielsen, 'EU Soft Power and the Capability–Expectations Gap', *Journal of Contemporary European Research* 9, no. 5 (2013), doi:10.30950/jcer.v9i5.479; Joseph S. Nye, *Soft Power: The Means to Success in World Politics*, first edition. (New York: Public Affairs, 2004).
[31] Alleanza Nazionale, 'Pensiamo l'Italia: Il Domani C'è Già. Valori, Idee e Progetti per l'Alleanza Nazionale'.
[32] Alleanza Nazionale, 'Elezioni Europee '99: Programma Politico' (retrieved from European Manifesto Project, 1999).
[33] Alleanza Nazionale, 'Valori e Idee Senza Compromessi: Manifesto Dei Valori', *Secolo d'Italia*, 2000.

To sum up, the MSI/AN relied on the notion of liberty to define Europe as a continent in need of autonomy in the 1980s, and to reflect on crucial issues of self-rule emerging from increased European integration in the 1990s. Most notably, however, the party maintained a strong continuity in its notion of Europe as a continent with a historical mission to project power in the external realm so as to ensure balance in the world. Thus, the concept of liberty as power was essential in its approach to Europe, insofar as it is through the prism of power that it understood its past, its nature, and its future mission.

From autonomy for Europe to self-rule against the EU: the Rassemblement National's sovereigntist evolution

As with the MSI/AN, the concept of liberty occupied a central place in the RN's definition of Europe. Equally, the party's use of the term evolved over time: while in the 1980s, the RN demanded a 'free and powerful' Europe, from the 1990s onwards it began claiming the need for the nation to re-establish (democratic) self-rule against an ever-encroaching EU.

The RN's early approach to Europe through the prism of liberty bears significant resemblance to that of the MSI. Like the Italian party, the RN observed a declining influence of Europe and identified the USSR and the USA as the main culprits in this situation. As Jean-Marie Le Pen put it in his programmatic book, *Français d'abord*, 'What appeared to post-war men is that, following the occupations of Europe by the Soviet army, the appearance of the two super-giants on the world scene, our European nations [...] had brusquely fallen to the status of, if one may say it, second-order nations'.[34] As with the MSI, this observation of the decline of Europe paved the way for an analysis that pushed for 'the right of the European peoples to rule themselves, to self-affirm and search for power and global reach in the respect of their roots'.[35] To achieve this, the RN advocated a 'European irredentism':[36] the reunification with the 'captive nations' of Eastern Europe, and the 'mooring' of Western Germany to the European Community, so as to avoid Germany 'falling prey to the temptation of being united under the authority of Moscow'.[37] Additionally, like the MSI, in the 1980s the RN also pushed for

---

[34] Jean-Marie Le Pen, *Les Français d'abord* (Paris: Carrère—Michel Lafon, 1984), 157.
[35] Jean-Marie Le Pen, *Pour La France: Programme Du Front National* (Paris: Albatros, 1985), 189.
[36] Carl Lang, 'Jeunesse Nation Europe', *La Lettre de Jean-Marie Le Pen*, 1987; Le Pen, *Les Français d'abord*.
[37] Le Pen, *Pour La France*, 190.

a common European defence policy as a means to ensure collective security and achieve European autonomy.³⁸

As was the case for the MSI, ideas of liberty were entwined with notions of European power because, as Bruno Mégret, the RN's number two at the time, highlighted, 'Europe will be free only if it is powerful'.³⁹ The RN claimed that the need for Europe to have power was because this would allow it to be truly autonomous and fulfil its historical, civilizing mission. Le Pen summarized this state of affairs in his 1984 book when he said that 'Europe retreats, and civilization and liberty retreat with it; Europe is no longer Europe because it has resigned itself to not being the world'.⁴⁰ This single sentence captures both the feeling of European decline and the assessment that this is problematic, because the retreat of Europe has negative implications for 'civilization and liberty'.

Underlying the RN's view was the idea that Europe had some form of 'historical mission' to make the world more European, a mission that its decline did not allow it to pursue. This was further stressed a few years later by Bruno Mégret, when he exhorted, 'let us [Europeans] stop announcing everywhere in the world that we have no design to expand, let us stop behaving like guilty and assisted parties'.⁴¹ Just as for the MSI, there was a view of Europe as a civilization 'in retreat', made to feel guilty by others, but which should, on the contrary, reclaim its heritage and acquire a more active role in the world in the name of its clear superiority. In other words, Europe should exert power in the external realm because it is in its nature, and its duty, to do so.

For the RN, power, as Mégret put it, was essential for Europe because (in a similar way to autonomy) it allowed one to 'be a master of one's own fate'.⁴² This point is well made in the RN's *Passeport pour la victoire* (Passport to victory). The *Passeport* is a short booklet detailing the party's organization and positions, and includes a 'glossary' of key terms and a number of memorable quotes associated with important party issues. The entry for 'power (European)' presents the following quote:

> One cannot build a true community except by affirming oneself as autonomous and different compared to others. Let us state clearly what objective the European construction must pursue. For us, it is [a] triple [objective]: firstly, power; secondly, power; thirdly, power.

---

³⁸ Le Pen, *Les Français d'abord*; Le Pen, *Pour La France*.
³⁹ Bruno Mégret, 'Construire l'Europe de La Puissance' (Paris: Cahiers Communication Interne, Bibliothèque Nationale de France, 1987).
⁴⁰ Le Pen, *Les Français d'abord*, 164.
⁴¹ Cited in Front National, *Passeport Pour La Victoire* (Paris: Front National, 1989).
⁴² Mégret, 'Construire l'Europe de La Puissance'.

Power, because without power, Europe will lose its independence, its identity and will cease to be a master of its own fate.

Power, because power is life and nations are like living beings: if they are not expanding, they are regressing.

Power, because, without it, nothing great can be done.[43]

The passage is extracted from a speech given by Mégret in the French parliament at the time of the debates on the Single European Act. Presenting an alternative, non-economic form of development for the EU, underlying the entire passage is the idea that a nation or continent which is not powerful cannot be free, as it is always going to depend on others to preserve its autonomy. This leads Mégret to assert the need for a European construction endowed with power. Power becomes a constitutive part of Europe, the condition for true autonomy, as a Europe which cannot express itself outside its own borders cannot be truly free.

While the argument that Mégret brought forward in the previous passage pushed for a more powerful European Union, it should also be noted that it was not unselfish. In the bipolar world of the 1980s, and the unipolar one of the early 1990s, the RN was unsure about individual nations' ability to exert power by themselves, although it also thought that France was stronger than others, and hence better placed to act as a guide for everyone else. As a result, Europe was seen as a necessary 'means for its Nation States to find together the power they have lost during the fratricidal wars they engaged in and that they left the USA and the USSR to arbitrate'.[44] The idea of power was also selected as key to the project of European unity because it was the only principle that 'respects the identity and sovereignty of European nations'.[45] Thus, power became central to the construction of Europe not only as a marker of its collective freedom, but also as a means to protect the internal freedom of the individual member states.

As was the case for identity, and for reasons similar to those discussed in Chapter 2, the RN's message on liberty shifted between the turn of the decade and the early 1990s. Following the emergence of a 'unipolar' world order dominated by the USA and the departure of Bruno Mégret (one of the architects of the party's position on European power) from the party in 1998, notions of European power all but disappeared in Jean-Marie Le Pen's RN. In Marine Le Pen's RN, the notion of power does make the occasional

---

[43] Front National, *Passeport Pour La Victoire*.
[44] Front National, *Militer au Front* (Paris: Editions Nationales, 1991), 118.
[45] Jean-Marie Le Pen, *Le Contrat Pour La France Avec Les Français* (Paris: Ed. Nationales, 1995), 41; Front National, *300 Mesures Pour La Renaissance de La France* (Paris: Editions Nationales, 1993).

comeback, but when power is mentioned, it is usually presented as one of the EU's 'broken promises',[46] or as something that 'Europe' (rather than the EU—see Chapter 2) and its nations should retrieve. For example, the RN's 2012 manifesto insists that France's power is being limited by the EU or, to be even more specific, by a political class that is 'subjugated' by a globalist ideology that reduced France's foreign policy to the European horizon by aligning it with the United States.[47] The RN's 2019 European electoral manifesto, for its part, stresses how the European Alliance of Nations, an alliance of European far-right parties, is interested in supporting the project of a 'Europe of nations and citizens'.[48] 'Faced with the great empires that want to structure the world in the 21st century', the manifesto continues, this Europe would 'assert its ambitions to be powerful and influential' and 'retrieve its historical position of primary agent for world peace'.[49] However, this would only be done by centring individual nations, rather than facilitating collective action through EU institutions.

Additionally, the exponential growth in the powers of the European Union that started with the Single European Act and continued through the Maastricht, Amsterdam, Nice, and Lisbon treaties led the RN to shift away from reclaiming 'European autonomy'. Instead, it brought the theme of liberty as domestic self-rule front and centre and developed its trademark critique of the EU as a construction stifling domestic sovereignty, defined in the 2002 manifesto as 'the collective form of liberty: the freedom of a people to decide about its future, that which is also known as independence, the freedom of individuals to live in the framework of laws they have consented to'.[50] Since the 1990s, the RN's radical critique of the EU through the prism of democracy and self-rule is built around two axes: that the EU is a body that shifts power away from the nation through encroachment and a questionable institutional architecture; and, as a result, that it is deeply unrepresentative of popular claims. The concept of liberty is thus redeployed to oppose the European construction and redefine it as a threat to the nation's ability to pass whatever measures it considers appropriate.

---

[46] Marine Le Pen, 'Metz—Discours de Marine Le Pen—1er Mai', May 2019, https://rassemblementnational.fr/discours/metz-discours-de-marine-le-pen-1er-mai; Rassemblement National, 'Pour Une Europe Des Nations et Des Peuples (Projet - Elections Européennes)', 2019, https://www.politique-animaux.fr/sites/www.politique-animaux.fr/fichiers/prises-de-positions/pieces-jointes/europeennes-projet-rn.pdf.

[47] Front National, 'Notre Projet: Programme Politique Du Front National' (retrieved from www.frontnational.com, 2012).

[48] Rassemblement National, 'Pour Une Europe Des Nations. Manifeste Pour Une Nouvelle Coopération En Europe: "L'Alliance Européenne Des Nations"', 2019.

[49] Ibid.

[50] Front National, 'Programme Du Front National' (retrieved from Comparative Manifesto Project, 2002).

If we start with the first axis of critique, the party's 2004 Euromanifesto offers a good illustration of the RN's opposition to the EU on grounds of institutional design and encroachment. Prepared in the context of the European elections of 2004, the manifesto claims that the history of the EU consists of 'depriving States of their sovereignty' because 'Europe has seen its areas of intervention becoming larger' and then 'because the organization and functioning of the European institutions, as well as their decision-making, tend more and more to lead the notion of Nation-State itself to disappear and to entrust power to technocrats in Brussels'.[51] Encroachment, as the passage suggests, expands the powers of the EU at the expense of the member states, potentially limiting their ability to take decisions freely. Its functioning, on the other side, tends to bypass the nation and empower 'technocrats' with no visible national allegiances or democratic legitimacy.

The link between encroachment and limits to self-rule is exemplified more clearly by Jean-Marie Le Pen in a campaign speech from 2007, where the then leader expressed the feeling that the centre of decision-making had 'quit the Elysée and Matignon to install itself in the European quarter of Brussels',[52] leaving France without much control over its own destiny. As the same speech detailed it further,

> They know that we no longer decide anything by ourselves, that all is decided elsewhere, most often against us, against our interests, against our traditions and our values. We no longer decide of our own laws, they are made in Brussels. We no longer decide by ourselves who comes in and out of our country [. . .]. We no longer decide what goods come into our country because there are no commercial barriers. We no longer decide by ourselves on our economic policies, because we no longer have a national currency, no more budgetary and monetary room for manoeuvre, no right to lead any industrial policy. We no longer have the right to make, by ourselves, our labour law, our commercial law, our environmental laws.[53]

The opposition to the EU's impingement on each of the types of sovereignty named above appears in several other places, with legal sovereignty and, increasingly since the introduction of the euro, economic sovereignty occupying particularly central roles. Both, in addition, also allow for a more thorough critique of political classes in general, drawing on populist tropes.

---

[51] Front National, 'Programme Pour Les Élections Européennes de 2004' (Retrieved from European Manifesto Project, 2004).
[52] Jean-Marie Le Pen, 'Discours à Toulouse Sur Le Thème de l'Europe' (Retrieved from Archives de l'Internet, Bibliothèque nationale de France, 2007).
[53] Ibid.

Thus, for example, the loss of legal sovereignty is associated with a critique of the national political class, which merely 'translates directives from Brussels', being 'reduced to the level of translators for laws coming from elsewhere'.[54] Similarly, the loss of economic sovereignty feeds into a discourse about the 'global elites' and the dominance of economic power over national decision-making. The RN's 2019 European election programme illustrates this well when advocating that 'European elites have delivered Europe to forces belonging to a fictitious world market, in which public and private powers, states or multinational corporations, use all means to defend their interests', with little regard for national decision-making. The manifesto further argues for the return to a 'primacy of politics' over economics and for placing states back at the heart of the EU's institutions.[55]

The result of the empowerment of the EU and the 'Brussels bureaucrats' feeds into the second line of criticism of the EU as a body that is deeply unrepresentative of popular claims and even opposed to recognizing them. Concerns over self-rule here merge with considerations on popular sovereignty, and further develop the party's criticism of the EU on grounds of liberty. Brussels is accused of pushing for the replacement of popular sovereignty with 'expert' decision-making,[56] or, even worse, with external domination by the 'EUSSR'. As Bruno Gollnisch put it in a speech, the 'European Soviet Union' is little more than 'an ensemble whose leaders are not picked by the people and are often unknown to them, meaning that they cannot control or revoke them, and who however tend to rule over all the domains of political, economic and social life'. In his view, attempting to resist it is futile because 'resistance, even when it has the law on its side, is systematically hidden, bypassed, despised'.[57] These critiques remain present to this day: in the 2019 EU election manifesto, the RN accused the European Commission of knowingly governing against the people and being ready to resort to all sorts of 'legal tricks and measures to prevent the people from taking

---

[54] Marc Langlois, 'Non à Bruxelles Oui à l'Europe Des Nations', *Nations Presses Magasine*, May 2014.
[55] Rassemblement National, 'Pour Une Europe Des Nations. Manifeste Pour Une Nouvelle Coopération En Europe: "L'Alliance Européenne Des Nations"', 25.
[56] Front National, 'Le Front National Pour Restaurer Notre Identité Nationale Face à l'Europe Fédérale', *Français d'Abord*, Novermber, no 1, 1999.
[57] Bruno Gollisch, 'A Propos de l'Union Soviétique Européenne—Discours de Bruno Gollnisch à l'occasion de l'université d'été Du FN' (retrieved from Archives de l'Internet, Bibliothèque nationale de France, 2008); For similar ideas, see also Bruno Mégret, 'Les Principes Fondateurs de Notre Europe', *La Lettre de Jean-Marie Le Pen*, May, no 2, 1989; Catherine Salagnac, 'L'engrenage de Maastricht', *La Lettre de Jean-Marie Le Pen*, May, no 1, 1992; Front National, 'Notre Projet: Programme Politique Du Front National'.

their own decisions'.[58] Elsewhere, Marine Le Pen defined the EU as 'a totalitarian power that controls, rules and regulates' from the outside and 'puts in place a prison-like view of Europe'.[59] All these elements lead the RN to reclaim sovereignty for the nation (a regular theme in party programmes and one which has survived two leadership changes),[60] because, as Jean-Marie Le Pen put it, 'no good is more precious than independence, the collective manifestation of the collective liberty of peoples'.[61]

Revisiting national and European narratives: legitimacy through shared narratives

Narratives of liberty, the previous sections have shown, were central to the MSI/AN and the RN's definition of Europe, but how did they contribute to their legitimation efforts? In the remainder of this chapter, I argue that the increased focus on questions of liberty helped the parties bring attention to elements of their ideology that are not exclusive to them, but part of the shared language of national politics. These shared narratives signalled acceptability, making the MSI/AN and RN look aligned with others but not like others.

To understand the significance of the growing focus on the concept of liberty, it is helpful to consider how it differs from that of identity discussed in the previous chapter. Chapter 1 suggested that political ideologies are constellations of concepts, in which some concepts occupy a central and frequently more visible place, and others occupy adjacent and peripheral positions. For far-right parties whose ideological core is defined by nationalism, identity occupies a uniquely central place. It is the 'coat-hanger' concept around which all others revolve.[62] Although other parties may occasionally appeal to it, they rarely do so with the intensity of the far right. Crucially, however, identity is frequently (albeit not always) negatively connotated,[63] and especially so when discussed by the far right. Because identity in their discourse is

---

[58] Rassemblement National, 'Pour Une Europe Des Nations Et Des Peuples (Projet—Elections Européennes)'.
[59] Marine Le Pen, 'Discours de Marine Le Pen à Kintzheim', February 2018, https://rassemblementnational.fr/discours/discours-de-marine-le-pen-a-kintzheim.
[60] Marta Lorimer, 'What Is It, and Why Does It Matter? The Meaning of Sovereignty in the Rassemblement National's Critique of European Integration', in *Sovereignty in Conflict—Political, Constitutional and Economic Dilemmas in the EU*, by Nathalie Brack et al. (Basingstoke, Hants: Palgrave, 2023), 165–182.
[61] Jean-Marie Le Pen, 'Aucun Bien N'est Plus Précieux Que l'Indépendance', *Français d'Abord*, October 2004: 3–4.
[62] Cas Mudde, *Populist Radical Right Parties in Europe* (Cambridge: Cambridge University Press, 2007), doi:10.1111/j.1478-9302.2009.00194.x.
[63] Amy Gutmann, *Identity in Democracy* (Princeton, NJ: Princeton University Press, 2003).

usually associated with dynamics of extreme exclusion (as the term 'nativism' captures), it is an unlikely contender for the construction of shared narratives. The concept of liberty discussed in this chapter is different from that of identity in at least two ways. Unlike the concept of identity, it carries a generally positive connotation. It is also less exclusive to the far right, and functions as a foundational concept in most (if not all) European societies.

The growing focus on liberty becomes consequential once these differences between the concepts of identity and liberty are acknowledged. When the MSI/AN and RN started speaking more consistently of European issues, they did two things. First, they altered the balance between (negatively connotated) identity-related themes and (positively connotated) liberty-related arguments in their ideology. The change in the balance of concepts enabled them to bring focus away from a more divisive topic to more acceptable ideas. Second, the increased focus on liberty opened up the possibility for the parties to stress elements that were not exclusive to them, but shared more widely across the polity. This applied both in the parties' views of power, and most strongly in their approach to questions of liberty as self-rule.

To develop this contention, it is helpful to look at how the MSI/AN and RN's focus on liberty testifies to a process of 'mainstreaming' that involves not the adoption of policy positions close to those of mainstream parties specifically, but rather the embracing of ideas that are shared across the polity. Starting with the idea of liberty as power in the external realm, the previous sections showed that the MSI/AN and the RN suggested that Europe and their respective nations had a duty to fulfil in the world. While this claim may be seen as problematic because of its imperialist undertones, it also shares some commonalities with national and EU narratives about what Europe is for, and what its role in the world should be. Thus, for example, the views expressed by the RN in the 1980s, about France leading a 'great power' Europe, appear as strongly aligned with French perceptions of Europe as 'France written large' and the EU as a means to project power lost following decolonization.[64] It is equally possible to find echoes of EU statements in the positions held by the parties in the 1970s and 1980s. For example, it may be worth noting the parallels between the 1970s declaration on European identity—which stated that

> the Europe of the Nine is aware that, as it unites, it takes on new international obligations. European unification is not directed against anyone, nor is it inspired by

---

[64] Robert Frank, 'The Meanings of Europe in French National Discourse: A French Europe or an Europeanized France?', in *The Meaning of Europe: Variety and Contention within and among Nations*, ed. Mikael af Malmborg and Bo Stråth (Oxford; New York: Berg, 2002), 311–326.

a desire for power. On the contrary, the Nine are convinced that their union will benefit the whole international community since it will constitute an element of equilibrium and a basis for co-operation with all countries, whatever their size, culture or social system[65]

—and our parties' claims to make Europe an 'element of equilibrium' in the world. While the EU declaration arguably rejects the concept of power so keenly espoused by the MSI/AN and RN (an element, however, which suggests that 'powerful' is how the EU is commonly perceived), it still expresses similar ideas about its need to take an active role in guaranteeing the international order. This awareness of a European 'mission' remains present in today's EU, when the Treaty on European Union insists on its role in seeking to advance key values such as 'democracy, the rule of law, the universality and indivisibility of human rights and fundamental freedoms, respect for human dignity, the principles of equality and solidarity, and respect for the principles of the United Nations Charter and international law'.[66] While the MSI/AN and RN no longer use this type of argument, this suggests that the EU maintains a mission to export its values beyond its borders, and project its power in the world. When the parties draw upon such ideas, then, they are drawing on ideas that are already there, and while they present them in a more radical fashion, they are not acting in a void but reinterpreting and expressing views that are shared with the mainstream. In this sense, what they have to say about national and European missions resonates with other narratives about European and national 'missions'.

If ideas of power in the hands of far-right parties always risk remaining deeply suspicious because of their possible association with the legacies of European imperialism (and these ideas did indeed appear in the MSI/AN and RN's views), their views on matters of self-rule, autonomy, and democracy presented less problematic features and chimed even more strongly with existing discourses on the nation.[67] This is particularly true when it comes to the concept of sovereignty. While the analysis so far has eschewed the term sovereignty in an attempt to reflect the parties' own language, the ideas expressed by the MSI/AN and RN on liberty as (democratic) self-rule and autonomy retrace the internal and external facets of national sovereignty.

---

[65] European Union, 'Declaration on European Identity', no. 12 (1973): 118–122.
[66] European Union, *Consolidated Version of the Treaty on European Union*, 2007, art. 21, https://eur-lex.europa.eu/legal-content/EN/TXT/?uri=CELEX%3A12012M%2FTXT.
[67] It is worth noting that the timing of the emergence of this discourse seems to broadly coincide with the moment in which these parties became more consistently successful. As noted above, concerns about autonomy, self-rule, and democracy acquired more centrality from the early 1990s, when the RN cemented its strength and the MSI/AN successfully entered government for the first time.

Internal sovereignty corresponds most clearly to the idea of self-rule, suggesting that 'the state has the absolute power to make decisions on every aspect of human life', whereas external sovereignty can be defined as indicating that the state is 'independent of every other external power',[68] and hence autonomous, as our parties would have it.

National sovereignty is far from being a principle that matters exclusively to far-right parties. While, given the place the nation occupies in their ideology, it may matter to them more than to others, it is also a key principle in the functioning of the state and part of a common way of thinking about the nation. Within the Italian and French contexts specifically, the relevance of the principle of sovereignty can be inferred by its presence in the opening sections of their constitutions: the French Constitution proclaims an attachment to the principle of 'national sovereignty' in the preamble and dedicates its second constitutional article to it, while the Italian Constitution consents to limitations of sovereignty 'in parity with other states' for the maintenance of peace and justice among nations. As a result, when the parties draw upon these concepts to define Europe and their policies on the EU, they are tapping into widely accepted constitutional principles to advance their claims.

Appropriating widely shared values of the state system in defining their positioning on the EU helped the parties present themselves as more aligned with what is considered legitimate. It allowed them to claim that they were committed to certain elements of politics that are not exceptional, but rather shared across the political spectrum. As was the case for their stated attachment to Europe discussed in the previous chapter, however, using the language of liberty also enabled them to maintain continuity with existing beliefs because it restated the core idea that a nation should be able to politically manifest its will.[69] In short, Europe functioned as an ideological resource because it facilitated their efforts to present themselves as broadly aligned with what is considered 'normal' in their own societies, all the while remaining faithful to their own beliefs because the ideas they draw upon are still consistent with their own ideology.

In the case of AN, this process of adopting shared values was flanked by a more traditional process of mainstreaming intended as adopting the

---

[68] Michel Troper, 'Sovereignty', in *The Oxford Handbook of Comparative Constitutional Law*, ed. Michel Rosenfeld and András Sajó, 2012, 354–356, doi:10.1093/oxfordhb/9780199578610.013.0019.

[69] Atsuko Ichijo, 'Sovereignty and Nationalism in the Twenty-First Century: The Scottish Case', *Ethnopolitics* 8, no. 2 (2009): 156, doi:10.1080/17449050902761624; Alan Patten, 'The Autonomy Argument for Liberal Nationalism', *Nations and Nationalism* 5, no. 1 (1999): 1, doi:10.1111/j.1354-5078.1999.00001.x; Elie Kedourie, *Nationalism* (Oxford: Blackwell, 1993), 1; see also Chapter 5 for a more thorough discussion.

positions of other mainstream parties. Discussions of subsidiarity and competences are common within mainstream right-wing parties,[70] so AN's approach to European integration through this prism indicates a move towards the positions held by other parties in the mainstream. For the RN, the story was different because the party adopted a more radical position concerning European integration than it had done before. However, it justified its radical stance in the name of mainstream principles such as autonomy, self-rule, and democracy. Rather than trying to look like a mainstream conservative party, the RN drew upon certain foundational ideas of politics to defend its positions on the EU.

At this point, it could be noted that the similarities between far-right parties and the mainstream of politics are not only present in their ideology of Europe, but are present in their ideology more generally.[71] If we accept that far-right parties are 'well connected to mainstream ideas and much in tune with broadly shared mass attitudes and policy positions',[72] why would what they have to say about liberty with respect to Europe make them any more legitimate than what they have to say about immigration, or economic policy?

The answer to this question is two-fold. First, we can see this as a case of *'repetita iuvant'*. Scholars have highlighted the importance of repeating messages for politicians.[73] Publics are frequently distracted, and are unlikely to be hanging on the every word of political actors. Repeating these points within a different context, and in a different arena, might alert to their presence those who had previously not noticed them, or bring them again to mind to those who had. In this context, what the parties say in general and what they say on Europe reinforce each other.

Most importantly, however, repeating them with respect to the European Union can make a difference because of the way in which the European Union is commonly seen to affect a nation's liberty. The EU challenges notions of autonomy, democracy, and self-rule in several ways. It (partially) displaces the nation as the natural space of politics. It creates legislation that is

---

[70] Carlo Invernizzi Accetti, *What Is Christian Democracy? Politics, Religion and Ideology* (Cambridge: Cambridge University Press, 2019); Michael Schneider, 'Europe Must Deliver at the Level Closest to the Citizens Subsidiarity: Past, Present and Future', *European View* 18, no. 1 (April 2019): 16–25, doi:10.1177/1781685819844466.

[71] Mudde. 'The Populist Radical Right'; Tim Bale, 'Cinderella and Her Ugly Sisters: The Mainstream and Extreme Right in Europe's Bipolarising Party Systems', *West European Politics* 26 (2003): 75.

[72] Mudde, 'The Populist Radical Right', 1178.

[73] William L. Benoit et al., 'Staying "On Message": Consistency in Content of Presidential Primary Campaign Messages Across Media', *American Behavioral Scientist* 55, no. 4 (April 2011): 457–468, doi:10.1177/0002764211398072; Michael J. Burton, William J. Miller, and Daniel M. Shea, *Campaign Craft: The Strategies, Tactics, and Art of Political Campaign Management* (Santa Barbara, CA: ABC-CLIO, LLC, 2015).

binding on its member states, although it is not made exclusively by nationals and is unlikely to respond to the ideal interest of any member state because it is the result of balancing the interests of several member states.[74] In legal terms, the principles of direct effect and supremacy of EU law indicate that in certain areas, no matter how much the 'popular will' desires it, a member state is unable to implement measures in conflict with EU law.[75] The limitations of the EU's legitimacy in these areas form part of a broader set of critical approaches to the status of democracy and sovereignty in the EU. Debates on the EU's 'democratic deficit' and its complex relationship with popular sovereignty,[76] and more recently, critical assessments of the EU's actions in times of crisis[77] are features of academic and political analyses of the EU beyond the far right. Within the French context, they also chime with strong levels of party-based and popular Euroscepticism.[78] These issues are not raised exclusively by parties such as the RN and in a more moderate form, by the MSI/AN—they are present well beyond them. Criticism of the EU on these grounds by the parties, then, can be particularly effective because it suggests the parties are not only holding positions that are acceptable, but also saying things that sound credible and consistent with the analyses of other actors around them: they bear the ring of a shared truth.

Conclusion

Mainstreaming can be a tricky strategy for far-right parties if it entails becoming like other parties. However, once mainstreaming is interpreted more broadly as the process of stressing views and values that belong to the mainstream of politics, a new path to legitimation opens. This chapter

---

[74] Fritz W. Scharpf, 'The Joint-Decision Trap Revisited', *JCMS: Journal of Common Market Studies* 44, no. 4 (2006): 845–864, doi:10.1111/j.1468-5965.2006.00665.x; Christine Reh, 'European Integration as Compromise', *Government and Opposition* 47, no. 3 (2012): 414–440.

[75] Karen J. Alter, *Establishing the Supremacy of European Law: The Making of an International Rule of Law in Europe* (Oxford: Oxford University Press, 2003).

[76] Nathalie Brack, Ramona Coman, and Amandine Crespy, 'Unpacking Old and New Conflicts of Sovereignty in the European Polity', *Journal of European Integration* 41, no. 7 (2019): 817–832, doi:10.1080/07036337.2019.1665657; Andreas Follesdal and Simon Hix, 'Why There Is a Democratic Deficit in the EU: A Response to Majone and Moravcsik', *JCMS: Journal of Common Market Studies* 44, no. 3 (2006): 533–562, doi:10.1111/j.1468-5965.2006.00650.x; Peter Mair, *Ruling the Void: The Hollowing of Western Democracy* (London; New York: Verso, 2013), 201.

[77] Diane Fromage and Ton van den Brink, 'Democratic Legitimation of EU Economic Governance: Challenges and Opportunities for European Legislatures', *Journal of European Integration* 40, no. 3 (April 2018): 235–248, doi:10.1080/07036337.2018.1450407; Jonathan White, *Politics of Last Resort: Governing by Emergency in the European Union* (Oxford: Oxford University Press, 2019).

[78] Gabriel Goodliffe, 'Europe's Salience and "Owning" Euroscepticism: Explaining the Front National's Victory in the 2014 European Elections in France', *French Politics* 13, no. 4 (December 2015): 324–345, doi:10.1057/fp.2015.19; Eurobarometer, '*Public Opinion in the European Union. Eurobarometer 92, Autumn 2019*' (Brussels: European Commission, 2019).

has shown how integrating Europe in their ideology unlocked this path for the MSI/AN and the RN. It demonstrated how the early MSI/AN and RN spoke of Europe as a place that needed to be free and powerful, and how in the 1990s they increasingly insisted on the need to protect self-rule and democracy within the EU. Speaking of Europe in these terms shifted the balance of their ideology away from the potentially more divisive topic of identity to the more consensual one of liberty, and enabled the parties to stress their attachment to ideas that are shared across the political spectrum, rather than exclusive to themselves. The ways in which European integration affects nations provided their arguments with additional purchase by giving them the ring of truth. In sum, speaking of Europe in terms of liberty allowed the MSI/AN and RN to pursue mainstreaming through shared narratives, without losing their distinctiveness vis-à-vis other parties.

References

Accetti, Carlo Invernizzi. *What Is Christian Democracy? Politics, Religion and Ideology* (Cambridge: Cambridge University Press, 2019).

Alleanza Nazionale. 'Pensiamo l'Italia: Il Domani C'è Già. Valori, Idee e Progetti per l'Alleanza Nazionale' (retrieved from https://webcache.googleusercontent.com/search?q=cache:ws3qnPVyqTwJ:web.tiscali.it/riformistiandreolesi/Tesi%2520AN.doc+&cd=10&hl=it&ct=clnk&gl=it, 1995).

Alleanza Nazionale. 'Elezioni Europee '99: Programma Politico' (retrieved from European Manifesto Project, 1999).

Alleanza Nazionale. 'Valori e Idee Senza Compromessi: Manifesto Dei Valori'. *Secolo d'Italia*, 2000.

Alleanza Nazionale. 'Vince La Patria, Nasce l'Europa. Bologna. 4–7 Aprile 2002'. *Secolo d'Italia*, 4 April 2002.

Alleanza Nazionale. 'Programma Elezioni Del Parlamento Europeo 12/13 Giugno 2004' (retrieved from European Manifesto Project, 2004).

Almirante, Giorgio. *Intervista Sull'Eurodestra*. Edited by Michele Rallo (Palermo: Edizioni Thule, 1978).

Alter, Karen J. *Establishing the Supremacy of European Law: The Making of an International Rule of Law in Europe* (Oxford: Oxford University Press, 2003).

Bale, Tim. 'Cinderella and Her Ugly Sisters: The Mainstream and Extreme Right in Europe's Bipolarising Party Systems'. *West European Politics* 26 (2003): 67–90.

Benoit, William L., Mark J. Glantz, Anji L. Phillips, Leslie A. Rill, Corey B. Davis, Jayne R. Henson, and Leigh Anne Sudbrock. 'Staying "On Message": Consistency in Content of Presidential Primary Campaign Messages Across Media'. *American Behavioral Scientist* 55, no. 4 (April 2011): 457–468. https://doi.org/10.1177/0002764211398072.

Bindi, Federiga M. *The Foreign Policy of the European Union: Assessing Europe's Role in the World* (Washington, DC: Brookings Institution Press, 2010).

Brack, Nathalie, Ramona Coman, and Amandine Crespy. 'Unpacking Old and New Conflicts of Sovereignty in the European Polity'. *Journal of European Integration* 41, no. 7 (2019): 817–832. https://doi.org/10.1080/07036337.2019.1665657.

Burton, Michael J., William J. Miller, and Daniel M. Shea. *Campaign Craft: The Strategies, Tactics, and Art of Political Campaign Management* (Santa Barbara, CA: ABC-CLIO, LLC, 2015).

Caciagli, Mario. 'The Movimento Sociale Italiano-Destra Nazionale and Neo-Fascism in Italy'. In *Right-Wing Extremism in Western Europe*, edited by Klaus Beyme (London: Frank Cass, 1988), 19–46.

Carrino, Agostino. 'Questa Europa Poco Amata Dagli Europei'. *Secolo d'Italia*, 12 June 2008.

Carse, Alisa L. 'The Liberal Individual: A Metaphysical or Moral Embarrassment?' *Noûs* 28, no. 2 (1994): 184–209. https://doi.org/10.2307/2216048.

Chiarini, Roberto, and Marco Maraffi. *La Destra Allo Specchio: La Cultura Politica Di Alleanza Nazionale* (Venezia: Marsilio, 2001).

Eurobarometer. 'Public Opinion in the European Union. Eurobarometer 92 Autumn 2019' (Brussels: European Commission, 2019).

European Union. 'Declaration on European Identity', no. 12 (1973): 118–122.

European Union. *Consolidated Version of the Treaty on European Union*, 2007. https://eur-lex.europa.eu/legal-content/EN/TXT/?uri=CELEX%3A12012M%2FTXT.

Fennema, Meindert, and Marcel Maussen. 'Dealing with Extremists in Public Discussion: Front National and "Republican Front" in France'. *Journal of Political Philosophy* 8, no. 3 (2000): 379–400. https://doi.org/10.1111/1467-9760.00108.

Follesdal, Andreas, and Simon Hix. 'Why There Is a Democratic Deficit in the EU: A Response to Majone and Moravcsik'. *JCMS: Journal of Common Market Studies* 44, no. 3 (2006): 533–562. https://doi.org/10.1111/j.1468-5965.2006.00650.x.

Frank, Robert. 'The Meanings of Europe in French National Discourse: A French Europe or an Europeanized France?' In *The Meaning of Europe: Variety and Contention within and among Nations*, edited by Mikael af Malmborg and Bo Stråth (Oxford; New York: Berg, 2002), 311–326.

Freeden, Michael. *Ideologies and Political Theory: A Conceptual Approach* (Oxford: Oxford University Press, 1998).

Fromage, Diane, and Ton van den Brink. 'Democratic Legitimation of EU Economic Governance: Challenges and Opportunities for European Legislatures'. *Journal of

European Integration 40, no. 3 (April 2018): 235–248. https://doi.org/10.1080/07036337.2018.1450407.

Front National. *Passeport Pour La Victoire* (Paris: Front National, 1989).

Front National. *Militer Au Front* (Paris: Editions Nationales, 1991).

Front National. *300 Mesures Pour La Renaissance de La France* (Paris: Editions Nationales, 1993).

Front National. 'Le Front National Pour Restaurer Notre Identité Nationale Face à l'Europe Fédérale'. *Français d'Abord*, Novermber, no 1, 1999.

Front National. 'Programme Du Front National' (Retrieved from Comparative Manifesto Project, 2002).

Front National. 'Programme Pour Les Élections Européennes de 2004' (Retrieved from European Manifesto Project, 2004).

Front National. 'Notre Projet: Programme Politique Du Front National' (Retrieved from www.frontnational.com, 2012).

Gasparri, Maurizio. 'Alla Logica Della Moneta Opporremo Storia e Cultura'. *Secolo d'Italia*, 7 April 1988.

Gollisch, Bruno. 'A Propos de l'Union Soviétique Européenne—Discours de Bruno Gollnisch à l'occasion de l'université d'été Du FN' (retrieved from Archives de l'Internet, Bibliothèque nationale de France, 2008).

Goodliffe, Gabriel. 'Europe's Salience and "Owning" Euroscepticism: Explaining the Front National's Victory in the 2014 European Elections in France'. *French Politics* 13, no. 4 (December 2015): 324–345. https://doi.org/10.1057/fp.2015.19.

Griffin, Roger. 'The "Post-Fascism" of the Alleanza Nazionale: A Case Study in Ideological Morphology'. *Journal of Political Ideologies* 1, no. 2 (1996): 123–145. https://doi.org/10.1080/13569319608420733.

Gutmann, Amy. *Identity in Democracy* (Princeton, NJ: Princeton University Press, 2003).

Ichijo, Atsuko. 'Sovereignty and Nationalism in the Twenty-First Century: The Scottish Case'. *Ethnopolitics* 8, no. 2 (2009): 155–172. https://doi.org/10.1080/17449050902761624.

Ignazi, Piero. *Postfascisti?: Dal Movimento Sociale Italiano Ad Alleanza Nazionale* (Bologna: Il Mulino, 1994).

Ignazi, Piero. *Il Polo Escluso: Profilo Storico Del Movimento Sociale Italiano* (Bologna: Il Mulino, 1998).

Kantar Public—EPOKA. 'Baromètre d'image Du Rassemblement National (Édition Décembre 2022)', 2022. https://www.kantarpublic.com/fr/barometres/barometre-d-image-du-rassemblement-national/barometre-d-image-du-rassemblement-national-2023.

Kedourie, Elie. *Nationalism* (Oxford: Blackwell, 1993).

Lang, Carl. 'Jeunesse Nation Europe'. *La Lettre de Jean-Marie Le Pen*, September, no 2, 1987.

Langlois, Marc. 'Non à Bruxelles Oui à l'Europe Des Nations'. *Nations Presses Magazine*, May 2014.

Le Pen, Jean-Marie. *Les Français d'abord* (Paris: Carrère—Michel Lafon, 1984).

Le Pen, Jean-Marie. *Pour La France: Programme Du Front National* (Paris: Albatros, 1985).

Le Pen, Jean-Marie. *Le Contrat Pour La France Avec Les Français* (Paris: Editions Nationales, 1995).

Le Pen, Jean-Marie. 'Aucun Bien N'est Plus Précieux Que l'indépendance'. Edited by Bernard Fontagnes. *Français d'Abord*, October 2004: 3–4.

Le Pen, Jean-Marie. 'Discours à Toulouse Sur Le Thème de l'Europe' (retrieved from Archives de l'Internet, Bibliothèque nationale de France, 2007).

Le Pen, Marine. 'Discours de Marine Le Pen à Kintzheim', February 2018. https://rassemblementnational.fr/discours/discours-de-marine-le-pen-a-kintzheim.

Le Pen, Marine. 'Metz—Discours de Marine Le Pen—1er Mai', May 2019. https://rassemblementnational.fr/discours/metz-discours-de-marine-le-pen-1er-mai.

Lorimer, Marta. 'What Is It, and Why Does It Matter? The Meaning of Sovereignty in the Rassemblement National's Critique of European Integration'. In *Sovereignty in Conflict—Political, Constitutional and Economic Dilemmas in the EU*, by Nathalie Brack, Amandine Crespy, Ramona Coman, and Julia Rone (Basingstoke, Hants: Palgrave, 2023): 165–182.

Mair, Peter. *Ruling the Void: The Hollowing of Western Democracy* (London; New York: Verso, 2013).

Mégret, Bruno. 'Construire l'Europe de La Puissance' (Paris: Cahiers Communication Interne, Bibliothèque Nationale de France, 1987).

Mégret, Bruno. 'Les Principes Fondateurs de Notre Europe'. *La Lettre de Jean-Marie Le Pen*, May, no 2, 1989.

Movimento Sociale Italiano. 'Continuare per Rinnovare. Mozione Congressuale XII Congresso Napoli' (Fondo Movimento Sociale Italiano (serie 1, busta 6, fascicolo 21). Archivio Fondazione Ugo Spirito, Roma, Italia, 1979).

Movimento Sociale Italiano. 'Spazio Nuovo. Mozione Congressuale XII Congresso Napoli' (Fondo Movimento Sociale Italiano (serie 1, busta 6, fascicolo 21). Archivio Fondazione Ugo Spirito, Roma, Italia, 1979).

Movimento Sociale Italiano. *Il Msi-Dn Dalla A Alla Zeta: Principii Programmatici, Politici e Dottrinari Esposti Da Cesare Mantovani, Con Presentazione Del Segretario Nazionale Giorgio Almirante* (Rome: Movimento Sociale Italiano-Destra Nazionale, Ufficio propaganda, 1980).

Movimento Sociale Italiano. 'Destra '80. Mozione Congressuale, XIII Congresso Roma'. *Secolo d'Italia*, 17 January 1982.

Movimento Sociale Italiano. 'Programma Elezioni 1987'. *Secolo d'Italia* (12 May 1987).

Mudde, Cas. *Populist Radical Right Parties in Europe* (Cambridge: Cambridge University Press, 2007). https://doi.org/10.1111/j.1478-9302.2009.00194.x.

Mudde, Cas. 'The Populist Radical Right. A Pathological Normalcy'. *West European Politics* 33, no. 6 (2010): 1167–1186.

Newell, James L. 'Italy: The Extreme Right Comes in from the Cold'. *Parliamentary Affairs* 53 (2000): 469–485.

Nielsen, Kristian L. 'EU Soft Power and the Capability–Expectations Gap'. *Journal of Contemporary European Research* 9, no. 5 (2013). https://doi.org/10.30950/jcer.v9i5.479.

Nye, Joseph S. *Soft Power: The Means to Success in World Politics*. First edition. (New York: Public Affairs, 2004).

Patten, Alan. 'The Autonomy Argument for Liberal Nationalism'. *Nations and Nationalism* 5, no. 1 (1999): 1–17. https://doi.org/10.1111/j.1354-5078.1999.00001.x.

Rassemblement National. 'Pour Une Europe Des Nations et Des Peuples (Projet—Elections Européennes)', 2019. https://www.politique-animaux.fr/sites/www.politique-animaux.fr/fichiers/prises-de-positions/pieces-jointes/europeennes-projet-rn.pdf.

Rassemblement National. 'Pour Une Europe Des Nations. Manifeste Pour Une Nouvelle Coopération En Europe: "L'Alliance Européenne Des Nations"', 2019.

Reh, Christine. 'European Integration as Compromise'. *Government and Opposition* 47, no. 3 (2012): 414–440.

Romualdi, Pino. *Intervista Sull'Europa* (Palermo: Edizioni Thule, 1979).

Salagnac, Catherine. 'L'engrenage de Maastricht'. *La Lettre de Jean-Marie Le Pen*, May, no 1, 1992.

Scharpf, Fritz W. 'The Joint-Decision Trap Revisited'. *JCMS: Journal of Common Market Studies* 44, no. 4 (2006): 845–864. https://doi.org/10.1111/j.1468-5965.2006.00665.x.

Schneider, Michael. 'Europe Must Deliver at the Level Closest to the Citizens Subsidiarity: Past, Present and Future'. *European View* 18, no. 1 (April 2019): 16–25. https://doi.org/10.1177/1781685819844466.

Tarchi, Marco. *Dal MSI Ad AN: Organizzazione e Strategie* (Bologna: Il Mulino, 1997).

Troper, Michel. 'Sovereignty'. In *The Oxford Handbook of Comparative Constitutional Law*, edited by Michel Rosenfeld and András Sajó (Oxford: Oxford University Press, 2012), 357–370. https://doi.org/10.1093/oxfordhb/9780199578610.013.0019.

Vasilopoulou, Sofia. *Far Right Parties and Euroscepticism: Patterns of Opposition* (London; New York: Rowman & Littlefield, 2018).

Vassallo, Salvatore, and Rinaldo Vignati. *Fratelli Di Giorgia: Il Partito Della Destra Nazional-Conservatrice* (Bologna: Il Mulino, 2023).

Vrakopoulos, Christos. 'Political and Ideological Normalization: Quality of Government, Mainstream-Right Ideological Positions and Extreme-Right Support'. *European Political Science Review* 14, no. 1 (2022): 56–73. https://doi.org/10.1017/S1755773921000308.

White, Jonathan. *Politics of Last Resort: Governing by Emergency in the European Union* (Oxford: Oxford University Press, 2019).

4

States of emergency

Europe under threat

The preceding chapters explored paths to legitimation demanding some form of conformism on the part of the far right, but adaptation is not the only way for far-right parties to pursue legitimation. Instead of 'mainstreaming', or passively waiting for others to do the dirty job of mainstreaming for them, far-right parties can also try to shape the boundaries of what is considered acceptable. Evidence of them doing so abounds. The presentation of their most extreme measures as 'common sense' or as representing the views of a 'silent majority' are amongst the most familiar, but this chapter explores a different claim these parties make: that there is a 'crisis' gripping the nation, which they hold solutions for.

A recurrent motif in far-right discourse is the idea that the nation is threatened by some kind of crisis in need of urgent addressing, be it a migrant invasion or the danger of the nation's disappearance.[1] The language used to present this crisis bears close resemblance to the standard language of emergency politics, defined as 'actions departing from conventional practice and rationalized as necessary responses to exceptional and urgent threats'.[2] Although generally regarded as the prerogative of national executives,[3] and,

---

[1] Benjamin Moffitt, *The Global Rise of Populism: Performance, Political Style, and Representation* (Stanford: Stanford University Press, 2017); Ruth Wodak, *The Politics of Fear: What Right-Wing Populist Discourses Mean* (Los Angeles: SAGE, 2015); Cas Mudde, *Populist Radical Right Parties in Europe* (Cambridge: Cambridge University Press, 2007), doi:10.1111/j.1478-9302.2009.00194.x; Laurie Beaudonnet and Henio Hoyo Prohuber, 'Being European, the Nationalist Way: Europe in the Discourse of Radical Right Parties', *Party Politics*, March 2023, 13540688231161208, doi:10.1177/13540688231161209.

[2] Jonathan White, 'Emergency Europe', *Political Studies* 63, no. 2 (2015): 300, doi:10.1111/1467-9248.12072; In the field of international relations, the similar concept of 'securitization' has received significant attention, highlighting how political elites may use the notion of an existential threat to impose emergency measures that go against the regular rules of political life, see e.g. Barry Buzan, Ole Wæver, and Jaap de Wilde, *Security: A New Framework for Analysis* (Boulder: Lynne Rienner Publishers, 1998); Claudia Aradau, 'Security and the Democratic Scene: Desecuritization and Emancipation', *Journal of International Relations and Development* 7, no. 4 (2004): 388–413, doi:10.1057/palgrave.jird.1800030; Paul Roe, 'Is Securitization a "negative" Concept? Revisiting the Normative Debate over Normal versus Extraordinary Politics', *Security Dialogue* 43, no. 3 (2012): 249–266.

[3] Clinton L. Rossiter, *Constitutional Dictatorship: Crisis Government* (Princeton: Princeton University Press, 1948); Giorgio Agamben, *State of Exception* (Chicago: University of Chicago Press, 2005); Bonnie Honig, *Emergency Politics: Paradox, Law, Democracy* (Princeton: Princeton University Press, 2009);

more recently, as a mode of action available to transnational institutions,[4] emergency politics is also a form of validation in use beyond these groups. As Ben Anderson notes, progressive organizations frequently make use of emergency politics as a mobilization strategy 'to generate urgencies with the hope of translating unbearable or barely bearable conditions into ethical or political scenes demanding response'.[5] Similarly, Roxanne Doty shows how notions of emergency response abounded in the justifications of actions by civilian border-patrol groups on the USA–Mexico border.[6] In this broader sense, emergency politics no longer refers exclusively to state practices that violate the rule of law, but to a rhetorical strategy founded on the 'interlocking of a provocative practice [...] with a particular form of validation, which often, though not always, bears the vocabulary of "emergency", "exceptional", "save", "rescue", "security".'[7] Thus conceived, emergency politics becomes a form of validation and legitimation available to far-right parties: far-right policies (and, by extension, the people promoting them) commonly understood as 'extreme' become the 'provocative practice' that needs to be validated, and the constant reference to exceptional or existential threats the mode of validation.

Like other far-right parties, the MSI and RN regularly drew on a register of emergency.[8] For most of its history, the MSI's opposition to communism was entangled with the belief that it presented an existential threat to Italy. The RN is most known for presenting migration as an existential threat. However, this is not the only danger it identifies or has identified throughout its history. Political elites, Islam, demographic decline, drug dealers, and globalization have all been presented as emergencies needing to be urgently addressed.

These threats reappear in the parties' definition of Europe, and the remainder of this chapter considers how the register of emergency they used to characterize Europe fed into their legitimation efforts. It shows how both the MSI and RN, but not AN, presented Europe as endangered by all sorts of

William E Scheuerman, 'Survey Article: Emergency Powers and the Rule of Law After 9/11', *Journal of Political Philosophy* 14, no. 1 (2006): 61–84, doi:10.1111/j.1467-9760.2006.00256.x.

[4] Christian Kreuder-Sonnen, *Emergency Powers of International Organizations: Between Normalization and Containment* (Oxford: Oxford University Press, 2020); Jonathan White, *Politics of Last Resort: Governing by Emergency in the European Union* (Oxford: Oxford University Press, 2019).

[5] Ben Anderson, 'Emergency Futures: Exception, Urgency, Interval, Hope', *The Sociological Review* 65, no. 3 (September 2017): 465, doi:10.1111/1467-954X.12447.

[6] Roxanne Lynn Doty, 'States of Exception on the Mexico–U.S. Border: Security, "Decisions," and Civilian Border Patrols', *International Political Sociology* 1, no. 2 (2007): 113–137, doi:10.1111/j.1749-5687.2007.00008.x.

[7] White, 'Emergency Europe', 303.

[8] As later parts of the chapter will show, the story is different for AN.

threats, and argues that the introduction of European issues in the parties' ideology provided additional occasions to claim the existence of actual or purported emergencies. This new space for emergency politics made it possible for them to present themselves and their measures as acceptable and necessary responses to the dangers being faced. AN, on the other hand, opted for a different strategy, by progressively moderating its tones and views on European dangers.

Anchoring the core: Europe in danger

The concept of threat occupies a prominent place in the MSI and RN's definition of Europe. It refers to the notion that something (or someone) cherished is placed in an unwelcome situation of danger which may, in the most extreme cases, lead to its disappearance. For the MSI, the main threats facing Europe were of an external nature, with the Soviet Union towering above all others. For the RN, dangers were of both an external and an internal nature, with the two frequently compounding each other.

Unlike the concepts of identity and liberty, which were self-standing concepts, the concept of threat is relational because it involves the identification of something (usually linked to the conceptual core) that is valued, of something (or someone) that threatens it, and the claim of a negative relationship linking the former and the latter. Because of this relational aspect, the concept of threat is best thought of as an 'adjacent' concept which colours the parties' nationalism by 'finessing the core and anchoring it—at least temporarily—into a more determinate and decontested semantic field'.[9] The field the parties' ideology is anchored in is one of emergency, where everything they care about is constantly endangered. It is a space populated by dangerous peoples and phenomena, in which politics is about not just policies or ideas, but the very survival of the political body. It is also a field that feels distinctive to the MSI and RN and to other far-right actors. While the language of emergency is by no means exclusive to them, the consistency with which they appeal to it is characteristic of their own form of politics—or at least it used to be, before the age of 'permacrisis'. As such, while being an adjacent concept, the concept of threat is key to the MSI and RN's ideology: it fleshes out what they care about, and presents a distinctive face to the world.

[9] Michael Freeden, 'The Morphological Analysis of Ideology', in *The Oxford Handbook of Political Ideologies*, ed. Michael Freeden and Marc Stears (Oxford: Oxford University Press, 2013), 125–126.

The Movimento Sociale Italiano/Alleanza Nazionale: from a threatened Europe to a pacified one

The MSI identified several different threats for Europe, but communism and its Soviet vehicle were by far the most dominant. In line with its broader opposition to communism discussed in earlier chapters, and in keeping with a historical context in which the Soviet Union did present the main threat to Europe's security, the MSI worried that international communism could 'extinguish and remove' European countries 'from the memory and hope of men',[10] and that the Soviet Union could annihilate the continent. In their view, the USSR endangered Europe by means of military power because of its imperial 'expansionist logic'[11] and its proximity to Europe, which would make the latter 'a target [. . .] the Soviets' SS-20 could and can destroy in a few minutes'.[12] It also limited Europe's power and autonomy by means of hostile politics aimed at neutralizing Europe, so as to have on its doorstep an 'immense, dead political bog and at the same time a formidable laboratory of goods made available to its proletarian collectivized markets'.[13] Interestingly, the Soviet Union and communism retained the qualification of threat even after the fall of the USSR. As late as 1995, the theses of the Fiuggi Congress which marked the transition from the MSI to AN still highlighted the need for the new democracies in the East to 'eradicate any residue of "real socialism" and even more so the recycling of the communist "nomenklatura", albeit under the label of "socialist" or "social-democratic"'.[14] Failure to do this, the passage insisted, would present a serious threat to the EU's future, suggesting that communism remained a threatening element even after the demise of the Soviet Union.

Beyond the Soviet Union, the MSI was also concerned by the United States of America. While less worrying than the USSR, the USA also threatened Europe because it clearly reduced Europe's power to make its own decisions, especially in the context of NATO, a body the MSI only reluctantly accepted. The MSI was divided between those (mainly associated with Pino Rauti's traditionalist current) who opposed the Alliance on political and cultural

---

[10] Pino Romualdi, *Intervista Sull'Europa* (Palermo: Edizioni Thule, 1979), 5.
[11] Movimento Sociale Italiano, 'Spazio Nuovo. Mozione Congressuale, XIII Congresso Roma', *Secolo d'Italia*, 16 January 1982.
[12] Movimento Sociale Italiano, 'Programma Elezioni 1987', *Secolo d'Italia*, 12 May 1987.
[13] Movimento Sociale Italiano, 'Destra '80. Mozione Congressuale, XIII Congresso Roma', *Secolo d'Italia*, 17 January 1982.
[14] Alleanza Nazionale, 'Pensiamo l'Italia: Il Domani c'è Già. Valori, Idee e Progetti per l'Alleanza Nazionale' (retrieved from https://webcache.googleusercontent.com/search?q=cache:ws3qnPVyqTwJ:web.tiscali.it/riformistiandreolesi/Tesi%2520AN.doc+&cd=10&hl=it&ct=clnk&gl=it. Last accessed 20 September 2023, 1995).

grounds, looking at the USA as the defeaters of fascism and as embodying an anti-spiritual lifestyle, and those (mainly associated with the party's more moderate currents) who considered that being in the Alliance was the only way to defend Western civilization and reframe the political battle in terms of communism versus anti-communism. While the latter imposed themselves, and the MSI declared its allegiance to NATO in 1951, the wisdom of the choice was frequently questioned in party debates.[15] The MSI's ambivalence on the USA and NATO more broadly is well captured by Romualdi in the *Intervista sull'Eurodestra*, when he says that 'that which has mortified and keeps mortifying Europe politically' was not the loss in the Second World War, but rather the 'harsh diktat of Yalta, which dividing it, has intended to destroy it politically, to make it on the one side the colonial empire of communism, and on the other side, the zone of influence of the democratic imperialism of the USA'.[16] While Romualdi was among the supporters of NATO within the party, he nonetheless displays clearly the belief that the USA and the USSR were both to blame for the partition of Europe after the Second World War and its subsequent political destruction. The fear that the USA might continue to limit European autonomy remained even after 1989, when the party began to be increasingly concerned about the advent of a 'second Yalta'.[17]

In addition to limiting Europe's power, the MSI thought the USA also imported a way of life that was threatening to European traditions. This cultural domination was perceived as a negative development because it imposed a new way of life 'based on the negation of all that Europeans have always considered as such [a mode of life], because it is founded on agnosticism, on materialism, on egoism, on hedonism, on a self-serving consumerism absurdly transformed into a "value"'.[18] In later documents, this was further tied in (albeit in a more idiosyncratic fashion)[19] with new

---

[15] Giuseppe Parlato, 'La Cultura Internazionale Della Destra Fra Isolamento e Atlantismo 1946–1954', in *Uomini e Nazioni: Cultura e Politica Estera Nell'Italia Del Novecento*, ed. Giorgio Petracchi and Gianluca Volpi (Udine: Gaspari, 2005), 144ff.

[16] Romualdi, *Intervista Sull'Europa*, 51.

[17] Movimento Sociale Italiano, 'Nuove Prospettive. Mozione Congressuale XVI Congresso Rimini'. (Roma: Archivio Fondazione Ugo Spirito, Fondo Movimento Sociale Italiano, serie 4, busta 22, fascicolo 64, 1990).

[18] Movimento Sociale Italiano, 'Andare Oltre. Mozione Congressuale XV Congresso Sorrento' (Fondo Movimento Sociale Italiano (serie 1, busta 7, fascicolo 25). Archivio Fondazione Ugo Spirito, Roma, Italia, 1987).

[19] Immigration was in fact conspicuously absent from the MSI's early documents, and only started appearing around the end of the 1980s as the result of cross-pollination with the RN and the emergence of immigration as an issue in Italian politics. However, the MSI's relationship with the issue was more complex than the RN's, with the party leadership being reluctant to embrace anti-immigration as an issue—see for example Piero Ignazi, *Postfascisti?: Dal Movimento Sociale Italiano Ad Alleanza Nazionale* (Bologna: Il Mulino, 1994), 85–86; Piero Ignazi, *Il Polo Escluso: Profilo Storico Del Movimento Sociale*

emerging issues such as immigration via the fear of Europe becoming like the USA, a 'melting pot' that has 'given up on its roots and origins', losing all 'national specificity' to replace it with an 'amorphous and indefinite' new model.[20]

Internal threats were somewhat less pervasive, but nonetheless present. Chief among them was national decline brought about by factors such as domestic communism, demographic decline, and the acquisition of consumerist behaviours which led Europeans to 'grow lazy and cowardly, ready only to avoid deciding, seeing, used to giving up and forgetting'.[21] The MSI also indicated a specific category of people as being partially to blame for Europe's decline: the political establishment. Considering the MSI's place as an anti-establishment party in permanent opposition (especially from the mid 1970s),[22] this attack on the political class should appear as consistent with both their beliefs and their position on the political spectrum. For them, European governments and the political class more broadly were guilty of weakness and lack of vision, unable to 'prepare it [Europe] for the great world challenges'[23] and, as Romualdi put it in an article in the *Secolo d'Italia*, 'speak of nothing but pacifism, disarmament, neutralism and operate as if every day they would like to ditch their commitments, to transform Europe in a denuclearized area, the soft belly of the world, exactly as the Soviets would like'.[24]

Although in the previous chapters, there was significant continuity in messaging between the MSI and AN, this was not the case in their approach to the notion of threat. Compared with the MSI and the RN (discussed below) the concept of threat occupied a marginal position in AN's ideology. The party progressively moved away from claiming that Europe was victim of a variety of threats, and started viewing issues once defined in that way as regular issues in day-to-day politics. Europe, as a result, no longer appeared as endangered or in decline, but merely faced with 'normal' political choices in

---

Italiano (Bologna: Il Mulino, 1998), 414–415; see also Jean-Yves Camus, *Le Front National: Histoire et Analyses* (Paris: O. Laurens, 1997), 202 on Rauti's break with the RN over immigration. AN also sought to maintain a more balanced position on immigration, although it still presented rather restrictive policy preferences—see Piero Ignazi, 'Legitimation and Evolution on the Italian Right Wing: Social and Ideological Repositioning of Alleanza Nazionale and the Lega Nord', *South European Society and Politics* 10, no. 2 (2005): 333–349, doi:10.1080/13608740500135058; Jessika ter Wal, 'The Discourse of the Extreme Right and Its Ideological Implications: The Case of the Alleanza Nazionale on Immigration', *Patterns of Prejudice* 34, no. 4 (2000): 37–51, doi:10.1080/003132200128810982.

[20] Movimento Sociale Italiano, 'Destra in Movimento. Mozione Congressuale XVI Congresso Rimini' (Fondo Movimento Sociale Italiano (serie 4, busta 22, fascicolo 64). Archivio Fondazione Ugo Spirito, Roma, Italia, 1990).
[21] Movimento Sociale Italiano, 'Spazio Nuovo Mozione Congressuale, XIII Congresso Roma'.
[22] Ignazi, *Il Polo Escluso: Profilo Storico Del Movimento Sociale Italiano*.
[23] Movimento Sociale Italiano, 'Destra '80. Mozione Congressuale, XIII Congresso Roma'.
[24] Pino Romualdi, 'Voglia d'Europa', *Secolo d'Italia*, 19 October 1986.

need of balanced solutions. For example, in issues of migration (an area in which far-right parties are typically prone to exaggerate), the party's Verona Congress documents recommended that 'reciprocally acceptable appropriate forms and ways of peaceful cohabitation' be found to address the potentially destabilizing issues posed by 'the quantitative weakening of certain peoples, the incremental explosion of others, the territorial transfers that tend to take on a mass character.'[25] Here, it is worth noting how the response to migration is couched in a moderate language rather than in one that draws on notions of emergency. Immigration was still presented as problematic, and the loss of identity as a possibility, but there was also an attempt to find a solution that did not involve presenting other identities as dangerous.[26] As the passage later adds, the protection of identity must respect all identities and take place within the understanding that mankind shares a common '*humanitas*'. In short, while references to dangers persisted in AN's definition of Europe, these were no longer existential or all encompassing, but merely in need of careful management. As far as external threats go, these occupied, at best, a marginal position. Thus, while the party may have criticized external actors such as the European Commission or fellow European partners, its position lacked the MSI's sense of urgency and did not suggest that it was the entire European civilization that was at risk from these external actors' actions. It also changed approach to the US, fully embracing the idea of the 'West'.[27]

One last external threat worth mentioning because of its relevance to the RN, which will be addressed later, is globalization. The MSI did not discuss it because it did not emerge as a relevant topic until the 1990s. AN did speak of globalization, but it approached it in a radically different manner compared to the RN. Typically it did not treat it as a threat, but rather as a process in need of management: the necessity was less to arrest it than to direct it 'as to avoid social and economic crises in this or that region, or in this or that sector.'[28] Within this context, it is also relevant to underline that in a striking contrast with the RN, AN saw the EU as a body that could help manage globalization. AN, in fact, while seeing the EU as a potential danger in this case, maintained a constructive attitude towards it. It typically

---

[25] Alleanza Nazionale, 'Conferenza Programmatica Di AN. Verona. 27 Febbraio – 1 Marzo', *Secolo d'Italia*, 27 February 1998, 11–12.

[26] Leonardo Puleo and Gianluca Piccolino, 'Back to the Post-Fascist Past or Landing in the Populist Radical Right? The Brothers of Italy Between Continuity and Change', *South European Society and Politics*, September 2022, 1–25, doi:10.1080/13608746.2022.2126247.

[27] Alleanza Nazionale, 'Programma Elezioni Del Parlamento Europeo 12/13 Giugno 2004' (retrieved from European Manifesto Project, 2004).

[28] Alleanza Nazionale, 'Elezioni Europee '99: Programma Politico' (retrieved from European Manifesto Project, 1999).

called for finding a balance between the national interest and the shared European interest, and advocated the creation of a 'more conscious political Europe, as the harmonious sum of sovereignties, in which the democratic nature of a responsible government prevails.'[29] A similar point was raised in a more critical 2008 article in the *Secolo d'Italia*, which highlighted that the EU Constitutional Treaty ended up making the EU 'an instrument of neoliberal globalization' because it was put at the service of 'free and undistorted competition'; at the same time, the article argued Europe was 'something too important to be abandoned to the decisions of a class of too often insufficiently forward-looking technocrats and eurobureaucrats'.[30] The implication, then, was not that national governments should reject the EU, but rather that they should keep engaging with it and make it less of an instrument of globalization and more of an instrument to find a balance between national interests.

Always in danger: the Rassemblement National's threatened Europe

Like the MSI, the RN considered Europe to be an endangered space. Internal threats occupied a prominent place in its ideology. In the 1980s, the party was particularly concerned about the internal decline of Europe, which it saw as threatened by a series of negative developments (presented elsewhere as 'the same that threaten France'.)[31] The main threats are summarized in the 1986 *La Lettre* article *L'Europe, d'abord une volonté* (Europe, a will first). The article, which presented the RN's freshly elected MPs' and MEPs' vision for Europe, defined the continent as 'struck by senility', 'blocked by unqualified immigrant labour', and 'led by governments that are happy to manage for the short term'.[32] These aspects of European decline are present across the history of the RN, although their relative weight changes over time, as does the extent to which these are European problems.

The fear of a 'Europe struck by senility' and unable to reproduce itself is one of the oldest concerns for the RN. It had already been discussed in the party's 1979 European election manifesto[33] which claimed that 'Europe,

---

[29] Alleanza Nazionale, 'Vince La Patria, Nasce l'Europa. Bologna, 4–7 Aprile 2002', *Secolo d'Italia*, 4 April 2002.
[30] Agostino Carrino, 'Questa Europa Poco Amata Dagli Europei', *Secolo d'Italia*, 12 June 2008.
[31] Jean-Marie Le Pen, *Les Français d'abord* (Paris: Carrère—Michel Lafon, 1984), 163.
[32] Front National, 'L'Europe, d'abord Une Volonté', *La Lettre de Jean-Marie Le Pen*, April, no 1, 1986.
[33] While the party produced a manifesto, it did not participate in the actual election because, following the failure to broker a deal with Tixier-Vignancour's *Parti des Forces Nouvelles* (the MSI's partner in the *Eurodestra*), the Front National withdrew its list (see Camus 1997: 43, Emmanuelle Reungoat 2015: 228).

as the rest of West, suffers from a drop in the birth rate that can lead to the enslavement and even the disappearance of its nations'.[34] In the party's logic, a smaller European community would not be able to defend its own freedom, and would also risk disappearing because of its inability to transmit its own heritage and the elements that constitute its identity to younger generations.

Immigration further reinforced demographic decline in the RN's view, especially because the party expected it to lead to the progressive replacement of native populations with foreign 'others', diluting and ultimately destroying Europe's distinctive culture. The link between the two is well-captured in a speech given by Jean-Marie Le Pen at the 2003 National Council of the RN.[35] In the speech, Le Pen notes how striking it is that even though many analyses observe the 'demographic difficulties Europe will face', they do not push for a relaunch of European fertility, but rather content themselves with planning the replacement of local populations with foreigners. According to Le Pen, this is based on the misguided assumption that 'men are interchangeable without consideration for identities, cultures and history' and will cause 'the "Old Europe" as the Americans call it by now [to] disappear as a homogeneous continent'.[36]

The dual discourse on Europe versus the EU observed in Chapter 2 reappears in the RN's considerations of immigration, as while the party was concerned with the effects of immigration on Europe, it remained critical of the EU's role in facilitating it. The EU had already been critiqued along these lines in the 1980s, with party members such as Le Chevallier accusing it of fostering pro-immigration policies because of its intention to allow immigrants to vote in local elections,[37] and in the 1990s and 2000s, when the question of Turkey in particular led party cadres to present the EU as set on transforming Europe into 'an ensemble devoid of unity, without a soul, without borders, subject to immigration from the entire world and to the sole rule of the market'.[38] Inserting herself into this lineage, Marine Le Pen

---

[34] Front National, 'Plateforme de l'Union Française Pour l'Europe Des Patries', *Le National*, May 1979.
[35] Jean-Marie Le Pen, 'Discours Au Conseil National Du Front National' (retrieved from Archives de l'Internet, Bibliothèque nationale de France, 2003).
[36] Demographic decline and population replacement remain concerns for the RN to this day, although they are articulated as national concerns first. See for example Franck Johannes, 'Jordan Bardella Reprend à Son Compte La Théorie Complotiste Du "Grand Remplacement"', *Le Monde*, August 2021, https://www.lemonde.fr/politique/article/2021/08/30/jordan-bardella-reprend-a-son-compte-la-theorie-complotiste-du-grand-remplacement_6092713_823448.html)de.
[37] Jean-Marie Le Chevallier, 'Un Nouveau Pas Vers l'Europe Du Tiers-Monde', *La Lettre de Jean-Marie Le Pen*, September, no 1, 1988.
[38] Carl Lang, 'Au Parlement Européen, Le Front National: Le Parti Qui Defend Les Francais d'abord', *Français d'Abord*, 2003.

has defined immigration as 'the child of the European Union'³⁹ and highlighted the role of freedom of movement in exposing European countries to the 'Islamist threat'.⁴⁰

Like the MSI, the RN identified the political class as an enabling factor of internal, national, and European decline. Unlike the MSI, however, this was also inserted within a populist narrative where the party claimed to represent 'the people' and to defend them from the 'corrupt elite'. The core elements of the critique to the political class as an internal threat are relatively stable over time. For example, in the 1992 article *L'engrenage de Maastricht* (the Maastricht spiral) published in *La Lettre de Jean-Marie Le Pen*, pro-Maastricht parties are homogeneously defined as 'Eurofederasts' who have 'met to sell off France to the Brussels technocrats'.⁴¹ More recently, in a speech delivered in Kintzheim, Marine Le Pen stated that for the French government, 'the only inviolable thing is not the will of the people, it is the Europeanist dogmas [...]. They want to keep these dogmas against all common sense and against the will of the people'.⁴² More generally, national elites are also accused of selling off France not only to Brussels but also to financial lobbies,⁴³ and of actively working to abandon national sovereignty and European autonomy, to which they do not attach importance.⁴⁴ In short, the 'mad' political class is accused of doing nothing, instead bringing the country (and Europe) towards a cliff edge where it incites the French to move 'Forwards!'⁴⁵

While external threats occupied a less prominent place in the RN's ideology than in the MSI's, in the 1970s and 1980s the RN also viewed the USSR as the main external threat to Europe—a fear which was further compounded by the presence of a strong domestic Communist party. In a similar way to the Italian party, the RN viewed the Soviet Union as endangering both Europe's

---

³⁹ Marine Le Pen, 'Discours de Fréjus' (retrieved from https://www.facebook.com/watch/?v=1466142073402112. Last accessed 20 September 2023, 2016).

⁴⁰ Rassemblement National, 'Pour Une Europe Des Nations et Des Peuples (Projet—Elections Européennes)', 2019, https://www.politique-animaux.fr/sites/www.politique-animaux.fr/fichiers/prises-de-positions/pieces-jointes/europeennes-projet-rn.pdf.

⁴¹ Catherine Salagnac, 'L'engrenage de Maastricht', *La Lettre de Jean-Marie* Le Pen, May, no 1, 1992, 199.

⁴² Marine Le Pen, 'Discours de Marine Le Pen à Kintzheim', February 2018, https://rassemblementnational.fr/discours/discours-de-marine-le-pen-a-kintzheim.

⁴³ Front National, 'Programme Pour Les Élections Européennes de 2004' (retrieved from European Manifesto Project, 2004); Jean-Marie Le Pen, 'Le Discours Du NON Au Référendum Sur La Constitution Européenne.' (retrieved from Archives de l'Internet, Bibliothèque nationale de France, 2005); Front National, 'Notre Projet: Programme Politique Du Front National' (retrieved from www.frontnational.com (now https://rassemblementnational.fr/), 2012); Rassemblement National, 'Pour Une Europe Des Nations et Des Peuples (Projet—Elections Européennes)'.

⁴⁴ Front National, 'Programme Du Front National' (retrieved from Comparative Manifesto Project, 2002); Front National, 'Notre Projet: Programme Politique Du Front National'; Rassemblement National, 'Pour Une Europe Des Nations et Des Peuples (Projet—Elections Européennes)'.

⁴⁵ Le Pen, 'Le Discours Du NON Au Référendum Sur La Constitution Européenne'.

material and its spiritual survival. The following passage, extracted from a document prepared by Bruno Mégret for Le Pen's 1988 presidential campaign and entitled *Construire l'Europe de la Puissance* (Creating a Powerful Europe), clearly illustrates this sentiment:

> 11. *Consider serenely the USSR as our main enemy*
> Soviet hegemony directly threatens our security, and, eventually, our identity and our liberty. It is thus necessary to consider it our enemy and oppose it [. . .]. This implies, in addition, not abandoning the countries of Europe subjugated to its imperialism.
>
> 12. *Cease financing international communism*
> It is necessary to stop financing directly or indirectly international communism [. . .]. It is also necessary to fight vigorously the Soviets' technological espionage.[46]

The RN's fear of the USSR did not survive the latter's fall. In fact, following the collapse of the USSR, the RN adopted a much less critical position towards its successor state, seeing it as a source of inspiration and country of interest,[47] a position that proved to be problematic following Russia's 2022 invasion of Ukraine.[48]

In addition to the USSR, the RN was also concerned about the USA's influence on Europe. While early documents of the RN acknowledged American influence on Europe as a negative feature, defining Europe as 'subject to the economic and cultural pressures of the USA',[49] the Cold War, along with a certain affinity with Reagan, ensured that levels of criticism of the USA were kept to a minimum. It was not until the fall of the Berlin Wall and the first Gulf War that the RN shifted to a more explicitly anti-American stance in its international relations[50] and that the USA acquired the more definite contours of a threat to Europe. In fact, the USA was accused of pushing for a 'New World Order' based on economic globalization, international

---

[46] Bruno Mégret, 'Construire l'Europe de La Puissance' (Paris: Cahiers Communication Interne, Bibliothèque Nationale de France, 1987).

[47] Front National, 'Programme Du Front National'; 'Notre Projet: Programme Politique Du Front National'.

[48] The RN's support for Russia mirrors a broader tendency among the European far right to view Russia positively, whether this be due to an affinity with Vladimir Putin's political leadership or, as some have claimed, as a result of Russian funding supporting their activity. For a discussion of the relationship between Russia and the far right in Western Europe, see Anton Shekhovtsov, *Russia and the Western Far Right: Tango Noir* (London and New York: Routledge, 2018).

[49] Front National, 'Plateforme de l'Union Française Pour l'Europe Des Patries'.

[50] Guy Birenbaum, *Le Front National En Politique* (Paris: Balland, 1992), 182–191; Jocelyn A Evans, '"La Politique Du Dehors Avec Les Raisons Du Dedans": Foreign and Defence Policy of the French Front National', in *Europe for the Europeans*, ed. Christina Schori Liang (Aldershot and Burlington: Ashgate, 2007), 125–138.

organizations, and American domination by imposing 'diktats' on European countries by means of the EU and ultimately 'depriving them of their liberty and sovereignty'.[51] The USA, however, was by itself less dangerous than the Soviet Union; what made the USA dangerous was its influence on the EU.

The EU emerged as a threat to Europe from the mid 1980s to 1990s onwards, in response to shifts discussed in previous chapters. In the RN's discourse, it was frequently associated with the threat of globalization, of which it was considered the 'Trojan Horse'.[52] The EU and globalization are presented as threats to Europe and its nations' identity and liberty. These forces are accused of removing key boundaries, thereby 'dissolving' national identities. This line of criticism emerged in the mid 1980s, following the Single European Act. The EU was presented in documents from the time as a 'levelling' construction which destroyed local identities and harmed national prosperity. For example, in the *Passeport*, it is criticized because 'instead of being the instrument of the construction of an authentic community, it becomes [. . .] a factor of destruction of identities. It opens Europe to the wild winds of all subversive influences'.[53] The RN also accused the EU of drastically limiting nations' freedoms, thereby leading to their disappearance. The introduction of the Maastricht Treaty fomented this line of argument, as the Treaty was accused of leading the French to, as Le Pen put it in a speech given in Reims (known as the *Résolution de Reims*, Reims Resolution),

> give up their national sovereignty in favour of a supra-national state with a federal mission, thus destroying in time our identity, our language, our culture.
>
> In a strictly materialist and mercantile perspective, it gives to a plutocratic oligarchy the upper hand on our six-century-old currency and thus allows it to govern our nation.
>
> It accepts, with little regard for our Constitution, with the complicity of the man who is its guardian and the body charged with defending it, the subordination of French laws to the European law.
>
> It gives to foreigners the right to vote and opens our borders to foreign immigration.

---

[51] Jean-Marie Le Pen, 'Pour l'Europe Des Patries—Sortons de Cette Europe La!', *La Lettre de Jean-*Marie Le Pen, October, no 1, 1993; see also Jean-Marie Le Pen, 'Discours, 17ème Fête Des Bleu-Blanc-Rouge' (retrieved from Archives de l'Internet, Bibliothèque nationale de France, 1997); Jean-Marie Le Pen, 'Fête de Jeanne d'Arc Du 1er Mai 1998' (retrieved from Archives de l'Internet, Bibliothèque nationale de France, 1998).
[52] Front National, 'Notre Projet: Programme Politique Du Front National'.
[53] Front National, *Passeport Pour La Victoire* (Paris: Front National, 1989), 95.

All these abandonments are contrary to the principles of the State, to the laws of the Republic and even more to the unwritten traditions, usages and customs of the Nation.

It thus initiates a process which it proclaims irreversible, regardless of the indissoluble rights of future generations, a process that will ineluctably lead to the loss of our liberties, to the dissolution of the State, to the eradication of our language, to the disappearance of the French Army and finally to the death of France.[54]

Steeped in the language of emergency and immediate threat, as well as in references to an oncoming battle for survival, the *Résolution de Reims* is interesting for two reasons. It underscores more than any other document the threatening character of the EU. The EU is shown as an existential threat to European nations, one that will destroy their individual identities and capacity for self-rule. In subsequent years, the speech will also form a part of the party's anti-EU narrative, being frequently cited as a symbol of its long-standing opposition to the European project.[55] As such, it presents a milestone in how the party thinks about Europe.

Criticism of the EU as a body dedicated to the destruction of national identities and liberties remains a constant within the party to this day. The RN has, in fact, been remarkably consistent in its positions on globalization and the EU, even when it changed leader. Thus, Jean-Marie Le Pen's 1998 claim that the EU had led to the loss of 'what is essential: sovereignty, independence, liberty, security, the right to make our own laws, to live according to our laws and traditions, to be able to elect those who govern us, to live in our own country, in a framework apt for human needs'[56] is echoed by the RN's 2012 message that 'the Europeanist caste' was 'ready to sacrifice democracy, the nations and our social models to save its mad ideology',[57] and by Marine Le Pen's recent claim that the 'representatives of the system' will continue to pursue the project of a 'federal Europe, which because of its globalist and mercantilist ideology, works towards the destruction of our nations, their diversity, their freedom, their identity'.[58] Although Marine Le Pen's RN stresses more the topic of democracy, the same concerns with loss of identity and control in favour of unelected bureaucrats remain present.

[54] Jean-Marie Le Pen, 'La Resolution de Reims', *La Lettre de Jean-Marie Le Pen*, September, No 2, 1992.
[55] Front National, 'Programme Du Front National'; Front National, 'Programme Pour Les Élections Européennes de 2004'; José Pedro Zúquete, *Missionary Politics in Contemporary Europe* (Syracuse, NY: Syracuse University Press, 2007), 92–94.
[56] Le Pen, 'Fête de Jeanne d'Arc Du 1er Mai 1998'.
[57] Front National, 'Notre Projet: Programme Politique Du Front National'.
[58] Marine Le Pen, 'Discours de Marine Le Pen Dans l'Orne', January 2018, https://rassemblementnational.fr/discours/discours-de-marine-le-pen-dans-lorne.

'Euro-globalism' is presented as a destructive force, which will leave Europe and its nations borderless and powerless.

Finally, along with Soviet communism, the USA, and the EU, the RN identified an additional threat that the MSI and AN did not appear to care much about: developing countries and Islam. In fact, the MSI did not see them as a particularly salient issue (if anything, a fraction of the MSI even supported further engagement with developing countries in the name of anti-capitalism),[59] while France's history of colonialism and its experience of immigration made this external threat more salient because of its domestic implications. Starting in the 1980s, the RN presented Europe as endangered by 'Islamo-revolutionary hegemony, in any case the hegemony of the Third World, borne out of the demographic explosion of the Third World'.[60] This concern with developing countries was helpful in linking together both external threats and internal ones, because the 'demographic explosion of the Third World' necessarily led to immigration, a threat discussed earlier. It also served to critique the European Parliament as 'an assembly responsive to Marxist dialectics and attentive to the Third-Worldist ideology'.[61] Steadily through time, the focus shifted from 'the Third World and Islam' in general to Islam more specifically. Islam was presented as a force that threatened Europe's deeply held Christian identities and traditions by seeking to impose 'Islamist' ways of life on European countries.[62] Islam also moved from being a clearly external threat to being one more firmly anchored within European nations because of immigration. Thus, Europe became in the party's words a continent 'moving towards islamization',[63] at the expense of its own native traditions and local identities.

'Desperate times call for desperate measures': legitimacy through boundary shaping

The MSI and RN's world, the previous sections have established, was a dangerous one in which threats were coming from all sides. Some of these threats

---

[59] Piero Ignazi, 'Changing the Guard on the Italian Extreme Right', *Representation* 40, no. 2 (2004): 146–156, doi:10.1080/00344890408523256.
[60] Le Pen, *Les Français d'abord*, 164; Mégret, 'Construire l'Europe de La Puissance'.
[61] Jean-Marie Le Pen, *Pour La France: Programme Du Front National* (Paris: Albatros, 1985), 188.
[62] Lang, 'Au Parlement Europeen, Le Front National: Le Parti Qui Defend Les Francais d'abord', 200; Marc Langlois, 'Non à Bruxelles Oui à l'Europe Des Nations', *Nations Presses Magasine*, May 2014; Rassemblement National, 'Pour Une Europe Des Nations et Des Peuples (Projet—Elections Européennes)'.
[63] Front National, 'Programme "Europe" Du Front National: Leur Europe n'est Pas La Notre! Voila l'Europe Que Nous Voulons' (retrieved from European Manifesto Project, 2009).

appeared to be more existential than others, but they contributed to a general sense of Europe being deeply endangered. When something or someone cherished is in danger, there is a need for urgent action to respond to this threat. The emergency demands and justifies action, and the remainder of this chapter considers how the MSI and RN's continued reference to existential threats provided them with ammunition to expand the realm of the politically acceptable and legitimize their own political action.

Emergencies are a tricky form of justification in politics. While they may help legitimize behaviours that would be considered inappropriate under normal circumstances, in the absence of an actual or obvious crisis they also run the risk of suggesting detachment between a leader or party's analysis of a situation, and the actual situation. However, crises and emergencies, whether real or purported, can also prove formidably useful because they convey the idea that an unprecedented emergency requires, or at the very least justifies, an unprecedented response. Doing so, they facilitate the altering of the normal boundaries of political life because they suggest that a situation is so dire that unconventional measures may be warranted.

Existing works on populism and the far right place significant attention on the role that the 'populist creation of crisis'[64] or the 'politics of fear'[65] play in legitimizing far-right policies. For Benjamin Moffitt, the 'populist performance of crisis' serves to legitimize populist parties by allowing them to present themselves as 'the voice of the people' and justify the simplification of the rules and procedures of liberal democracy as a result. Although Moffitt's argument speaks to populism more generally, it is applicable to the specific subset of the far right that is also populist. In a similar vein, Ruth Wodak shows how far-right parties employ a 'politics of fear' to justify radical policies in the name of protecting the nation from some dangerous threat. The works of Moffitt and Wodak both suggest that far-right parties draw on the notion of exceptional circumstances to validate measures that under normal circumstances would not be considered acceptable—a procedure similar to that employed by executives appealing to emergency politics to justify a departure from the rules and conventions of political life.

In a similar vein, the MSI and RN's use of a rhetoric of emergency to describe Europe may be viewed as serving the purpose of legitimizing them and their policies. Implicitly, by constantly referring to threats facing Europe in the manner described in previous sections, the parties could contribute to the altering of social understandings of the situation around them, and create

[64] Moffitt, *The Global Rise of Populism: Performance, Political Style, and Representation*.
[65] Wodak, *The Politics of Fear: What Right-Wing Populist Discourses Mean*.

the sense that conditions were so extremely threatening that 'normal rules' no longer applied. When societal groups feel that their survival is threatened, they become more prone to accepting extraordinary emergency measures.[66] As a result, the parties' description of Europe as facing exceptional dangers created the space for others to consider things that would normally be considered unacceptable (such as the far-right parties' positions) as appropriate and commensurate to the danger being faced.

More explicitly, the parties' identification of threats and their association with an urgent sense of temporality created an opportunity to identify actors well-placed to intervene for the protection of Europe. When the MSI made claims along the lines of 'the defence of the part of Europe free from Soviet imperialism [. . .] is today a topic of such burning urgency that it does not allow hesitations of sorts',[67] and when the RN said that 'the massive waves of migrants that the EU allows to crash on our shores, these millions of migrants that the EU installs in our countries [. . .] this irresponsible policy determines the disappearance of Europe, unless we stop it',[68] they were not simply relating a state of affairs or 'constructing' a crisis, they were also advocating for appropriate solutions, commensurate to the urgency and size of the threat being faced.

Once the need to intervene was established, the parties could openly position themselves as the harbingers of the unprecedented action that was needed to respond to the emergency.[69] Marine Le Pen provided a good example of what this looks like in a speech given in 2019, in which she presented her party's measures as 'a revolution. A pacific, democratic revolution, but a true revolution of common sense' against the 'economic and social, demographic and identitarian Chernobyl' created by the EU.[70]

To strengthen their claim of being the best placed to intervene, the MSI and RN drew on various justifications. They demarcated themselves from other political actors by suggesting that they were the only ones who were aware of the true dangers facing Europe, an argument made for example by the RN in its party guide *Militer au Front* (Being an activist in the Front) in

---

[66] Tobias Theiler, 'Societal Security and Social Psychology', *Review of International Studies* 29, no. 2 (June 2003): 249–268.
[67] Giorgio Almirante, *Intervista Sull'Eurodestra*, ed. Michele Rallo (Palermo: Edizioni Thule, 1978), 10–11.
[68] Marine Le Pen, 'Discours de Marine Le Pen Au Luc-En-Provence', 2018, https://rassemblementnational.fr/discours/discours-de-marine-le-pen-au-luc-en-provence/.
[69] Moffitt, *The Global Rise of Populism: Performance, Political Style, and Representation*; see also Zúquete, *Missionary Politics in Contemporary Europe* on far right 'missionary politics'.
[70] Marine Le Pen, 'Metz—Discours de Marine Le Pen—1er Mai', May 2019, https://rassemblementnational.fr/discours/metz-discours-de-marine-le-pen-1er-mai.

which it claimed to be the only party interested in fighting for the survival and renaissance of the nations of Europe.[71] The parties also claimed to represent some higher interest, as Romualdi did when saying the *Eurodestra* had the job of 'interpreting much higher, broader and more important interests, concerning the political health and the guarantee of liberty and development of the entire EEC'.[72] These assertions were also frequently associated with the idea that the parties had some kind of prophetic ability, as they could see something which others could not. This point is well captured by Jean-Marie Le Pen in a piece titled *Ma verité sur l'Europe* (My Truth on Europe) in which he claims that 'in all fields, our most pessimist predictions have come true. [. . .] We said "Maastricht will bring more taxes, more immigration, more insecurity, more unemployment". We were right.'[73]

In sum, through these European politics of emergency the MSI and RN could seek legitimation by advancing the notion that society is faced with some sort of state of exception where normal rules no longer apply, and more radical solutions of the type they advocate are needed. Put briefly, they advanced the idea that 'desperate times call for desperate measures' of the type they presented. In this process, their limited experience with government potentially helped. Not having been empowered, and claiming that their calls for timely action had been ignored by those who were in power (a politics of 'we told you so'),[74] enabled their solutions to appear as truly radical and new, all the while making them appear as the most credible actors to address and overcome the crisis.

Although this account concurs with Wodak and Moffitt in identifying far-right parties as living in a state of 'permanent ideational emergency'[75] which they employ to validate their action, it also differs from their analyses in two important respects. Compared with Wodak, it shows how dynamics other than migration can give rise to a 'politics of fear'. Emergencies may have a wider scope than that offered by a narrow focus on issues of migration, and encompass not just peoples, but also processes and institutions.

As far as Moffitt's work is concerned, it draws on a different logic of validation. Moffitt is specifically concerned with populism as a political style that pits a 'pure people' against a 'corrupt elite'. As such, central to his account is

---

[71] Front National, *Militer Au Front* (Paris: Editions Nationales, 1991), 115.
[72] Romualdi, *Intervista Sull'Europa*, 17.
[73] Jean-Marie Le Pen, 'Ma Verité Sur l'Europe', *La Lettre de Jean-Marie* Le Pen, June, no 1, 1994.
[74] Nicholas Startin, '"Euromondialisme" and the Growth of the Radical Right', in *Routledge Handbook of Euroscepticism*, ed. Benjamin Leruth, Nicholas Startin, and Simon Usherwood (London: Routledge, 2018), 85.
[75] Michael Freeden, 'After the Brexit Referendum: Revisiting Populism as an Ideology', *Journal of Political Ideologies* 22, no. 1 (2017): 6, doi:10.1080/13569317.2016.1260813.

the understanding that populists construct crises to establish a representative link between themselves and the electorate. The populist leader, in this case, seeks to construct legitimacy by arguing that their policies are what the people want (and the elite will not give them). In the account brought forward here, the mode of legitimation is not based on the creation of a representative claim,[76] but rather, on a politics of necessity. The people and what they want (or vote for) are secondary, a point noticeably made by Jean-Marie Le Pen in the *Resolution de Reims*, when he claimed that 'if the totalitarian methods of power did manage to mislead the people' and convince them to adopt the Maastricht Treaty in a referendum, his party would still 'fight against the execution of the Maastricht plot'.[77] What the people need is much more central to this account. It is less a 'politics of volition'[78] or representation and more of a far-right brand of TINA (there is no alternative) politics in which it is claimed that the far-right party will do what is necessary to 'save the nation'. As such, this form of legitimation is also available to non-populist actors, because it requires not the creation of an opposition between the people and the elite, but merely an appeal to the concept of necessity.

These strategies need not be mutually exclusive, and parties that are both populist and far right (such as the RN) may indeed rely on claims of representation and claims of necessity depending on what aspect of their ideology they wish to foreground. For example, representative claims, or a politics of volition, may be particularly relevant if what they are trying to do is suggest that someone else's emergency is going against what the people want, and what they might be able to give them. Conversely, a politics of necessity may be most useful if the emergency they are foregrounding is one created by them or one they have an interest in promoting.

Although, as the opening sections of this chapter showed, the use of politics of emergency is a broader feature of the MSI and RN which is not limited to what they have to say about Europe, there is reason to believe that Europe gave their message more resonance. In a similar way to their positions on Europe's identity and liberty, it offered an opportunity to transnationalize their message and restate it in a new context. For the MSI, for whom opposition to communism presented an important domestic legitimation strategy,[79] the latter point might have been particularly useful. For the RN, the notion of a European crisis may have proven particularly effective with respect to Europe and the EU in recent years. Given the multiple crises of the

---

[76] Michael Saward, *The Representative Claim* (Oxford: Oxford University Press, 2010).
[77] Le Pen, 'La Resolution de Reims'.
[78] White, *Politics of Last Resort: Governing by Emergency in the European Union*.
[79] Ignazi, *Postfascisti?: Dal Movimento Sociale Italiano Ad Alleanza Nazionale*.

European Union, the rhetoric of emergency would have come across as in line with what was actually happening, thereby providing it additional purchase. Furthermore, the fact that the RN had not been given a chance to 'test' its solutions may have served to suggest that, given the circumstances and the mainstream parties' apparent failures to conclusively deal with the eurozone and migration crises, it should be given an opportunity to implement its own solutions.[80]

Before concluding, it is worth noting how different this mode of politics appeared from that of AN. A common thread in these three empirical chapters has been the observation of AN's pragmatic approach to politics. In this chapter in particular, this manifested itself in an absence of the concept of threat and an approach to problems that involved the identification of issues and the advancement of balanced solutions to approach them. Instead of identifying issues, linking them together, and reading them through a temporal frame aimed at creating a sense of emergency, AN limited itself to the identification of issues without claiming the need to address them urgently. Furthermore, it did not present itself as the only holder of simple and straightforward solutions (or, indeed, as a representative of 'the people' against the elite that had created the issues), but acknowledged a level of complexity in political decision-making. As a result, AN's Europe was not deeply immersed in emergency, and AN did not appear as a 'prophetic' or 'providential' force, but rather as a moderate and careful manager.

There are two plausible explanations for the absence of emergency politics in AN. The first, more strategic in nature, points to AN's willingness to appear 'coalitionable' and moderate. Following its transformation, AN was keen to stress its nature as a 'conservative' party able to govern and ally with other mainstream parties. Drawing excessively on the concept of emergency would have placed it more firmly in the far-right area it was seeking to leave, suggesting the party may have adopted a different language to mark the change from far-right to mainstream actor. Abandoning radicalism would also have had the added benefit of helping it distinguish itself from its far-right contemporary, the Lega. Unlike AN, the Lega maintained a strongly crisis-driven vocabulary, especially concerning the issue of immigration. Abandoning

[80] For empirical investigations on the relationship between crisis and Euroscepticism, see for example Sara B. Hobolt and Catherine de Vries, 'Turning against the Union? The Impact of the Crisis on the Eurosceptic Vote in the 2014 European Parliament Elections', *Electoral Studies* 44 (2016): 504–514, doi:https://doi.org/10.1016/j.electstud.2016.05.006; Andrea L. P. Pirro and Paul Taggart, 'The Populist Politics of Euroscepticism in Times of Crisis: A Framework for Analysis', *Politics* 38, no. 3 (2018): 253–262, doi:10.1177/0263395718770579; Paul Taggart and Aleks Szczerbiak, 'Putting Brexit into Perspective: The Effect of the Eurozone and Migration Crises and Brexit on Euroscepticism in European States', *Journal of European Public Policy* 25, no. 8 (2018): 1–21, doi:10.1080/13501763.2018.1467955.

such language would have helped AN stress its distinctive (non-radical) profile. A second, more ideology-driven explanation concerns precisely AN's ideological evolution from a party of the far right to one of the conservative right. Its progressive abandonment of far-right themes and ideas would have included leaving behind the notion of emergency and the view of politics as an activity where survival was at stake. Instead, politics became a 'regular' exercise in interest representation and pragmatic problem-solving, indicating a complete party transformation.

Conclusion

This chapter has explored how the MSI and RN used the concept of threat to present Europe and its nations as endangered. It argued that this far-right version of emergency politics made it possible for the parties to validate their own 'exceptional' political action. By identifying a threat, advocating for the need to address it, and identifying themselves as the most appropriate actors to do so, the parties promoted the idea that given the circumstances, their own 'extreme' positions were a commensurate response to the dangers being faced. As the adage goes, 'desperate times call for desperate measures', and since it is the survival of the polity that is at stake in cases of emergency, it becomes acceptable to pursue measures that would not normally be considered legitimate. Engaging in emergency politics helped the MSI and RN present themselves and their own policies as the 'unconventional measures' needed in a dire situation.

References

Agamben, Giorgio. *State of Exception* (Chicago: University of Chicago Press, 2005).
Alleanza Nazionale. 'Pensiamo l'Italia: Il Domani C'è Già. Valori, Idee e Progetti per l'Alleanza Nazionale' (retrieved from https://webcache.googleusercontent.com/search?q=cache:ws3qnPVyqTwJ:web.tiscali.it/riformistiandreolesi/Tesi%2520AN.doc+&cd=10&hl=it&ct=clnk&gl=it. Last accessed 23 July 2019, 1995).
Alleanza Nazionale. 'Conferenza Programmatica Di AN. Verona. 27 Febbraio – 1 Marzo'. *Secolo d'Italia*, 27 February 1998.
Alleanza Nazionale. 'Elezioni Europee '99: Programma Politico' (retrieved from European Manifesto Project, 1999).

Alleanza Nazionale. 'Vince La Patria, Nasce l'Europa, Bologna. 4–7 Aprile 2002'. *Secolo d'Italia*, 4 April 2002.

Alleanza Nazionale. 'Programma Elezioni Del Parlamento Europeo 12/13 Giugno 2004' (retrieved from European Manifesto Project, 2004).

Almirante, Giorgio. *Intervista Sull'Eurodestra*. Edited by Michele Rallo (Palermo: Edizioni Thule, 1978).

Anderson, Ben. 'Emergency Futures: Exception, Urgency, Interval, Hope'. *The Sociological Review* 65, no. 3 (September 2017): 463–477. https://doi.org/10.1111/1467-954X.12447.

Aradau, Claudia. 'Security and the Democratic Scene: Desecuritization and Emancipation'. *Journal of International Relations and Development* 7, no. 4 (2004): 388–413. https://doi.org/10.1057/palgrave.jird.1800030.

Beaudonnet, Laurie, and Henio Hoyo Prohuber. 'Being European, the Nationalist Way: Europe in the Discourse of Radical Right Parties'. *Party Politics*, March 2023, 13540688231161208. https://doi.org/10.1177/13540688231161209.

Birenbaum, Guy. *Le Front National En Politique* (Paris: Paris: Balland, 1992).

Buzan, Barry, Ole Wæver, and Jaap de Wilde. *Security: A New Framework for Analysis* (Boulder: Lynne Rienner Publishers, 1998).

Camus, Jean-Yves. *Le Front National: Histoire et Analyses* (Paris: O. Laurens, 1997).

Carrino, Agostino. 'Questa Europa Poco Amata Dagli Europei'. *Secolo d'Italia*, 12 June 2008.

Doty, Roxanne Lynn. 'States of Exception on the Mexico–U.S. Border: Security, "Decisions", and Civilian Border Patrols'. *International Political Sociology* 1, no. 2 (2007): 113–137. https://doi.org/10.1111/j.1749-5687.2007.00008.x.

Evans, Jocelyn A. '"La Politique Du Dehors Avec Les Raisons Du Dedans": Foreign and Defence Policy of the French Front National'. In *Europe for the Europeans*, edited by Christina Schori Liang (Aldershot and Burlington: Ashgate, 2007), 125–138.

Freeden, Michael. 'The Morphological Analysis of Ideology'. In *The Oxford Handbook of Political Ideologies*, edited by Michael Freeden and Marc Stears (Oxford: Oxford University Press, 2013), 115–137.

Freeden, Michael. 'After the Brexit Referendum: Revisiting Populism as an Ideology'. *Journal of Political Ideologies* 22, no. 1 (2017): 1–11. https://doi.org/10.1080/13569317.2016.1260813.

Front National. 'Plateforme de l'Union Française Pour l'Europe Des Patries'. *Le National*, May 1979.

Front National. 'L'Europe, D'abord Une Volonté'. *La Lettre de Jean-Marie Le Pen*, April, no 2, 1986.

Front National. *Passeport Pour La Victoire* (Paris: Front National, 1989).

Front National. *Militer Au Front* (Paris: Editions Nationales, 1991).

Front National. 'Programme Du Front National' (retrieved from Comparative Manifesto Project, 2002).
Front National. 'Programme Pour Les Élections Européennes de 2004' (retrieved from European Manifesto Project, 2004).
Front National. 'Programme "Europe" Du Front National: Leur Europe n'est Pas La Notre! Voila l'Europe Que Nous Voulons' (retrieved from European Manifesto Project, 2009).
Front National. 'Notre Projet: Programme Politique Du Front National' (retrieved from www.frontnational.com (now https://rassemblementnational.fr/), 2012).
Hobolt, Sara B., and Catherine de Vries. 'Turning against the Union? The Impact of the Crisis on the Eurosceptic Vote in the 2014 European Parliament Elections'. *Electoral Studies* 44 (2016): 504–514. https://doi.org/10.1016/j.electstud.2016.05.006.
Honig, Bonnie. *Emergency Politics: Paradox, Law, Democracy* (Princeton: Princeton University Press, 2009).
Ignazi, Piero. *Postfascisti?: Dal Movimento Sociale Italiano Ad Alleanza Nazionale* (Bologna: Il Mulino, 1994).
Ignazi, Piero. *Il Polo Escluso: Profilo Storico Del Movimento Sociale Italiano* (Bologna: Il Mulino, 1998).
Ignazi, Piero. 'Changing the Guard on the Italian Extreme Right'. *Representation* 40, no. 2 (2004): 146–156. https://doi.org/10.1080/00344890408523256.
Ignazi, Piero. 'Legitimation and Evolution on the Italian Right Wing: Social and Ideological Repositioning of Alleanza Nazionale and the Lega Nord'. *South European Society and Politics* 10, no. 2 (2005): 333–349. https://doi.org/10.1080/13608740500135058.
Johannes, Franck. 'Jordan Bardella Reprend à Son Compte La Théorie Complotiste Du "Grand Remplacement"'. *Le Monde*, August 2021. https://www.lemonde.fr/politique/article/2021/08/30/jordan-bardella-reprend-a-son-compte-la-theorie-complotiste-du-grand-remplacement_6092713_823448.html)de.
Kreuder-Sonnen, Christian. *Emergency Powers of International Organizations: Between Normalization and Containment* (Oxford: Oxford University Press, 2020).
Lang, Carl. 'Au Parlement Europeen, Le Front National: Le Parti Qui Defend Les Francais d'abord'. *Français d'Abord*, 2003.
Langlois, Marc. 'Non à Bruxelles Oui à l'Europe Des Nations'. *Nations Presses Magasine*, May 2014.
Le Chevallier, Jean-Marie 'Un Nouveau Pas Vers l'Europe Du Tiers-Monde'. *La Lettre de Jean-Marie Le Pen*, September, no 1, 1988.
Le Pen, Jean-Marie. *Les Français d'abord* (Paris: Carrère—Michel Lafon, 1984).

Le Pen, Jean-Marie. *Pour La France: Programme Du Front National* (Paris: Albatros, 1985).
Le Pen, Jean-Marie. 'La Resolution de Reims'. *La Lettre de Jean-Marie Le Pen*, September, no 1, 1992.
Le Pen, Jean-Marie. 'Pour l'Europe Des Patries. Sortons de Cette Europe La!' *La Lettre de Jean-Marie Le Pen*, October, no 1, 1993.
Le Pen, Jean-Marie. 'Ma Verité Sur l'Europe'. *La Lettre de Jean-Marie Le Pen*, June, no 1, 1994.
Le Pen, Jean-Marie. 'Discours, 17ème Fête Des Bleu-Blanc-Rouge' (retrieved from Archives de l'Internet, Bibliothèque nationale de France, 1997).
Le Pen, Jean-Marie. 'Fête de Jeanne d'Arc Du 1er Mai 1998' (retrieved from Archives de l'Internet, Bibliothèque nationale de France, 1998).
Le Pen, Jean-Marie. 'Discours Au Conseil National Du Front National' (retrieved from Archives de l'Internet, Bibliothèque nationale de France, 2003).
Le Pen, Jean-Marie. 'Le Discours Du NON Au Référendum Sur La Constitution Européenne' (retrieved from Archives de l'Internet, Bibliothèque nationale de France, 2005).
Le Pen, Marine. 'Discours de Fréjus' (retrieved from https://www.facebook.com/watch/?v=1466142073402112. Last accessed 20 September 2023, 2016).
Le Pen, Marine. 'Discours de Marine Le Pen à Kintzheim', February 2018. https://rassemblementnational.fr/discours/discours-de-marine-le-pen-a-kintzheim.
Le Pen, Marine. 'Discours de Marine Le Pen Au Luc-En-Provence', 2018. https://rassemblementnational.fr/discours/discours-de-marine-le-pen-au-luc-en-provence/.
Le Pen, Marine. 'Discours de Marine Le Pen Dans l'Orne', January 2018. https://rassemblementnational.fr/discours/discours-de-marine-le-pen-dans-lorne.
Le Pen, Marine. 'Metz—Discours de Marine Le Pen - 1er Mai', May 2019. https://rassemblementnational.fr/discours/metz-discours-de-marine-le-pen-1er-mai.
Mégret, Bruno. 'Construire l'Europe De La Puissance' (Paris: Cahiers Communication Interne, Bibliothèque Nationale de France., 1987).
Moffitt, Benjamin. *The Global Rise of Populism: Performance, Political Style, and Representation* (Stanford: Stanford University Press, 2017).
Movimento Sociale Italiano. 'Destra '80. Mozione Congressuale, XIII Congresso Roma'. *Secolo d'Italia*, 17 January 1982.
Movimento Sociale Italiano. 'Spazio Nuovo. Mozione Congressuale, XIII Congresso Roma'. *Secolo d'Italia*, 16 January 1982.
Movimento Sociale Italiano. 'Andare Oltre. Mozione Congressuale XV Congresso Sorrento' (Fondo Movimento Sociale Italiano (serie 1, busta 7, fascicolo 25). Archivio Fondazione Ugo Spirito, Roma, Italia, 1987).

Movimento Sociale Italiano. 'Programma Elezioni 1987'. *Secolo d'Italia* (12 May 1987).
Movimento Sociale Italiano. 'Destra in Movimento. Mozione Congressuale XVI Congresso Rimini' (Fondo Movimento Sociale Italiano (serie 4, busta 22, fascicolo 64). Archivio Fondazione Ugo Spirito, Roma, Italia, 1990).
Movimento Sociale Italiano. 'Nuove Prospettive. Mozione Congressuale XVI Congresso Rimini'. (Roma: Archivio Fondazione Ugo Spirito, Fondo Movimento Sociale Italiano, serie 4, busta 22, fascicolo 64, 1990).
Mudde, Cas. *Populist Radical Right Parties in Europe* (Cambridge: Cambridge University Press, 2007). https://doi.org/10.1111/j.1478-9302.2009.00194.x.
Parlato, Giuseppe. 'La Cultura Internazionale Della Destra Fra Isolamento e Atlantismo 1946–1954'. In *Uomini e Nazioni: Cultura e Politica Estera Nell'Italia Del Novecento*, edited by Giorgio Petracchi and Gianluca Volpi (Udine: Gaspari, 2005): 134–154.
Pirro, Andrea L. P., and Paul Taggart. 'The Populist Politics of Euroscepticism in Times of Crisis: A Framework for Analysis'. *Politics* 38, no. 3 (2018): 253–262. https://doi.org/10.1177/0263395718770579.
Puleo, Leonardo, and Gianluca Piccolino. 'Back to the Post-Fascist Past or Landing in the Populist Radical Right? The Brothers of Italy between Continuity and Change'. *South European Society and Politics*, September 2022, 1–25. https://doi.org/10.1080/13608746.2022.2126247.
Rassemblement National. 'Pour Une Europe Des Nations et Des Peuples (Projet— Elections Européennes)', 2019. https://www.politique-animaux.fr/sites/www.politique-animaux.fr/fichiers/prises-de-positions/pieces-jointes/europeennes-projet-rn.pdf.
Reungoat, Emmanuelle. Mobilizing Europe in national competition: The case of the French Front National. *International Political Science Review* 36, no. 3 (2015): 296–310. https://doi.org/10.1177/0192512114568816.
Roe, Paul. 'Is Securitization a "negative" Concept? Revisiting the Normative Debate over Normal versus Extraordinary Politics'. *Security Dialogue* 43, no. 3 (2012): 249–266.
Romualdi, Pino. *Intervista Sull'Europa* (Palermo: Edizioni Thule, 1979).
Romualdi, Pino. 'Voglia d'Europa'. *Secolo d'Italia*, 19 October 1986.
Rossiter, Clinton L. *Constitutional Dictatorship: Crisis Government* (Princeton: Princeton University Press, 1948).
Salagnac, Catherine. 'L'engrenage de Maastricht'. *La Lettre de Jean-Marie Le Pen*, May, no 1, 1992.
Saward, Michael. *The Representative Claim* (Oxford: Oxford University Press, 2010).

Scheuerman, William E. 'Survey Article: Emergency Powers and the Rule of Law After 9/11'. *Journal of Political Philosophy* 14, no. 1 (2006): 61–84. https://doi.org/10.1111/j.1467-9760.2006.00256.x.

Shekhovtsov, Anton. *Russia and the Western Far Right: Tango Noir* (London and New York: Routledge, 2018).

Startin, Nicholas. '"Euromondialisme" and the Growth of the Radical Right'. In *Routledge Handbook of Euroscepticism*, edited by Benjamin Leruth, Nicholas Startin, and Simon Usherwood (London: Routledge, 2018): 75–85.

Taggart, Paul, and Aleks Szczerbiak. 'Putting Brexit into Perspective: The Effect of the Eurozone and Migration Crises and Brexit on Euroscepticism in European States'. *Journal of European Public Policy* 25, no. 8 (2018): 1–21. https://doi.org/10.1080/13501763.2018.1467955.

ter Wal, Jessika. 'The Discourse of the Extreme Right and Its Ideological Implications: The Case of the Alleanza Nazionale on Immigration'. *Patterns of Prejudice* 34, no. 4 (2000): 37–51. https://doi.org/10.1080/003132200128810982.

Theiler, Tobias. 'Societal Security and Social Psychology'. *Review of International Studies* 29, no. 2 (June 2003): 249–268.

White, Jonathan. 'Emergency Europe'. *Political Studies* 63, no. 2 (2015): 300–318. https://doi.org/10.1111/1467-9248.12072.

White, Jonathan. *Politics of Last Resort: Governing by Emergency in the European Union* (Oxford: Oxford University Press, 2019).

Wodak, Ruth. *The Politics of Fear: What Right-Wing Populist Discourses Mean* (Los Angeles: SAGE, 2015).

Zúquete, José Pedro. *Missionary Politics in Contemporary Europe* (Syracuse, NY: Syracuse University Press, 2007).

5
For the nation and for Europe
European and national interests

Consistency has many merits for political parties, and the previous chapter explored how presenting Europe as endangered enabled the MSI/AN and the RN to remain true to their message, while attempting to shape perceptions concerning the acceptability of themselves and their measures. This chapter digs deeper into the idea that Europe enabled far-right parties to stay on message by considering how it made it possible for them to restate their commitment to existing nationalist values, thereby helping them perform a balancing act between acquiring wider appeal and keeping the fidelity of their core supporters.

To understand why renewing commitments may have been important for the MSI/AN and the RN, it helps to briefly consider what political parties are and what holds them together.[1] At their most basic, political parties are institutions involved in political competition.[2] Their participation may be geared towards winning votes[3] or gaining access to political office,[4] but will usually be accompanied by a commitment to achieve some kind of policy connected to the party's ideas of what the 'good society'[5] would look like. In this latter sense, parties are not only electoral machines, but also groups united by interests, purposes, common projects, and a shared view of the world—in short, an ideology. Ideology guides their political action (or is at least used to justify it, provoking a strong incentive to behave as if it actually did motivate them),[6]

---

[1] Given the vastness of the subject, it will be impossible to do it justice in a few paragraphs. For more detailed discussions of this topic, see John Kenneth White, 'What Is a Political Party?', in *Handbook of Party Politics*, ed. R. S. Katz and W. Crotty (London: SAGE, 2006), 5–15, doi:10.4135/9781848608047; Jonathan White and Lea Ypi, *The Meaning of Partisanship* (Oxford: Oxford University Press, 2016), 10ff.

[2] Anthony Downs, *An Economic Theory of Democracy* (New York: Harper & Row, 1985), 24–25; Leon D. Epstein, *Political Parties in Western Democracies* (New Brunswick: Transaction Books, 1980), 9; Peter Mair, *Party System Change: Approaches and Interpretations* (Oxford: Clarendon Press; Oxford University Press, 1997), 21.

[3] Downs, *An Economic Theory of Democracy*.

[4] William H. Riker, *The Theory of Political Coalitions* (New Haven, CT: Yale University Press, 1962).

[5] Diane Sainsbury, *Swedish Social Democratic Ideology and Electoral Politics 1944–1948: A Study of the Functions of Party Ideology* (Stockholm: Almqvist & Wiksell International, 1980).

[6] Quentin Skinner, 'Some Problems in the Analysis of Political Thought and Action', *Political Theory* 2, no. 3 (1974): 299, doi:10.1177/009059177400200303.

Europe as Ideological Resource. Marta Lorimer, Oxford University Press. © Marta Lorimer (2024).
DOI: 10.1093/oso/9780198892366.003.0006

defines how they place themselves with respect to other political actors, and provides the parties with a narrative, a way to explain why certain policies are more desirable than others and how they are consistent with a party's overall goals.

Because ideology forms the basis of the promises that parties bring forward in programmatic terms, and of their political appeal, it also creates a bond between the party and its voters and activists, based on a commitment to pursue those promises. Voters, sympathizers, and activists will reasonably expect a level of consistency between the parties' (claimed) beliefs and their policies, or between their beliefs and intended political action when they are not in a position to advance policies. This constraint equally applies to the addition of new issues (such as the European one), which may be expected to somehow fit in with the party's overall narrative if the party wishes to maintain the fidelity of its core electorate and of its activists. A party wishing to appear as credibly committed and 'internally' legitimate will then need to convince activists, members, and followers that 'it still remains true to established partisan goals and traditions'.[7]

Both the MSI/AN and RN have by and large been 'ideological' parties for whom demonstrating attachment to core values was important. Lacking for most of their political history any true chance of becoming parties of government, it was their political identity and sense of community that held them together.[8] In this context, Europe became an ideological resource enabling them to stress 'internal' consistency. By introducing a new issue, they were offered an opportunity to restate their existing commitments, and apply old lenses to present a new issue. This factor may have proved particularly important in times of change. To analyse this dynamic, the following sections move away from studying the conception of 'Europe' broadly intended and focus specifically on how the MSI/AN and RN constructed their position on the principle, practice, and future of European integration.[9] It shows how their claims to act in the name of the national interest in response to varied threats to identity and liberty allowed them to restate their attachment to long-held beliefs and reinforce their image as committed actors who could be trusted to defend their principles.

---

[7] Raphael Zariski, 'The Legitimacy of Opposition Parties in Democratic Political Systems: A New Use for an Old Concept', *Political Research Quarterly* 39, no. 1 (1986): 29–47, doi:10.1177/106591298603900104.

[8] Although both parties tended towards leader-centrism, the leaders did not create or dictate the party line by themselves. Both parties also demonstrated their ability to survive leadership changes, suggesting that while charismatic leadership may have mattered to them, the person of the leader was also supported by a relatively strong organization.

[9] The tripartite division between 'principle', 'practice', and 'future' of EU integration comes from Sofia Vasilopoulou, 'European Integration and the Radical Right: Three Patterns of Opposition', *Government and Opposition* 46, no. 2 (2011): 223–244, doi:10.1111/j.1477-7053.2010.01337.x.

Thought into action: defending and promoting the national interest

The final concept that the MSI/AN and RN use to define Europe is the concept of national interest. This concept foregrounds the importance of the nation in the parties' ideological landscape, and appears most clearly in their definition of the 'programme for action'[10]—that is, their concrete views concerning what should be done in matters of European integration. It guides their understanding of what the EU is for and whether it should exist at all (the 'principle' of EU integration), helps them define whether they think that the EU fulfils the objectives they set for it (the 'practice' of EU integration), and informs their views of what ideal form they think the EU should take (the 'future' of EU integration).[11] The following sections show how the MSI/AN and RN weaved together the concept of national interest and the concepts explored in the previous chapters to define their own views on what should be done, and how, concerning European integration. While the concept of national interest is no less important than the others considered so far, its study is best carried out in relation to the other concepts of identity, liberty, and threat because the definition of what constitutes the national interest is related to what the parties consider to be most important in general (e.g., considering it to be in the national interest to work collectively against a threat).

Defending Europe, restoring power, serving the national interest: the Movimento Sociale Italiano/Alleanza Nazionale's cautious support for European integration

The MSI was favourable to the principle of European integration. Because it saw Europe as endangered, it espoused European unity as a way to fend off various threats to its identity and liberty. This view of European integration's purpose was well captured by Romualdi, when in an article in the party newspaper *Secolo d'Italia* he argued in favour of the creation of a nation called Europe 'as a defence against the false myths and false philosophies, the brutality of the force that sustains them and the assault on our liberties and our lives'.[12] Uniting Europe, in the MSI's view, would also restore its power, a point

---

[10] Michael Freeden, *Ideologies and Political Theory: A Conceptual Approach* (Oxford: Oxford University Press, 1998), 3.
[11] Petr Kopecky and Cas Mudde, 'The Two Sides of Euroscepticism: Party Positions on European Integration in East Central Europe', *European Union Politics* 3, no. 3 (2002): 297–326; Vasilopoulou, 'European Integration and the Radical Right'.
[12] Pino Romualdi, 'Le Nostre Radici', *Secolo d'Italia*, 19 April 1981.

well made in the 1979 minority congress motion *Spazio Nuovo* (New Space), which insisted that 'the concept of Europe' would have to be

> a 'myth' based on the observation that only a united, independent and strong Europe [. . .] will be able to, in front of the current superpowers, not only re-establish order, but also make it possible for the world to exist without the duopolistic logic [sic] in which it has been enclosed for years.[13]

The commitment to restoring European power through unity was not entirely guided by marked Europeanism, but also by the view that this was somewhat necessary to preserve the power of the individual nations. As Adriano Romualdi, son of Pino and, albeit only briefly,[14] party intellectual, put it:

> de Gaulle's mistake was to speak in the name of France, and not of Europe. It was to think that France could still be great as France. But Italians, the French and even Germans will no longer be able to be great as Italians, French, Germans; they could be so as Europeans.[15]

In light of this view, the MSI claimed that the goal of European unity was also perfectly compatible with the party's broader commitment to serving the nation. The 1982 congress motion *Destra '80* (Right '80s), brought forward by Romualdi's faction, illustrates this point well. The motion starts by holding that 'the guiding line of Italy's foreign policy must be the defence of its interests of all types' and identifies 'promoting with any initiative an ever-growing political integration within the European community' as a way to achieve that goal. As the motion explains, in the face of Soviet imperialism, 'there is no other possibility to defend oneself than integrating and fully coordinating our interests and our initiatives with those of the other free and independent countries that wish to stay so'.[16]

While AN maintained a commitment to European integration, its narrative centred on the idea of European integration as a process that served the national interest. Like the MSI, AN viewed European integration as a way

[13] Movimento Sociale Italiano, 'Spazio Nuovo. Mozione Congressuale XII Congresso Napoli' (Fondo Movimento Sociale Italiano (serie 1, busta 6, fascicolo 21). Archivio Fondazione Ugo Spirito, Roma, Italia, 1979); for similar points, see also Movimento Sociale Italiano, 'Continuare per Rinnovare. Mozione Congressuale XII Congresso Napoli' (Fondo Movimento Sociale Italiano (serie 1, busta 6, fascicolo 21). Archivio Fondazione Ugo Spirito, Roma, Italia, 1979); Movimento Sociale Italiano, 'Proposta Italia. Mozione Congressuale XV Congresso Sorrento' (Fondo Movimento Sociale Italiano (serie 1, busta 7, fascicolo 25). Archivio Fondazione Ugo Spirito, Roma, Italia, 1987).
[14] Adriano Romualdi died in a car accident in 1973, aged 32.
[15] Cited in Pino Romualdi, *Intervista Sull'Europa* (Palermo: Edizioni Thule, 1979), 53.
[16] Movimento Sociale Italiano, 'Destra '80. Mozione Congressuale, XIII Congresso Roma', *Secolo d'Italia*, 17 January 1982.

to solve issues that nations alone could not solve. It was thus presented, at various stages, as a key supporting mechanism allowing member states to tackle issues such as globalization,[17] complex foreign policy issues,[18] and even long-standing national issues such as the gap between the North and South of Italy.[19] In this sense, it served the national interest by performing a crucial problem-solving role for the nation. This assessment was further reinforced by the understanding that the EU was an arena where the national interest should be pursued. The 2004 programme highlighted this point when it suggested that previous Italian governments wrongly thought that fidelity to the European ideal 'meant renouncing the protection of legitimate political, social and economic interests of the Italian nation', while both could be pursued together at the European level, as the successful experience of countries such as France, Great Britain, and Germany demonstrated.[20]

If the MSI/AN was broadly positive about the principle of European integration, it was more critical about the practice of European integration. The MSI built its assessment of the European Union as a concrete project by referring to the idea that European unity should be aimed at the three interlinked objectives of defending Europe, restoring its power, and serving Italy. It found the EU wanting on all counts. Starting with the view that the EU should allow for the common defence of Europe and the pursuit of power, the EU's form was considered by the party as largely inadequate. This was imputed to a variety of factors, including the replacement of 'nationalisms' with 'low and petty particular interests. The interests of individuals, of economic groups or multinational companies, and especially of parties and their internationals', 'the bad European leading classes', and the 'Europe of technocracy, experts and employees answerable only to themselves.'[21] The prevalence of such localized interests most clearly limited the EU's ability to unite in front of a common threat because it limited Europe's ability to present itself as a unified bloc in the face of the East,[22] leaving it largely 'non-existent' in world politics.[23]

---

[17] Alleanza Nazionale, 'Elezioni Europee '99: Programma Politico' (Retrieved from European Manifesto Project, 1999); Agostino Carrino, 'Questa Europa Poco Amata Dagli Europei', *Secolo d'Italia*, 12 June 2008.
[18] Alleanza Nazionale, 'Programma per Le Elezioni Politiche', *Secolo d'Italia*, 27 February 1994; Alleanza Nazionale, 'Vince La Patria, Nasce l'Europa. Bologna. 4–7 Aprile 2002', *Secolo d'Italia*, 4 April 2002.
[19] Alleanza Nazionale, 'Seconda Conferenza Programmatica Di AN. Napoli 23–25 Febbraio', *Secolo d'Italia*, 23 February 2001.
[20] Alleanza Nazionale, 'Programma Elezioni Del Parlamento Europeo 12/13 Giugno 2004' (Retrieved from European Manifesto Project, 2004).
[21] Romualdi, *Intervista Sull'Europa*, 54.
[22] Movimento Sociale Italiano, 'Per La Nuova Repubblica, Contro Il Sistema. Mozione Congressuale, XIII Congresso Roma', *Secolo d'Italia*, 14 January 1982.
[23] Movimento Sociale Italiano, 'Programma Elezioni 1987', *Secolo d'Italia*, 12 May 1987.

The MSI also considered that the EU's institutional structure was inadequate to pursue true European unity. The main lines of this opposition were well expressed by Michele Rallo in the introduction to Almirante's *Intervista sull'Eurodestra*, when he said that although the current structures of the community were a step in the right direction, the MSI and the *Eurodestra* 'did not identify' with them because in their view,

> Europe is something rather different than a mere super-parliament destined to be the mouthpiece for the internal contradictions of member States; because it believes that Europe is something more than a common market that at times disregards the economic interests of the associated peoples, creating in addition dangerous anti-European moods in certain Countries in our Continent. Equally, the Eurodestra does not identify with old federalism, as Europe cannot be a jumble of semi-powerful states, deprived of a true unifying glue, open to the political and financial speculations of foreign powers.[24]

The 1987 Congress motion *Proposta Italia* (Proposition Italy) struck a familiar chord when it said that the MSI could not 'share the utilitarian and mercantile level on which the life of the European organisms is developed' and did not 'approve its political structures, inspired by a type of parliamentarism in which inconclusiveness and partisan offshoots and subjections coming from different countries end up dominating.'[25]

The MSI's main area of critique of the EU concerned its predominantly economic character which, in the MSI's view, limited its ability to address the real threats that faced Europe. In particular, a purely economic form of integration did not make Europe free in any meaningful way (see also Chapter 3), and failed to provide the necessary tools to defend it from external enemies. Criticism of the EU as a purely economic construction which limited the pursuit of more important political goals is well expressed by Maurizio Gasparri, leader of the youth branch of the MSI (FUAN) and subsequently MP, who claimed that

> we, who have always believed in Europe, will certainly not oppose integration processes. But we do not want a Europe of free trade—we do not want a Europe of

---

[24] Giorgio Almirante, *Intervista Sull'Eurodestra*, ed. Michele Rallo (Palermo: Edizioni Thule, 1978), 9.
[25] Movimento Sociale Italiano, 'Proposta Italia. Mozione Congressuale XV Congresso Sorrento'; Movimento Sociale Italiano, 'Programma Elezioni 1987'; Movimento Sociale Italiano, 'Destra Italiana. Mozione Congressuale XVI Congresso Rimini' (Fondo Movimento Sociale Italiano (serie 4, busta 22, fascicolo 64). Archivio Fondazione Ugo Spirito, Roma, Italia, 1990).

monetary systems and finance only. [. . .] We look at political integration, at the military defence of our Europe, to the cultural identity of our land.[26]

Even though the MSI criticized the EU as being a victim of petty interests, it should be noted that they were not unfamiliar with critiques based on Italy's national interest. For example, a 1982 minority motion criticized the Common Agricultural Policy because it forced Italy's South to compete with a more productive northern Europe.[27] This point was included in the 1983 programme, although, rather than blaming the EU itself, the programme blamed the Italian political class for being unable to protect Italian goods.[28] Further along the line, Maastricht was also heavily criticized by the party as having negative implications for Italy because it created an unequal relationship with European partners and had negative effects on the Italian economy, all the while not presenting a sufficiently 'political' form of integration.[29] In this sense, the MSI was also clearly concerned with ensuring that European integration did not harm Italy.

The MSI also discussed how Europe should be reformed to address these shortcomings. For example, while remaining sceptical of parliamentarism,[30] they suggested at various points strengthening the European Parliament,[31] creating a European executive,[32] establishing an independent foreign and defence policy,[33] and promoting social measures to protect European workers living in countries different from their own.[34] While it is obvious that many of these measures would have served their own political interests

[26] Maurizio Gasparri, 'Alla Logica Della Moneta Opporremo Storia e Cultura', *Secolo d'Italia*, 7 April 1988.
[27] Movimento Sociale Italiano, 'Spazio Nuovo. Mozione Congressuale, XIII Congresso Roma', *Secolo d'Italia*, 16 January 1982.
[28] Movimento Sociale Italiano, 'Il Messaggio Degli Anni '80. Programma Elettorale' (Retrieved from Comparative Manifesto Project, 1983).
[29] Maurizio Gasparri, 'La Crisi Politica Travolge Maastricht', *Secolo d'Italia*, 3 August 1993; P. Toppi, 'Nuova Europa. E Chi Se Ne e' Accorto?', *Secolo d'Italia*, 7 November 1993; Alleanza Nazionale, 'Programma per Le Elezioni Politiche'.
[30] Almirante, *Intervista Sull'Eurodestra*, 46.
[31] Movimento Sociale Italiano, 'Continuare per Rinnovare. Mozione Congressuale XII Congresso Napoli'; Movimento Sociale Italiano, 'Per La Nuova Repubblica, Contro Il Sistema. Mozione Congressuale, XIII Congresso Roma'.
[32] Movimento Sociale Italiano, 'Elezioni 10 Giugno 1979: Il Programma Del MSI-DN per Il Parlamento Europeo', *Secolo d'Italia*, 11 May 1979; Movimento Sociale Italiano, 'Impegno Unitario. Mozione Congressuale XVI Congresso Rimini' (Roma: Archivio Fondazione Ugo Spirito, Fondo Movimento Sociale Italiano, serie 4, busta 22, fascicolo 64, 1990).
[33] Movimento Sociale Italiano, 'Elezioni 10 Giugno 1979: Il Programma Del MSI-DN per Il Parlamento Europeo'; Movimento Sociale Italiano, 'Programma Elezioni 1987'; Gasparri, 'Alla Logica Della Moneta Opporremo Storia e Cultura'; Movimento Sociale Italiano, 'Destra Italiana. Mozione Congressuale XVI Congresso Rimini'.
[34] Almirante, *Intervista Sull'Eurodestra*, 49–50.

or were guided by their national battles,[35] they also demonstrate a will to engage with the existing structures of the EU to pursue the national interest.

Like the MSI, AN was critical of the EU's current form. Although AN generally viewed the EU as a body which should be preserved[36] and even defined it in its 2004 programme as having achieved 'perhaps [the] most extraordinary result of the 20th century' of 'removing the bloody borders which for centuries had separated the peoples and economies of Western Europe',[37] it considered that in many cases the EU did not fulfil its role of problem-solver, and even violated key values. Like the MSI, AN criticized the EU's 'neo-Enlightenment' and '*dirigiste*' form which focused on economics while ignoring key political principles such as democracy and national cultures.[38] More importantly, it questioned the extent to which the EU served Italy's (or even Europe's) interests in a balanced manner. It suggested that Italy was compromising much more than other countries, leading to negative consequences for the country's social and economic development.[39]

The tensions in AN's position on EU integration are captured in an editorial in the *Secolo d'Italia* by Gustavo Selva, an MP and president of the parliamentary committee in charge of foreign policy and EU integration.[40] In the editorial, tellingly called *Se il sogno Europeo diventa incubo* (If the European dream becomes a nightmare), Selva confesses to feeling like a 'defrocked priest' who has to review 'the dream of a Community seeking to become the United States of Europe' after losing faith in 'this Europe'. Following the Dutch and French 'No' votes in the 2005 referendums on the European Constitution, Selva identifies 'the conflict that is ever more evident between the European institutions and the political will of European peoples' as one reason to review the original idea of where European integration should go. He continues, identifying other issues in the project of European integration such as 'the bureaucratization of the institutions' that

---

[35] For example, the focus on the protection of workers in the community can be seen as part of the MSI's long-standing commitment to protecting Italian nationals abroad, while the focus on a stronger Parliament can be seen as guided by their will to have an impact on the decisions of the community through their MEPs.

[36] Mirko Tremaglia, 'Destra Vuol Dire Europa', *Secolo d'Italia*, 2 March 1996; Lucilla Parlato, 'Fini: "Vogliamo Un'Europa Dei Popoli"', *Secolo d'Italia*, 22 March 2002.

[37] Alleanza Nazionale, 'Programma Elezioni Del Parlamento Europeo 12/13 Giugno 2004'.

[38] Alleanza Nazionale, '12 Giugno La Nuova Europa' (retrieved from European Manifesto Project, 1994); Alleanza Nazionale, 'Programma Elezioni Del Parlamento Europeo 12/13 Giugno 2004'.

[39] Tremaglia, 'Destra Vuol Dire Europa'; Gianni Alemanno, 'Rapporti Più Chiari Con l'UE', *Secolo d'Italia*, 29 November 2000; Alleanza Nazionale, 'Vince La Patria, Nasce l'Europa. Bologna. 4–7 Aprile 2002'; Alleanza Nazionale, 'Programma Elezioni Del Parlamento Europeo 12/13 Giugno 2004'.

[40] Gustavo Selva, 'Se Il Sogno Europeo Diventa Incubo', *Secolo d'Italia*, 5 June 2005.

has 'become not a simplification of the relationship between the community and individual citizens, but an obstacle'. Most critically, he considers that Italians need to review their positions on the EU as it is no longer serving their national interests. As he says,

> Following the rhetoric of a 'political Europe of the future' [...] we Italians did the opposite of the French and Germans, and especially of the English: we privileged European politics over the defence of the national interest. I do not mean to say that this has not given us some advantages [...], but I do say that we must no longer talk about European 'unity' without first defending the 'diversity' of interests and of the national 'values'.

Written at a difficult time for the EU—following, as mentioned, the French and Dutch 'No' votes on the Constitutional Treaty—this passage helps highlight the tension between what AN saw as the goal of European integration and the EU's ability to fulfil it. It was stated earlier that AN viewed European integration as necessary to protect the national interest through action at the European level. This would be done by protecting the cultures and nations of Europe—its identity—something which the passage above suggests the EU was no longer able to do. This also leads, in Selva's view, to a break between the EU and its constituent nations, raising issues of democracy. What is perhaps most interesting about the article, however, is the perspective from which it is delivered. Even though Selva criticizes the EU on a wide range of grounds, the overwhelming sense is one of disappointment, the regret of a former convert in seeing that the project one had been pursuing has fallen short. This suggests that AN, even when being critical, remained committed to European integration as a project.

Finally, the MSI/AN had views concerning what a united Europe should look like in the future. In this case, the parties diverge in terms of the language they use to define it. For the MSI, the objective was '*Europa Nazione*' (Nation Europe). To the MSI, the ideal Europe should be 'One, free, self-sufficient',[41] guided by the imperative of power in the external world, but respectful of national individualities. When speaking of the endpoint of European integration, the MSI argued that Europe should become a 'political' and united 'Nation Europe', able to act decisively on the world stage. In the MSI's view, only such a form of European unity would allow the EU to fulfil its goals. As the party's 1987 programme most clearly put it, the MSI wanted 'a politically, economically and militarily integrated Europe, a united Europe as

---

[41] Movimento Sociale Italiano, 'Per La Nuova Repubblica, Contro Il Sistema. Mozione Congressuale, XIII Congresso Roma'.

an influencing factor for peace and stability; it will compete with the USA in maintaining freedom and civilization'.[42] The MSI's 'Nation Europe', then, could be seen primarily as a foreign policy actor, able to project power in the external realm and expected, with time and further political integration, to become 'an equal pole of the USA and the USSR'.[43]

As far as the form that integration should take, while adopting the language of a 'Nation Europe', the MSI viewed the ideal form of integration as a confederal one. MSI activist Michele Rallo discussed this most clearly in the opening sections of the *Intervista sull'Eurodestra*, when he highlighted that the party's 'Nation Europe' was neither a centralized project of European integration nor a federal 'levelling' one, but a confederal project in which Europe would be 'united and integrated' while 'maintaining intact the national individualities that make it up'.[44]

In contrast to the MSI, AN spoke of a *'Europa delle patrie'* (Europe of the Homelands), a confederal but integrated union. While it maintained the MSI's commitment to a confederal and more 'political' Europe, in which the sovereignty and national interests of individual nations would be respected, it also broke with tradition by distancing itself from the idea that European integration should be guided by action against external enemies, and by shifting the intellectual references for its ideal of Europe.

The presence of both breaks and continuities could already be observed in the party's first manifestoes, in which the ideas of the MSI remained present, but were repackaged to fit in with a more standard conservative political lineage. As far as continuity was concerned, the programmes stressed the need for the EU to become a more political confederation of states. At the same time, the party abandoned the language of 'Nation Europe' and adopted the Gaullist formula of 'Europe of the Homelands'.[45] Thus, the 1994 EU manifesto stressed that the party drew its inspiration from de Gaulle's project, while the national programme presented AN's view of an ideal Europe as a 'Confederation of diverse and sovereign states' able to 'find together the strength and will to give themselves a foreign or security policy, a unity of aims, of directives and laws that guarantee the primary efficacy of "politics", not subordinated to economics as a system that is an end in itself'.[46]

---

[42] Movimento Sociale Italiano, 'Programma Elezioni 1987'.
[43] Movimento Sociale Italiano, 'Destra Italiana. Mozione Congressuale XVI Congresso Rimini'.
[44] Almirante, *Intervista Sull'Eurodestra*, 9–10.
[45] It is worth noting that, at least in the 1970s, the MSI was not overly enthused by de Gaulle's vision, which Romualdi defined as 'positively grand' but 'chauvinistic' (1979: 52).
[46] Alleanza Nazionale, '12 Giugno La Nuova Europa'.

AN remained attached to this confederal and political project even in the years that followed, viewing it as the form of collaboration most respectful of national identities. The 2002 Congress expressed this view clearly when presenting the ideal EU as 'an institution that, preserving the specificities of individual States as an element of richness in the Union, can synergistically unite their contributions, not annulling the national States but constituting a confederation of nation-states'.[47] Other documents stressed that it should also seek to be closer to the citizens and to the peoples of Europe,[48] an innovation which brought the party more in line with the EU itself. Importantly and, as we shall see, in stark opposition to the RN, this confederal Europe remained a variation of the EU that kept intact its key structures, rather than an entirely new project based on radically different forms of collaboration.

EU-optimist to EU-phobic: the Rassemblement National's changing views on European integration

The RN's position on the desirability of European integration, and especially on the form it should take, shifted visibly over time. In its early years, the RN (like the MSI) constructed its positions on the principle of European integration against the backdrop of a threat to the continent, viewing European unity as a form of protection from the outside world. This point is well illustrated in Jean-Marie Le Pen's 1984 campaign book, in which he suggests that, after decades of war between Europeans,

> one can now accept the creation of a united Europe in the face of external threats. When one creates a society, it is because one does not have the means to act alone. It is certain that the threat of Soviet Communism (and the dangers of disintegration by subversion it entails) is also Europe's great chance. It can allow it to define itself precisely against a certain form of danger.[49]

Far from being an isolated case of support for European integration, this vision was pervasive in party documents at the time. Thus, Le Pen repeated the same point in a more succinct fashion later in the book, when he claimed that 'there will be no Europe unless it is destined to become a Nation. Now this nation cannot be created if not to defend itself (and God knows that

---

[47] Alleanza Nazionale, 'Vince La Patria, Nasce l'Europa. Bologna. 4–7 Aprile 2002'.
[48] Parlato, 'Fini: "Vogliamo Un'Europa Dei Popoli"'; Alleanza Nazionale, 'Programma Elezioni Del Parlamento Europeo 12/13 Giugno 2004'.
[49] Jean-Marie Le Pen, *Les Français d'abord* (Paris: Carrère—Michel Lafon, 1984), 155–156.

Europe is threatened) against external dangers',⁵⁰ and again in other documents, such as the 1989 *La Lettre* editorial *Pour Une Europe Des Peuples* (For a Europe of the Peoples) in which he insisted that 'the unity of Europe is necessary because what is at stake is our survival, our independence, our identity and our culture, our economic and social capacity'.⁵¹

Because the RN also saw Europe as in decline, it followed the MSI in its assessment of European integration as a means to restore European power. Combining the concepts of liberty and threat, this view was brought forward particularly by Bruno Mégret, who insisted on the need for Europeans to unite in the name of the 'common benefit' of 'power'.⁵² European unity was considered desirable as a way to create a European *'pôle de puissance'* (power centre), which would be able to stand up to the USA and the USSR and ensure that Europe and its nations 'find anew the power they have lost in the fratricidal wars they fought against one another and that they left the USA and the USSR to arbitrate'.⁵³

Underlying the RN's commitment to the principle of European integration was a belief that this would serve France's national interest. Restoring European power and defending Europe were equivalent to defending France—or so the party thought, at least until the end of the 1980s when it concluded that in fact further ambitious European integration would not serve the national interest.⁵⁴ This, in turn, led the RN to propose increasingly less ambitious measures to adopt at the European level and to focus exclusively on European integration as a means to pursue mutually beneficial projects. While this could occasionally lead to proposing measures such as a common currency (but not a shared one),⁵⁵ European integration only made sense, in the words of the 2009 programme, 'if it creates jobs, riches; if it creates the conditions for more security and for peace for the peoples of Europe first'.⁵⁶ Therefore, while the party did not turn against the principle of European collaboration, it certainly recalibrated its expectations concerning how far it should go.

---

⁵⁰ Ibid., 164.
⁵¹ Jean-Marie Le Pen, 'Pour Une Europe Des Peuples', *La Lettre de Jean-Marie* Le Pen, May, no 1 1989.
⁵² Bruno Mégret, 'Les Patries Contre Maastricht: Notre Europe', *La Lettre de Jean-Marie Le Pen*, July 1992.
⁵³ Front National, *Militer Au Front* (Paris: Editions Nationales, 1991), 118.
⁵⁴ On the reasons for this shift, see Chapter 2 and Marta Lorimer, 'The Rassemblement National and European Integration', in *A Critique of Europe. Nationalist, Sovereignist and Right-Wing Populist Attitudes to the EU*, ed. Francesco Berti and Joanna Sondel-Cedarmas (London: Routledge, 2022), 49–59.
⁵⁵ Jean-Marie Le Pen, 'Fête de Jeanne d'Arc Du 1er Mai 1998' (retrieved from Archives de l'Internet, Bibliothèque nationale de France, 1998); Front National, 'Le Front National Pour Restaurer Notre Identité Nationale Face à l'Europe Fédérale', *Français d'abord*, November, no 1, 1999.
⁵⁶ Front National, 'Programme "Europe" Du Front National: Leur Europe n'est Pas La Notre! Voila l'Europe Que Nous Voulons' (retrieved from European Manifesto Project, 2009).

For the nation and for Europe: European and national interests   151

If the RN's positions on the principle of integration shifted over time, it is worth noting that its assessment of the EU's form was always more critical. While the party adopted a more nuanced stance in the early 1980s,[57] and occasionally welcomed specific EU initiatives such as the single market,[58] overall it has tended to see the EU as a deeply flawed project which did not conform with its view of what European unity should achieve. In the 1980s, the RN expressed this criticism by presenting the EU as insufficiently ambitious in its political aims. For example, in the 1985 programmatic book *Pour la France* (For France), Jean-Marie Le Pen criticized the EU for neither 'solving issues' nor giving itself proper 'financial and regulatory means'. He also presented the European Parliament as 'an assembly responsive to Marxist dialectics and to Third-Worldist ideology' and the Commission as 'an organism influenced by bureaucratic socialism', concluding that

> this is not what Europe is, it is not only the Europe of merchants, of trade unions, of theoreticians and of technocrats. It is an extra-millenary community of destiny, whose construction, the last great design of the 20th century, can give our youth a future commensurate to its legitimate ambitions.[59]

In line with its shift of view on the principle of European integration, from the end of the 1980s and early 1990s RN criticism of the practice of EU integration truly exploded and the party became hyper-critical of the EU on three grounds. First, the EU was assessed negatively as a body that harmed identities by removing (or shifting) established physical and symbolic boundaries between 'Us' and 'Them'. Under this heading, the EU was presented, for example, as a force that facilitated immigration (both intra-EU and extra-EU),[60] empowered regions,[61] and destroyed national diversity through harmonization.[62] Second, the RN opposed the current form of European integration by claiming that the EU violated the fundamental principle

---

[57] Front National, 'Manifesto de La Campagne de Jean-Marie Le Pen', *Le National*, May 1981; Le Pen, *Les Français d'abord*; Jean-Marie Le Pen, *Pour La France: Programme Du Front National* (Paris: Albatros, 1985).
[58] Mégret, 'Les Patries Contre Maastricht: Notre Europe'.
[59] Le Pen, *Pour La France: Programme Du Front National*, 188–189.
[60] Jean-Marie Le Chevallier, 'Un Nouveau Pas Vers l'Europe Du Tiers-Monde', *La Lettre de Jean-Marie Le Pen*, September, no 1, 1988; Front National, 'Programme Du Front National' (retrieved from Comparative Manifesto Project, 2002); B. Gollnisch, 'Des Plombiers Polonais', *Français d'abord.*, March 2006; Marine Le Pen, 'Discours de Fréjus' (retrieved from https://www.youtube.com/watch?v=7SduAX4knp4, 2016). See also Chapter 4.
[61] Front National, 'Programme Du Front National'; Jean-Marie Le Pen, 'Discours Au Conseil National Du Front National' (retrieved from Archives de l'Internet, Bibliothèque nationale de France, 2003).
[62] Bruno Mégret, 'Les Principes Fondateurs de Notre Europe', *La Lettre de Jean-Marie Le Pen*, May, no 2, 1989; Front National, *Militer Au Front*, 116; Front National, '2007: Programme de Gouvernement de Jean-Marie Le Pen', ed. Front National (Retrieved from Comparative Manifesto Project, 2007).

of liberty by removing power from its rightful holders. Drawing on the notions of autonomy and self-rule, this form of opposition encompassed attacks on the primacy of EU law, on the 'unelected Brussels bureaucrats', and on the EU more generally as diminishing the sovereignty of its constituent members.[63] Finally, the RN also developed an economic line of critique which suggested that the EU created poverty in its members, thus violating their national interest and harming their long-term chances of survival. This was built by criticizing both generic and specific aspects of EU policy such as its flair for liberalization, the Common Agricultural Policy, and especially the euro, defined in a speech as an 'occupation currency'.[64]

All three lines of critique are well summarized in a 2011 article by Louis Aliot, RN politician, former partner of Marine Le Pen, and at the time of writing mayor of Perpignan. The article, published in the party magazine *Nations Presse Magazine* (created in 2010 to support Marine Le Pen's candidacy for the leadership of the party), holds that:

> Faced with this situation, while they could have been an anchor to safeguard our jobs, our social protection, our public services and our cultures, Europe and its Brussels Commission have forced upon the people a European model:
> - drifting geographically, first East, up to Asia Minor with the desired accession of Turkey;
> - drifting economically towards unfettered free trade;
> - drifting politically through the slow construction of a EUSSR.[65]

These three lines of critique as presented by Aliot are in continuity with the party's message prior to Le Pen's arrival at the helm of the party and have remained overall constant, albeit with some shift in focus. For example, in the aftermath of the 2007 financial crisis and the 2009 sovereign debt crisis, Marine Le Pen gave more resonance to the economic critique of the European Union.[66] The essentials, however, remain the same and since the end of the 1980s and early 1990s in particular, the EU is assessed negatively as a

---

[63] Front National, 'Le Front National Pour Restaurer Notre Identité Nationale Face à l'Europe Fédérale'; Front National, 'Notre Projet: Programme Politique Du Front National' (Retrieved from www.frontnational.com, 2012); Marine Le Pen, 'La Révision Constitutionnelle Que Je Propose Aux Français' (2017).

[64] Le Pen, 'Fête de Jeanne d'Arc Du 1er Mai 1998'; on this third line of critique, see also Front National, 'Le Front National Pour Restaurer Notre Identité Nationale Face à l'Europe Fédérale'; Jean-Marie Le Pen, 'Discours à Toulouse Sur Le Thème de l'Europe' (retrieved from Archives de l'Internet, Bibliothèque nationale de France, 2007).

[65] Louis Aliot, 'L'autre Europe', *Nations Presse Magazine*, July 2011.

[66] Gilles Ivaldi, 'Towards the Median Economic Crisis Voter? The New Leftist Economic Agenda of the Front National in France', *French Politics* 13, no. 4 (December 2015): 346–369, doi:10.1057/fp.2015.17.

body with unclear boundaries (and which removes the ones that are present), an economically unprosperous area, and a bureaucratic nightmare removing political power from its rightful holders.

One area of change in the RN's criticism of the EU is how it proposes to deal with it, with the party oscillating between leaving the EU and reforming it. The party has been ambivalent on this, supporting in turn exit from the EU project as a whole,[67] a simple renegotiation with no mention of exit,[68] and a renegotiation with a possibility of exit if this does not go in the right direction.[69]

If the EU is so inadequate, what does the RN propose to supplant it with? Over the years, the RN's answer to this question appears to have become increasingly less ambitious. Although the chosen terminology has remained relatively similar, with the party swaying between 'Europe of the Nations', 'Europe of the Homelands', and 'Europe of the Peoples', the type of project it has suggested has not remained quite as static. To observe the evolution in the RN's positions, it is worth comparing three different documents spanning a 20-year period. The first one is an excerpt from the 1991 party guide *Militer au Front* (Being an activist in the Front) in which the 'Europe of the Homelands' is presented as 'a community of civilization founded on the renewal of European nations, each preserving its identity and integrity within a confederal entity' based on 'a political, and not economic, project. [. . .] The common denominator must be specific to European countries; therefore, it must be founded on European identity and civilization'. This confederal entity should, the document continues, be based on the Swiss model and aim to do 'what states cannot do themselves: find the means for a shared defence, develop great projects such as Ariane, Hermes or Airbus', all the while remaining a 'European Europe' free from non-European immigration.[70] To some extent, what is suggested is a fairly ambitious approach: a 'political Europe' based on a common civilization rather than a mere economic project, and aimed primarily at protecting Europe from threats such as decline.

Whereas in *Militer au Front* the project of European unity appeared as having to take a confederal form, later documents seemed to suggest less structured forms of ad hoc cooperation as preferable. This is well illustrated

---

[67] Front National, 'Programme Du Front National'.
[68] Front National, '2007: Programme de Gouvernement de Jean-Marie Le Pen'; Rassemblement National, 'Pour Une Europe Des Nations et Des Peuples (Projet—Elections Européennes)', 2019, https://www.politique-animaux.fr/sites/www.politique-animaux.fr/fichiers/prises-de-positions/pieces-jointes/europeennes-projet-rn.pdf.
[69] Front National, 'Notre Projet: Programme Politique Du Front National'; Front National, '144 Engagements Présidentiels' (retrieved from www.rassemblementnational.fr, 2017).
[70] Front National, *Militer Au Front*, 118–119.

in the second document considered here, an article by Carl Lang, an MEP and Secretary-General of the party, in party magazine *Français d'abord*. For Lang, 'the only Europe worth building is that in which free cooperation between fully independent and totally sovereign nations reinforces each one of them. This cooperation can only be carried out at the intergovernmental level'. Instead of having a confederation that somehow works together, in this configuration, which Lang calls a Europe of 'the Nations, of the Homelands and of the Peoples', 'the States would be able to pick freely the domains in which they wish to act together'. What do not change are the geographical limits of this project, which would, as Lang explicitly says 'welcome all European countries, but only European countries'.[71]

More recent iterations of the RN's project for a future Europe are closer in line with Lang than with the early RN's party guide. For example, in the 2012 electoral programme, the party called for a renegotiations of EU treaties, so as to make it possible for France 'to regain control of its borders, preferably in the context of a free association of European States sharing the same vision and the same interests on subjects such as immigration or the rules regulating foreign exchanges and the movement of capital', and start a new period of 'great innovative European projects to come, at the service of the peoples, built by starting from voluntary partnerships'. This, the party concludes, would 'return to its rightful place the useful European cooperation: in projects, cooperation, but removing the tutelage of a Eurocratic Super-State'.[72]

While the above projects varied in ambition, it is worth noting that they all stressed a commitment to the (endangered) concepts of identity and liberty discussed in previous chapters. The party, in fact, viewed European unity as guided by the principle of identity among Europeans, in a form that would respect their individual sovereignty, and aimed at their collective defence and the pursuit of mutually beneficial projects where nations alone would not be able to act. The next section explores the value of this commitment further.

Consistently nationalist: legitimacy through renewed commitments

Political parties change. Members, personnel, and leaders change, as do their ideas and policy prescriptions.[73] On the topic of European integration alone,

---

[71] C. Lang, 'Indépendance', *Français d'abord*, October, no 2, 2000.
[72] Front National, 'Notre Projet: Programme Politique Du Front National'.
[73] James Adams, 'Causes and Electoral Consequences of Party Policy Shifts in Multiparty Elections: Theoretical Results and Empirical Evidence', *Annual Review of Political Science* 15, no. 1 (June 2012):

for example, socialist,[74] green,[75] and far-right parties[76] have all changed their positions. Change happens for a variety of good reasons,[77] but it is not a cost- or risk-free process. Sudden or dramatic change can create fractures that hamper the internal cohesion of the party.[78] Change too much and parties also risk becoming unrecognizable to their members and supporters, losing a precious reserve of support and allegiance.[79] Change is particularly dangerous for niche parties such as those of the far right. Voters for these parties tend to be strongly ideologically oriented, and may view any shift as a betrayal of a party's core commitments.[80]

One under-appreciated fact about party change, however, is that it can also be an opportunity to restate one's commitment to existing principles. The introduction of new issues in party ideology, for example, provides an opportunity for political parties to say something about how 'old' principles and concepts matter to the understanding of new issues. Similarly, rather than becoming a moment in which a party distances itself completely from its previous views, changing positions on certain issues provides an opportunity to justify those changes in the name of previous beliefs. Developing the link between old and new enables parties to commit themselves anew to their ideological core, and creates continuity between the party's past and present by showing that the same principles keep applying over time and across issues. In turn, this continuity contributes to an overall sense of consistency—the idea that a party will stand for what it believes in.

The addition of Europe to their ideological framework provided the MSI/AN and RN with this kind of opportunity. As the previous chapters

401–419, doi:10.1146/annurev-polisci-031710-101450; Jelle Koedam, 'A Change of Heart? Analysing Stability and Change in European Party Positions', *West European Politics* 45, no. 4 (June 2022): 693–715, doi:10.1080/01402382.2021.1915659.

[74] Fabio Wolkenstein, 'The Social Democratic Case against the EU', *Journal of European Public Policy* 27, no. 9 (September 2020): 1349–1367, doi:10.1080/13501763.2020.1753229.

[75] Elizabeth Bomberg, *Green Parties and Politics in the European Union* (London; New York: Routledge, 1998).

[76] Cas Mudde, *Populist Radical Right Parties in Europe* (Cambridge: Cambridge University Press, 2007), doi:10.1111/j.1478-9302.2009.00194.x; Marta Lorimer, 'What Do They Talk about When They Talk about Europe? Euro-Ambivalence in Far Right Ideology', *Ethnic and Racial Studies* 44, no. 11 (2021): 202, doi:10.1080/01419870.2020.1807035.

[77] See Andreas Fagerholm, 'Why Do Political Parties Change Their Policy Positions? A Review', *Political Studies Review*, 2015: 501–511, doi:10.1111/1478-9302.12078 for a review.

[78] Adam Przeworski and John Sprague, *Paper Stones: A History of Electoral Socialism* (Chicago: University of Chicago Press, 1986).

[79] Adams, 'Causes and Electoral Consequences of Party Policy Shifts in Multiparty Elections'; Ian Budge, David Robertson, and Derek Hearl, *Ideology, Strategy and Party Change: Spatial Analyses of Post-War Election Programmes in 19 Democracies* (Cambridge: Cambridge University Press, 1987).

[80] James Adams et al., 'Understanding Change and Stability in Party Ideologies: Do Parties Respond to Public Opinion or to Past Election Results?', *British Journal of Political Science* 34, no. 4 (2004): 589–610, doi:10.1017/S0007123404000201; James Adams et al., 'Are Niche Parties Fundamentally Different from Mainstream Parties? The Causes and the Electoral Consequences of Western European Parties' Policy Shifts 1976–1998', *American Journal of Political Science* 50, no. 3 (2006): 513–529.

and the sections above have shown, the parties mobilized four concepts to conceptualize Europe and define their positions on the EU: identity, liberty, threat, and national interest. These four concepts all belong to the ideological realm of far-right nationalism. The concept of identity is key to nationalism because it performs a 'boundary-building' function, defining who belongs and who does not belong to the nation. The concept of liberty expresses the need for the nation thus defined to have its will expressed politically and institutionally. The concept of threat, while not as central as the other two, 'colours' these concepts in a way that is distinctive to the far right, in that while other parties may appeal to ideas of identity and liberty, few also present them as deeply endangered in the way the far right does. It also has the merit of restating the importance of the core concepts of identity and liberty precisely because it presents them as something that is cherished and in need of defending. Finally, pursuing the national interest may be viewed as a logical implication of nationalism, with the appeal to the national interest constituting a linkage between the party's ideological core and its political practice.

The MSI/AN and RN's appeal to these key concepts in defining their positions on European integration enabled them to renew their commitment to long-held principles and stressed the parties' nature as 'communities of belief'.[81] When the MSI/AN and RN made Europe a part of their ideology and justified their positions by referring to key concepts, they did not simply stress their commitment to certain principles; they also showed more clearly how this plays out in different contexts. They created a narrative about how what matters to them matters everywhere, not simply in selected areas. In short, Europe functioned as an ideological resource by helping them signal that they could be trusted to defend the principles that they (and their supporters) stood for in all matters.

One might be sceptical about the value of consistency for political parties. It could be objected that voters are motivated by a variety of factors that have relatively little to do with ideological consistency, such as cost-benefit analyses, long-standing social cleavages, and short-term factors such as campaigns and issue attitudes.[82] Activists display a similar level of complexity in joining parties for a variety of reasons, including furthering party objectives

---

[81] White and Ypi, *The Meaning of Partisanship*.
[82] Downs, *An Economic Theory of Democracy*; Stein Rokkan and Seymour Martin Lipset, *Party Systems and Voter Alignments: Cross-National Perspectives* (New York: Free Press, 1967); Sara B. Hobolt, *Europe in Question: Referendums on European Integration* (Oxford: Oxford University Press, 2009); Ruth Dassonneville, 'Volatile Voters, Short-Term Choices? An Analysis of the Vote Choice Determinants of Stable and Volatile Voters in Great Britain', *Journal of Elections, Public Opinion and Parties* 26, no. 3 (2016): 273–292, doi:10.1080/17457289.2016.1158181.

and collective interests, finding like-minded people, and taking advantage of the material benefits offered by membership.[83] Complexity of motives should not, however, lead to a discounting of the importance of consistency. Consistency may not be all that matters, but constancy of message serves a crucial role in injecting a measure of predictability to political engagement because it ensures that, whatever the reasons one comes to politics for, the message makes sense as part of a coherent whole that can be 'meaningfully endorsed'.[84] The message is what binds the party together and what is presented to voters, so it needs to be somewhat consistent in time and space if the party does not want to appear to be betraying its own principles and lose credibility in the process.

Being able to show some form of continuity may have proven to be particularly valuable for the parties in times of change. By demonstrating conceptual continuity, the MSI/AN and RN could signal that their message could still be backed even at times in which they were changing—either as parties, or in their positions—and counterbalance any view that they might be forgetting who they were. To develop this point, it is worth looking in depth at two very visible instances of change: the RN's U-turn on European integration, and the MSI's transition to AN.

The RN's shift from support for European integration to opposition to it has been discussed at various points in this book.[85] However, even when the RN changed positions, it displayed significant levels of continuity in the terms it used to justify its positions. The degree of continuity in concepts (if not in positions) is well captured by a comparison of the two following quotes, one from the early RN's pro-EU period and the latter from its anti-EU years:

> Europe can only be built in the fight for its liberty, even more than that, for its liberation. We will never accept the amputation and slavery of the sister nations captured by communism [. . .].
>
> For there to be a Europe, there needs to be a European sentiment, and that is why we have wanted to transcend patriotism, our national patriotisms, in a European patriotism. That means that there will be no Europe unless it is likely to become a Nation. Now, this nation cannot be created if not to defend itself (and God knows that Europe is menaced) from foreign dangers. [. . .]

---

[83] Michael Bruter and Sarah Harrison, *The Future of Our Democracies: Young Party Members in Europe*, 2009, doi:10.1057/9780230245426; Monica Poletti, Paul Webb, and Tim Bale, 'Why Do Only Some People Who Support Parties Actually Join Them? Evidence from Britain', *West European Politics* 42, no. 1 (2019): 156–172, doi:10.1080/01402382.2018.1479921.

[84] Jonathan White, 'The Party in Time', *British Journal of Political Science* 47, no. 4 (2017): 854, doi:10.1017/S0007123415000265.

[85] See Chapter 2 and Lorimer, 'The Rassemblement National and European Integration'.

> The fight for Europe is a fight for France, and the fight for France is a fight for Europe. Build Europe, yes! But by reconstructing France first. Help Europeans, yes! But by helping the French first![86]

> The European Union, created at the beginning between countries sharing similar civilizations, with comparable levels of economic and social development, founded on the principle of 'Community preference', is today diverted from its aims. The results are well known: opening of borders leading to offshoring, unemployment, the dictatorship of the markets, destruction of public services, precariousness, poverty, massive immigration. Installation of a Super-State, with its Constitution, its indefinite borders where one would like to allow Turkey to become a member, its ultra-liberal and globalist ideology, its ecstasy of new competences.[87]

The two passages reproduced here illustrate the positions held by the same party but separated by roughly thirty years. In the first, extracted from the chapter *Une patrie forte dans une Europe forte* (A strong homeland in a strong Europe) of Jean-Marie Le Pen's 1984 programmatic book *Français d'abord*, Le Pen discusses his (mostly) favourable view of European integration. The second passage heads the 'Europe' sections of the RN's 2012 electoral programme, where, in its original form, it is duly followed by a discussion of the EU's democratic deficit, its role as a body that was built 'without the people' and working 'against the people', and the ways in which it harms France; it also ends with the call to leave the EU and 'lay the foundations for a Europe that will respect popular sovereignties, national identities, languages and cultures, and that will truly be at the service of the peoples through concrete actions'.[88]

What is remarkable about these passages is that while the party changed position on the EU, the core concepts it relied upon remained the same, albeit interpreted differently. In the first passage, identity appears through ideas of a shared heritage and European patriotism; in the second, it is something that the EU has ceased to respect when it abandoned the idea of 'Community preference' and clear borders. In the first passage, there is a call for the liberty of Europe; in the second, it is claimed that the EU is some 'Super-State' which always seeks new powers and violates sovereignty. In both cases there is a threat lurking in the background: in the first passage, it is not named; in the second, it is the EU itself. Finally, the first passage advances the idea that what is good for Europe is good for France (and vice-versa), and may as a result be viewed as serving the national interest; while, in parts of the second passage

[86] Le Pen, *Les Français d'abord*, 162–165.
[87] Front National, 'Notre Projet: Programme Politique Du Front National'.
[88] Front National, 'Notre Projet: Programme Politique Du Front National'.

not reproduced here, the EU is presented as something that actively harms it. Overall, then, while the policy changed, the presence of similar guiding principles ensured continuity between past and present.

In the case of the MSI/AN, maintaining the use of similar concepts in its positions on Europe fostered a sense of continuity with the past in times of change for the party. The MSI's transition to AN was not a risk-free process. For a party held together by a strong sense of identity, transitioning to 'something else' was always going to be tricky: how could it change its principles, without losing the support of its cadres, members, activists, and voters?

Defining Europe in broadly similar terms to those adopted by the MSI provided AN with the sense that even in times of change, certain principles remain unaltered. Its continued references to a 'powerful' Europe, its attachment to a European civilization and to an EU dedicated to defending the national interest ensured conceptual and policy continuity between the MSI and its successor party, even as other concepts such as threat disappeared. The notion of Europe as a topic that stresses continuity between past and present is also explicitly referred to by the party. A 1996 article by Mirko Tremaglia in the *Secolo d'Italia* illustrates this well. The article, titled *Destra vuol dire Europa* (Right means Europe), retraces the party's history of support for Europe from the 1970s onwards. Tremaglia presents the MSI as 'on the front line' for the defence of Europe, and AN as continuing in that tradition.[89] Similar points were made in AN's 2004 party manifesto. The manifesto presents Europe as 'one of the most qualifying ideals of the Italian right' and further stresses how since its inception, 'when others were looking at Soviet internationalism, the Italian Right responded by affirming the identity of the united Europe'.[90] Following that lineage, the party claims that it now understands that 'the Union could not only be a simple and sole sum of economic and commercial agreements, but should base itself on a spiritual yearning able to recall its tradition'. Europe, in sum, was presented as a topic that tied together the past and the present of the party, making it possible to anchor a different present in a familiar past.

Conclusion

This chapter has explored the value of consistency as a factor contributing to the MSI/AN and the RN's legitimation. It has argued that Europe provided the MSI/AN and RN with a new arena in which to present and restate their

---

[89] Tremaglia, 'Destra Vuol Dire Europa'.
[90] Alleanza Nazionale, 'Programma Elezioni Del Parlamento Europeo 12/13 Giugno 2004'.

values, and stress continuity between the past and present of the parties. It has shown how the MSI/AN and RN positioned themselves on the principle, practice, and future of European integration, and how the parties repurposed the concepts of identity, liberty, threat, and national interest to define their views on the EU as a concrete political project. This contributed to their legitimation by enabling them to strike a balance between old and new. Even as the parties were changing, or as they were seeking to attract new voters, displaying attachment to existing principles enabled them to stress continuity in times of change and show their traditional voters and activists that they still cared about the core principles that had first led these supporters to back the party. In summary, Europe worked as an ideological resource for the MSI/AN and RN because it helped them strike a balance between the old and the new, and keep old voters on board as they sought to win new ones.

References

Adams, James. 'Causes and Electoral Consequences of Party Policy Shifts in Multiparty Elections: Theoretical Results and Empirical Evidence'. *Annual Review of Political Science* 15, no. 1 (June 2012): 401–419. https://doi.org/10.1146/annurev-polisci-031710-101450.

Adams, James, Michael Clark, Lawrence Ezrow, and Garrett Glasgow. 'Understanding Change and Stability in Party Ideologies: Do Parties Respond to Public Opinion or to Past Election Results?' *British Journal of Political Science* 34, no. 4 (2004): 589–610. https://doi.org/10.1017/S0007123404000201.

Adams, James, Michael Clark, Lawrence Ezrow, and Garrett Glasgow. 'Are Niche Parties Fundamentally Different from Mainstream Parties? The Causes and the Electoral Consequences of Western European Parties' Policy Shifts, 1976–1998'. *American Journal of Political Science* 50, no. 3 (2006): 513–529.

Alemanno, Gianni. 'Rapporti Più Chiari Con l'UE'. *Secolo d'Italia*, 29 November 2000.

Aliot, Louis. 'L'autre Europe'. *Nations Presse Magazine*, July 2011.

Alleanza Nazionale. '12 Giugno La Nuova Europa' (retrieved from European Manifesto Project, 1994).

Alleanza Nazionale. 'Programma per Le Elezioni Politiche'. *Secolo d'Italia*, 27 February 1994.

Alleanza Nazionale. 'Elezioni Europee '99: Programma Politico' (retrieved from European Manifesto Project, 1999).

Alleanza Nazionale. 'Seconda Conferenza Programmatica Di AN. Napoli 23–25 Febbraio'. *Secolo d'Italia*, 23 February 2001.

Alleanza Nazionale. 'Vince La Patria, Nasce l'Europa. Bologna. 4–7 Aprile 2002'. *Secolo d'Italia*, 4 April 2002.

Alleanza Nazionale. 'Programma Elezioni Del Parlamento Europeo 12/13 Giugno 2004' (retrieved from European Manifesto Project, 2004).

Almirante, Giorgio. *Intervista Sull'Eurodestra*. Edited by Michele Rallo (Palermo: Edizioni Thule, 1978).

Bomberg, Elizabeth. *Green Parties and Politics in the European Union* (London; New York: Routledge, 1998).

Bruter, Michael, and Sarah Harrison. *The Future of Our Democracies: Young Party Members in Europe*, 2009. https://doi.org/10.1057/9780230245426.

Budge, Ian, David Robertson, and Derek Hearl. *Ideology, Strategy and Party Change: Spatial Analyses of Post-War Election Programmes in 19 Democracies* (Cambridge: Cambridge University Press, 1987).

Carrino, Agostino. 'Questa Europa Poco Amata Dagli Europei'. *Secolo d'Italia*, 12 June 2008.

Dassonneville, Ruth. 'Volatile Voters, Short-Term Choices? An Analysis of the Vote Choice Determinants of Stable and Volatile Voters in Great Britain'. *Journal of Elections, Public Opinion and Parties* 26, no. 3 (2016): 273–292. https://doi.org/10.1080/17457289.2016.1158181.

Downs, Anthony. *An Economic Theory of Democracy* (New York: Harper & Row, 1985).

Epstein, Leon D. *Political Parties in Western Democracies* (New Brunswick: Transaction Books, 1980).

Fagerholm, Andreas. 'Why Do Political Parties Change Their Policy Positions? A Review'. *Political Studies Review*, 14, no 4, 2015: 501–511. https://doi.org/10.1111/1478-9302.12078.

Freeden, Michael. *Ideologies and Political Theory: A Conceptual Approach* (Oxford: Oxford University Press, 1998).

Front National. 'Manifesto de La Campagne de Jean-Marie Le Pen'. *Le National* (May 1981).

Front National. *Militer Au Front* (Paris: Editions Nationales, 1991).

Front National. 'Le Front National Pour Restaurer Notre Identité Nationale Face à l'Europe Fédérale'. *Français d'abord*, November, no 1, 1999.

Front National. 'Programme Du Front National' (retrieved from Comparative Manifesto Project, 2002).

Front National. '2007: Programme de Gouvernement de Jean-Marie Le Pen'. Edited by Front National (retrieved from Comparative Manifesto Project, 2007).

Front National. 'Programme "Europe" Du Front National: Leur Europe n'est Pas La Notre! Voila l'Europe Que Nous Voulons' (retrieved from European Manifesto Project, 2009).

Front National. 'Notre Projet: Programme Politique Du Front National' (retrieved from www.frontnational.com, 2012).

Front National. '144 Engagements Présidentiels' (retrieved from www.rassemble mentnational.fr, 2017).

Gasparri, Maurizio. 'Alla Logica Della Moneta Opporremo Storia e Cultura'. *Secolo d'Italia*, 7 April 1988.

Gasparri, Maurizio. 'La Crisi Politica Travolge Maastricht'. *Secolo d'Italia*, 3 August 1993.

Gollnisch, B. 'Des Plombiers Polonais'. *Français d'abord*, March 2006.

Hobolt, Sara B. *Europe in Question: Referendums on European Integration* (Oxford: Oxford University Press, 2009).

Ivaldi, Gilles. 'Towards the Median Economic Crisis Voter? The New Leftist Economic Agenda of the Front National in France'. *French Politics* 13, no. 4 (December 2015): 346–369. https://doi.org/10.1057/fp.2015.17.

Koedam, Jelle. 'A Change of Heart? Analysing Stability and Change in European Party Positions'. *West European Politics* 45, no. 4 (June 2022): 693–715. https://doi.org/10.1080/01402382.2021.1915659.

Kopecky, Petr, and Cas Mudde. 'The Two Sides of Euroscepticism: Party Positions on European Integration in East Central Europe'. *European Union Politics* 3, no. 3 (2002): 297–326.

Lang, Carl. 'Indépendance'. *Français d'abord*, October, no 2, 2000.

Le Chevallier, Jean-Marie. 'Un Nouveau Pas Vers l'Europe Du Tiers-Monde'. *La Lettre de Jean-Marie Le Pen*, 1988.

Le Pen, Jean-Marie. *Les Français d'abord* (Paris: Carrère—Michel Lafon, 1984).

Le Pen, Jean-Marie. *Pour La France: Programme Du Front National* (Paris: Albatros, 1985).

Le Pen, Jean-Marie. 'Pour Une Europe Des Peuples'. *La Lettre de Jean-Marie Le Pen*, July, no 1, 1989.

Le Pen, Jean-Marie. 'Fête de Jeanne d'Arc Du 1er Mai 1998' (retrieved from Archives de l'Internet, Bibliothèque nationale de France, 1998).

Le Pen, Jean-Marie. 'Discours Au Conseil National Du Front National' (retrieved from Archives de l'Internet, Bibliothèque nationale de France, 2003).

Le Pen, Jean-Marie. 'Discours à Toulouse Sur Le Thème de l'Europe' (retrieved from Archives de l'Internet, Bibliothèque nationale de France, 2007).

Le Pen, Marine. 'Discours de Fréjus' (retrieved from https://www.youtube.com/watch?v=7SduAX4knp4, 2016).

Le Pen, Marine. 'La Révision Constitutionnelle Que Je Propose Aux Français' (2017).

Lorimer, Marta. 'What Do They Talk about When They Talk about Europe? Euro-Ambivalence in Far Right Ideology'. *Ethnic and Racial Studies* 44, no. 11 (2021): 2016–2033. https://doi.org/10.1080/01419870.2020.1807035.

Lorimer, Marta. 'The Rassemblement National and European Integration'. In *A Critique of Europe. Nationalist, Sovereignist and Right-Wing Populist Attitudes to the EU*, edited by Francesco Berti and Joanna Sondel-Cedarmas (London: Routledge, 2022), 49–59.

Mair, Peter. *Party System Change: Approaches and Interpretations* (Oxford: Clarendon Press; Oxford University Press, 1997).

Mégret, Bruno. 'Les Principes Fondateurs de Notre Europe'. *La Lettre de Jean-Marie Le Pen*, May, no 2, 1989.

Mégret, Bruno. 'Les Patries Contre Maastricht: Notre Europe'. *La Lettre de Jean-Marie Le Pen*, July 1992.

Movimento Sociale Italiano. 'Continuare per Rinnovare. Mozione Congressuale XII Congresso Napoli' (Fondo Movimento Sociale Italiano (serie 1, busta 6, fascicolo 21). Archivio Fondazione Ugo Spirito, Roma, Italia, 1979).

Movimento Sociale Italiano. 'Spazio Nuovo. Mozione Congressuale XII Congresso Napoli' (Fondo Movimento Sociale Italiano (serie 1, busta 6, fascicolo 21). Archivio Fondazione Ugo Spirito, Roma, Italia, 1979).

Movimento Sociale Italiano. 'Destra '80. Mozione Congressuale, XIII Congresso Roma'. *Secolo d'Italia*, 17 January 1982.

Movimento Sociale Italiano. 'Per La Nuova Repubblica, Contro Il Sistema. Mozione Congressuale, XIII Congresso Roma'. *Secolo d'Italia*, 14 January 1982.

Movimento Sociale Italiano. 'Spazio Nuovo. Mozione Congressuale, XIII Congresso Roma'. *Secolo d'Italia*, 16 January 1982.

Movimento Sociale Italiano. 'Il Messaggio Degli Anni '80. Programma Elettorale' (retrieved from Comparative Manifesto Project, 1983).

Movimento Sociale Italiano. 'Programma Elezioni 1987'. *Secolo d'Italia* (12 May 1987).

Movimento Sociale Italiano. 'Proposta Italia. Mozione Congressuale XV Congresso Sorrento' (Fondo Movimento Sociale Italiano (serie 1, busta 7, fascicolo 25). Archivio Fondazione Ugo Spirito, Roma, Italia, 1987).

Movimento Sociale Italiano. 'Destra Italiana. Mozione Congressuale XVI Congresso Rimini' (Fondo Movimento Sociale Italiano (serie 4, busta 22, fascicolo 64). Archivio Fondazione Ugo Spirito, Roma, Italia, 1990).

Movimento Sociale Italiano. 'Impegno Unitario. Mozione Congressuale XVI Congresso Rimini' (Roma: Archivio Fondazione Ugo Spirito, Fondo Movimento Sociale Italiano, serie 4, busta 22, fascicolo 64, 1990).

Movimento Sociale Italiano. 'Elezioni 10 Giugno 1979: Il Programma Del MSI-DN per Il Parlamento Europeo'. *Secolo d'Italia*, 11 May 1979.

Mudde, Cas. *Populist Radical Right Parties in Europe* (Cambridge: Cambridge University Press, 2007). https://doi.org/10.1111/j.1478-9302.2009.00194.x.

Parlato, Lucilla. 'Fini: "Vogliamo Un'Europa Dei Popoli"'. *Secolo d'Italia*, 22 March 2002.

Poletti, Monica, Paul Webb, and Tim Bale. 'Why Do Only Some People Who Support Parties Actually Join Them? Evidence from Britain'. *West European Politics* 42, no. 1 (2019): 156–172. https://doi.org/10.1080/01402382.2018.1479921.

Przeworski, Adam, and John Sprague. *Paper Stones: A History of Electoral Socialism* (Chicago: University of Chicago Press, 1986).

Rassemblement National. 'Pour Une Europe Des Nations et Des Peuples (Projet—Elections Européennes)', 2019. https://www.politique-animaux.fr/sites/www.politique-animaux.fr/fichiers/prises-de-positions/pieces-jointes/europeennes-projet-rn.pdf.

Riker, William H. *The Theory of Political Coalitions* (New Haven, CT: Yale University Press, 1962).

Rokkan, Stein, and Seymour Martin Lipset. *Party Systems and Voter Alignments: Cross-National Perspectives* (New York: Free Press, 1967).

Romualdi, Pino. *Intervista Sull'Europa* (Palermo: Edizioni Thule, 1979).

Romualdi, Pino. 'Le Nostre Radici'. *Secolo d'Italia*, 19 April 1981.

Sainsbury, Diane. *Swedish Social Democratic Ideology and Electoral Politics 1944–1948: A Study of the Functions of Party Ideology* (Stockholm: Almqvist & Wiksell International, 1980).

Selva, Gustavo. 'Se Il Sogno Europeo Diventa Incubo'. *Secolo d'Italia*, 5 June 2005.

Skinner, Quentin. 'Some Problems in the Analysis of Political Thought and Action'. *Political Theory* 2, no. 3 (1974): 277–303. https://doi.org/10.1177/009059177400200303.

Toppi, P. 'Nuova Europa. E Chi Se Ne è Accorto?' *Secolo d'Italia*, 7 November 1993.

Tremaglia, Mirko. 'Destra Vuol Dire Europa'. *Secolo d'Italia*, 2 March 1996.

Vasilopoulou, Sofia. 'European Integration and the Radical Right: Three Patterns of Opposition'. *Government and Opposition* 46, no. 2 (2011): 223–244. https://doi.org/10.1111/j.1477-7053.2010.01337.x.

White, John Kenneth. 'What Is a Political Party?' In *Handbook of Party Politics*, edited by R. S. Katz and W. Crotty (London: SAGE, 2006), 5–15. https://doi.org/10.4135/9781848608047.

White, Jonathan. 'The Party in Time'. *British Journal of Political Science* 47, no. 4 (2017): 851–868. https://doi.org/10.1017/S0007123415000265.

White, Jonathan, and Lea Ypi. *The Meaning of Partisanship* (Oxford: Oxford University Press, 2016).

Wolkenstein, Fabio. 'The Social Democratic Case against the EU'. *Journal of European Public Policy* 27, no. 9 (September 2020): 1349–1367. https://doi.org/10.1080/13501763.2020.1753229.

Zariski, Raphael. 'The Legitimacy of Opposition Parties in Democratic Political Systems: A New Use for an Old Concept'. *Political Research Quarterly* 39, no. 1 (1986): 29–47. https://doi.org/10.1177/106591298603900104.

Conclusion

How did political parties that were beyond the pale until a few decades ago go from the margins to the mainstream, and what did what they had to say about Europe have to do with it? In response to this question, this book has argued that Europe constituted a valuable ideological resource for far-right parties looking for legitimation. An ideological resource was conceived of as a device that offers political parties an opportunity to revise and reframe their political message and belief system. Europe functioned as one such resource for far-right parties because it provided them with an opportunity to reframe their political message in a manner that enabled them to widen their appeal, but without losing the support of their core electorate.

The book's core argument has been developed by unfolding the concept of an ideological resource through reference to two case studies, the MSI/AN in Italy and the RN in France. The empirical chapters have traced the concepts the parties used to define Europe and have shown how integrating Europe in their ideology made it possible for them to expand their appeal without alienating their existing members and supporters.

Chapter 2 has shown how the MSI/AN and the RN drew on the concept of identity to integrate Europe in their ideology. Both parties acknowledged the existence of a civilization called 'Europe' and presented themselves as belonging to it. Drawing on the concept of identity to define Europe, the chapter has argued, enabled the parties to transnationalize their message and distance themselves from portrayals of them as dangerous, closed nationalists. It also made it possible for them to associate themselves with the concept of Europe and draw upon its mystique.

Chapter 3 has considered how the MSI/AN and RN defined Europe through the concept of liberty. It has shown how the parties presented Europe as a continent needing to recover its freedom and project power beyond its borders. It has also traced the evolution from thinking of freedom as an external quality of Europe as a whole to its being an internal one belonging to individual nations. The use of the concept of liberty to define Europe enabled the parties to construct a more legitimate image by shifting focus away from the controversial concept of identity to the more positively connoted concept of liberty. It also gave them the possibility to draw upon shared narratives of the nation and 'mainstream' by stressing their attachment to widely shared values and ideas.

Chapter 4 has studied how the MSI and RN employed the concept of threat to characterize Europe. It has demonstrated how the MSI and RN identified threats of different nature to define Europe as an endangered space. It has advanced the view that the use of the concept of threat to define Europe amounted to a far-right variant of emergency politics in which the parties used the notion of an emergency to shift the boundaries of acceptable politics and present themselves as the best-placed actors to address the crises facing their countries. In this, they were not followed by AN who eschewed emergency politics, preferring a narrative of themselves as pragmatic problem-solvers.

Finally, Chapter 5 has analysed how the MSI/AN and RN employed the concept of national interest and those of identity, liberty, and threat to approach the principle, practice, and future of the European Union. It has illustrated how integrating Europe in their ideology made it possible for the parties to restate their commitment to the guiding principles of far-right ideology. This was important in ensuring that they could appear as truly committed and consistent political actors and maintain the allegiance of their core voters and supporters.

These findings add one piece to the puzzle of far-right mainstreaming. Against the view that far-right positions on European integration usually work as markers of marginalization, this book has shown how party positions on EU integration, both oppositional and supportive, contributed to the MSI/AN and RN legitimation efforts. The strength of Europe as an ideological resource derived from its ability to get them not only to discuss a new issue, but to do so in a way that appeared appealing to new voters and consistent with their pre-existing commitments to old ones.

The remainder of this chapter considers some broader implications of the findings presented in the book. It considers whether Europe still functions as an ideological resource today, and what the findings of this book can tell us about Euroscepticism, far-right attempts to construct 'nationalist internationals', and the future of the EU. The chapter concludes with a postscript on Fratelli d'Italia (Brothers of Italy, FdI), the MSI/AN's successor party.

Ideological resources old and new

This book has focused on Europe's function as an ideological resource in the far right's past, but can anything be said about whether it still functions as an ideological resource today? And if Europe is no longer an ideological resource, are there any other issues that could replace it?

At first sight, one could expect Europe to have lost some of its power as an ideological resource. For starters, it is no longer a new issue on which the far right has no established profile. Contemporary far-right parties, including the RN and the MSI/AN's successor, Fratelli d'Italia, have more defined positions on Europe. As such, the leeway they have in defining their positions is reduced. Similarly, although European integration remains divisive today, after Brexit there is a consensus, even amongst far-right parties,[1] that 'hard' Euroscepticism may not be a viable proposition. Additionally, far-right parties today are moving in a significantly different context compared to the one the MSI/AN and the RN were acting in for most of their political lives. At a time when the parties were being shunned by other parties and voters and struggling to gain legitimacy, having something to help them widen their appeal without losing the faithfulness of their existing supporters would have been particularly valuable. However, the far right is no longer an illegitimate fringe, kept out of power. The MSI/AN's successor is currently leading the government in Italy. The RN secured an unprecedented number of MPs in the French 2022 legislative elections. Elsewhere in Europe, far-right parties have joined in government or secured parliamentary representation. Their ideas have been appropriated and spread by mainstream actors, and have acquired growing levels of media coverage.[2] Europe may, therefore, no longer work as an ideological resource for legitimation because there is little left to legitimize—and much of the legitimation is performed by actors other than the far right.

There is some truth to all these arguments, and Europe's role as an ideological resource appears weaker today than in the past. However, it is worth noting that many of the legitimation mechanisms observed in this book remain in use in the far right to this day, suggesting it may still carry some value for the parties involved. Marine Le Pen happily flaunts her 'pro-European, anti-EU' credentials, as do far-right leaders such as FdI's Giorgia Meloni, Fidesz's Viktor Orban, and Law and Justice's Mateusz Morawiecki. These parties also construct their opposition to European integration on

---

[1] Stijn van Kessel et al., 'Eager to Leave? Populist Radical Right Parties' Responses to the UK's Brexit Vote', *British Journal of Politics & International Relations* 22, no. 1 (2020): 65–84, doi:10.1177/1369148119886213.

[2] Lise Esther Herman and James B. Muldoon, *Trumping the Mainstream: The Conquest of Mainstream Democratic Politics by the Populist Radical Right* (London; New York: Routledge, 2019); Benjamin Moffitt, 'How Do Mainstream Parties "Become" Mainstream, and Pariah Parties "Become" Pariahs? Conceptualizing the Processes of Mainstreaming and Pariahing in the Labelling of Political Parties', *Government and Opposition*, 2021, 1–19, doi:10.1017/gov.2021.5; Léonie de Jonge, 'The Populist Radical Right and the Media in the Benelux: Friend or Foe?', *The International Journal of Press/Politics* 24, no. 2 (2019): 189–209, doi:10.1177/1940161218821098.

arguments about the national interest and the importance of defending shared elements such as (domestic) popular and legal sovereignty from outside threats. As such, while Europe may have lost some of its power as an ideological resource, it remains a tool in the arsenal of far-right legitimation.

If Europe has exhausted at least some of its power as an ideological resource, are there any other new topics that could perform a similar function? Could issues such as COVID-19 or climate change, for example, become new ideological resources?

The case for climate change seems particularly strong. Most far-right parties (and not only these) do not have a particularly well-established agenda on environmental issues,[3] and climate change is a divisive subject, especially once one considers questions of how it is best addressed. As such, it carries similar characteristics of 'newness' and 'divisiveness' as Europe did. It could also make it possible for far-right parties to both speak to their traditional voters and appeal beyond them. Similar to Europe, it would enable them to transnationalize their message, draw on notions of emergency, and stress the importance of shared topics such as liberty and the national interest through an insistence on the domestic repercussions of international climate change legislation. At the same time, it would enable them to renew their commitment to existing values by, for example, using the opportunity to highlight the value of the environment for identity, or insisting on how the nation should remain in charge of determining policy on climate change. Some of these approaches could potentially clash with one another, but they need not. If on one hand one could expect issues of environmental protection to clash with arguments about a nation's freedom to legislate on its own on climate change, on the other they could be employed together, with the 'national way' of protecting the environment being presented as the most fitting way forwards. Given these characteristics, it is at least plausible that climate change could in the future perform a similar role as ideological resource that Europe did in the past.

Revisiting Euroscepticism

The findings from this book also tell us something about the far right and Europe more broadly. Far-right parties are usually branded as 'Eurosceptics', their opposition to EU integration taking centre stage in analyses of their

---

[3] Bernhard Forchtner and Balša Lubarda, 'Scepticisms and beyond? A Comprehensive Portrait of Climate Change Communication by the Far Right in the European Parliament', *Environmental Politics* 32, no. 1 (January 2023): 43–68, doi:10.1080/09644016.2022.2048556; Bernhard Forchtner, 'Climate Change and the Far Right', *WIREs Climate Change* 10, no. 5 (September 2019): e604, doi:10.1002/wcc.604.

relationship to Europe. The analysis is not incorrect, but there are enough shades in the far right's approach to Europe that should caution against any simplistic view of its Euroscepticism.

A first element of complexity directly linked to the notion of Europe as an ideological resource concerns the complex relationship that far-right parties have with a process that many of them dislike, but that brings them significant benefits. As the book has shown, even when the RN and, to a lesser extent, the MSI/AN criticized the European Union, they were still able to benefit from it as an ideological resource. Nor were they the only far-right parties to directly benefit from European integration and the opportunities for legitimation it offered.[4] Although this may not directly question the view of them as 'Eurosceptics', the term does obscure the benefits that far-right parties have derived from the process of European integration. While these parties may have opposed the construction and consolidation of the EU, they have also been beneficiaries of it, suggesting at least some likely measure of ambivalence.

A second element of complexity is introduced once one separates 'Europe' from the 'EU'. As this book has shown, the MSI/AN and RN distinguished between the two, and the RN was strongly inclined to demonstrate allegiance to the former but not the latter. Playing with the duality of Europe is not exclusive to the MSI/AN or the RN; rather, it is a recurrent motif in the discourse of the far right (and beyond).[5] The term Eurosceptic captures this duality poorly, at least when taken in the standard form of scepticism as opposition. 'Eurosceptic' as a term only applies to the extent that Europe and the EU are taken to be the same thing. However, separating them allows an interpretation of the far right's position on Europe that is more nuanced.

Finally, the observation of positional changes on Europe over time, and particularly the noticeable shift from support to opposition in the RN, suggests that there is nothing 'natural' about the far right's ideological opposition to the EU. As the book has shown, the MSI did not reject the process of European integration, while the RN only came to oppose it from the late 1980s onwards. Their early support for the EU made sense from an ideological perspective because the parties were strongly anti-communist, placed

---

[4] Duncan McDonnell and Annika Werner, *International Populism: The Radical Right in the European Parliament* (London: Hurst, 2019).

[5] Joseph Cerrone, 'Reconciling National and Supranational Identities: Civilizationism in European Far-Right Discourse', *Perspectives on Politics* 21, no. 3 (2023): 951–66, doi:10.1017/S1537592722002742; Laurie Beaudonnet and Henio Hoyo Prohuber, 'Being European, the Nationalist Way: Europe in the Discourse of Radical Right Parties', *Party Politics*, March 2023, 13540688231161208, doi:10.1177/13540688231161209; Fabio Wolkenstein, 'Christian Europe Redux', *JCMS: Journal of Common Market Studies* 61, no. 3 (May 2023), doi:10.1111/jcms.13400.

in a situation where they realized individual European nations would not be able to achieve their national interest by themselves, and acting in the context of a certain type of European Union—one that did not impinge as strongly on a nation's liberty. This informed a position in which nationalism and Europeanism were compatible. Once the context changed, their positions were revised to adapt, although as the book has shown, the concepts they relied upon did not. Neither were they the only parties to follow a trajectory from support to opposition: the Italian Lega and the Austrian Freiheitliche Partei Österreichs, for example, followed a similar trajectory.[6] In this sense, while there were certainly good reasons to expect that the parties' ideology could lead them to oppose European integration, this was not inevitable, but instead the result of a combination of factors shifting their positions in that direction. As Christopher Flood pertinently noted, ideology is flexible and Europe is complex, and there is no party family that is naturally bound to oppose European integration.[7] Far-right parties are no exception, and this should act as a reminder of why it is important to 'take ideology seriously' in studies of Euroscepticism.[8] The links between positions on the EU and ideology are complex and need to be studied in depth to be fully understood.

These points suggest that the far right's approach to Europe is more complex than terms such as 'Eurosceptic' or 'Europhobic' capture. Mixed within opposition to the EU project are several points of ambivalence, as far-right parties display elements of both support and opposition in their approach to 'Europe' and in their relationship with the EU. Taken together, these points suggest that it may be worth redefining the far right's relationship with Europe as being of an ambivalent, and not just sceptic or 'phobic', nature.[9]

The return of Euronationalism and the future of the EU

Recent years have seen a marked increase in far-right transnational collaboration. The creation of far-right groups in the European Parliament and a growing number of summits in European capitals including Prague, Warsaw,

---

[6] Benedicte Williams, 'Electoral Strategy Trumps Political Ideology', in *Varieties of Right-Wing Extremism in Europe*, ed. Andrea Mammone, Emmanuel Godin, and Brian Jenkins (Abingdon, Oxon: Routledge, 2013), 134–148.

[7] Chris Flood, 'Euroscepticism: A Problematic Concept', UACES 32nd Annual Conference, 2002, 7–11; see also Aleks Szczerbiak and Paul A. Taggart, *Opposing Europe? The Comparative Party Politics of Euroscepticism. Volume 2* (Oxford: Oxford University Press, 2008), 257.

[8] Chris Flood and Rafal Soborski, 'Euroscepticism as Ideology', in *Routledge Handbook of Euroscepticism*, ed. Benjamin Leruth, Nicholas Startin, and Simon Usherwood (London: Routledge, 2018), 38.

[9] Marta Lorimer, 'What Do They Talk about When They Talk about Europe? Euro-Ambivalence in Far Right Ideology', *Ethnic and Racial Studies* 44, no. 11 (2021): 2016–2033, doi:10.1080/01419870.2020.1807035.

and Madrid attest to this.[10] While far-right transnational links are nothing new,[11] media, political, and academic commentators often look at these 'nationalist internationals' with a mixture of concern and bewilderment.[12] Bewilderment because nationalists appear as the most unlikely actors to build transnational links; concern because they worry about what a united far-right front could do, especially to the European Union.

The findings from this book offer a few cues concerning both whether surprise is justified and how concerned one should be about the rise of far-right transnational collaboration. On the first count, they suggest that these forms of collaboration are less puzzling than might appear at first glance. Like the MSI/AN and RN, many far-right parties today will acknowledge some form of European identity that could be used to facilitate the construction of common interests, especially when faced with common enemies. Not unlike the RN and the MSI in the 1980s (but now replacing the USSR with the new threats of 'Brussels' and 'Islam'), these parties have been able to justify their transnational activities as part of a project to defend Europe from the EU and foreign immigration. Additionally, they have been able to collaborate because they find cooperation beneficial. Europe, as this book has shown, is a provider of multiple resources, be they ideological, financial, or symbolic. Developing transnational links served to portray the parties as a unified and growing movement, carrying ever-greater political weight and forming the main axis of opposition to cosmopolitan elites. 'Euronationalism,'[13] in short, makes eminent sense as a political strategy that the far right can benefit from.

However, Euronationalism also has some serious limitations, which suggests one should not assume that a far-right takeover or destruction of the EU institutions is in the making or ever likely to happen. While far-right parties

---

[10] Robert Tait, 'Far Right to Gather in Prague as Fears Grow of Rising Czech Populism', *The Guardian*, December 2017, https://www.theguardian.com/world/2017/dec/15/far-right-conference-prague-czech-republic-populism-marine-le-pen; Lili Bayer, Maia De la Baume, and Hannah Roberts, 'European Far-Right Leaders Fail to Tie the Knot', *Politico*, December 2021, https://www.politico.eu/article/viktor-orban-marine-le-pen-jaroslaw-kaczynski-europe-far-right-parties-coalition/; Euronews, 'Europe's Far-Right Meets in Madrid for Two-Day Summit Led by Spain's Vox', *Euronews*, January 2022, https://www.euronews.com/2022/01/29/europe-s-far-right-meets-in-madrid-for-two-day-summit-led-by-spain-s-vox.

[11] Matteo Albanese and Pablo Del Hierro, *Transnational Fascism in the Twentieth Century: Spain, Italy and the Global Neo-Fascist Network* (London; New York: Bloomsbury Academic, 2016); Andrea Mammone, *Transnational Neofascism in France and Italy* (Cambridge: Cambridge University Press, 2015); José Pedro Zúquete, 'The New Frontlines of Right-Wing Nationalism', *Journal of Political Ideologies* 20, no. 1 (2015): 69–85, doi:10.1080/13569317.2015.991492.

[12] Charlemagne, 'Europe's Hard-Right Is Pitching Voters a Contradictory Fantasy', *The Economist*, 2019, https://www.economist.com/charlemagnes-notebook/2019/05/18/europes-hard-right-is-pitching-voters-a-contradictory-fantasy Last accessed 23 July 2019.

[13] McDonnell and Werner, *International Populism*.

do benefit from some ideological flexibility, the nation and the national interest remain their guiding principles. They may be invoked in the service of a higher European interest, but this strategy will only be effective so long as there is some convergence between the European and the national interest, and where no fundamental trade-offs are required between the two. Thus, while far-right parties may be able to argue that they are both nationalists and Europeans in the current political context, in case of conflict it is unlikely that their commitment to Europe will ever trump the nation. In the improbable event that far-right parties did engineer a takeover of EU institutions, it is also doubtful that they would actively seek to dismantle them. Europe, after all, has its uses, and it is likely that the far right will be willing to take advantage of some of them. More likely, it would try to transform the EU into something more compatible with its own world view. However, what this 'Europe of the Nations' would look like, or how (and if) it would function, remains mostly unclear.

This does not mean that the far right's discourses on Europe carry no dangers and that all is well for the EU. What is more problematic for the EU in the short term is that much of the far right's criticism contests core assumptions about the EU institutions, and runs counter to some of the solutions brought forward to tackle its own legitimacy deficit. For example, the centrality of the concept of identity to the parties' definition of Europe raises questions about the feasibility of promoting a European identity as a solution to the EU's legitimacy issues. In fact, while both the MSI and the RN defined themselves as belonging to Europe, for the RN this did not seem to involve supporting the EU, but rather, became a reason to oppose it in the name of a different, truer Europe. European identity could in this sense become an additional challenge for the EU, rather than a solution.

This points towards another factor worth noting, namely the continued contestedness of the concept of Europe. What this book has shown is that, for all the EU's attempts to monopolize the meaning of Europe,[14] Europe and the EU remain separate concepts, making it possible for parties to pit one against the other. This creates a counter-narrative of Europe which questions the very premise that the EU is the embodiment of Europe. Reopening that equation to contestation removes one of its legitimizing narratives, suggesting that the way ahead for the EU will remain paved with opposition. In that regard, even if far-right parties may not be able to coalesce to dismantle the

---

[14] Andrew Glencross, '"Love Europe, Hate the EU": A Genealogical Inquiry into Populists' Spatio-Cultural Critique of the European Union and Its Consequences', *European Journal of International Relations* 26, no. 1 (2020): 116–136, doi:10.1177/1354066119850242.

EU or orchestrate a takeover of its institutions from the inside, they can still lead public opinion against it and hinder further institution-building.

There is, however, also a silver lining for the European Union here. One point made by this book and by existing literature is that the EU seems to have empowered some of its worst critics. For a body frequently accused of having a 'democratic deficit', the empowering of antagonistic voices may be seen as an unexpectedly democratic outcome, and one that could foster further EU-level democratization. By providing the far right with various types of resources, the EU may have given ammunition to its enemies. However, it has also brought into the conversation more critical voices, who have been able to scrutinize it and foster a conversation concerning its ideal form and shape. Although one could have hoped for better messengers of a critical approach to the European institutions, these parties do have the merit of having opened up European integration to further discussion. Contestation is the beginning of democratization, and it can be hoped that more constructive voices feel empowered by the possibility of responding to these critiques to shape a better EU.

This leads to a further point on what might actually constitute a danger for the EU, and for European societies more broadly going forwards. The aim of this book has been to analyse how far-right parties were makers of their own success. It showed how they could present themselves at their best. However, what 'their best' looks like may have still differed from the political beauty standards of the time, and their efforts would have been unlikely to succeed had they not been helped by others along the way. Mainstream parties certainly played a role in making sure that the messages brought forward by the far right resonated. The role of the mainstream and other actors including the media in normalizing the far right has not been studied here, but presents one of the most critical issues for European countries going forward. Suffice it to refer to Brexit—a vote that would not even have happened had a mainstream conservative party not brought it about. Mainstream parties play a key role in maintaining the floodgates that hold the far right out of power. Once the centre succumbs to far-right rhetoric, even those dams show cracks, ultimately pushing the far right from the margins to the mainstream.

Postscript: after the MSI/AN

The research for this book started in 2015 and ended in 2019. At that time, FdI, the political heirs of the MSI/AN, were not faring too well. FdI was founded in 2012, a few years after the merger of AN and Berlusconi's

Forza Italia.¹⁵ Following Berlusconi's refusal to hold a primary election for the leadership of the Popolo delle Libertà, Giorgia Meloni (former MSI activist, AN minister for youth policies, and current Italian PM), Ignazio la Russa (longstanding MSI/AN politician, former defence secretary and current President of the Italian Senate), and Guido Crosetto (former Forza Italia under-secretary in the Ministry of Defence and now defence minister) created a new splinter party initially called 'Fratelli d'Italia-Alleanza Nazionale' (it dropped 'Alleanza Nazionale' in 2014). In its first elections in 2013, the party obtained less than 2% of the vote, securing a meagre nine mandates. In the 2014 European Parliament elections, it did not get enough votes to get into the parliament. The 2018 elections provided the party with a few more mandates, but it was still hovering in the low single digits, with most of the far-right vote being taken up by Matteo Salvini's Lega.

The party's fortunes changed around 2019.¹⁶ The formation of the Movimento Cinque Stelle-Lega government in 2018, and Salvini's subsequent failed gamble to overturn his own government to force new elections led to a progressive loss of consensus for his party. Many disillusioned Lega voters turned to Meloni's FdI, improving its ratings. However, FdI's opposition to Mario Draghi's technocratic government proved to be the real game-changer. In 2021 Draghi, a former president of the European Central Bank, took the helm of a grand coalition including most parties in the Italian Parliament. FdI decided not to join the government and effectively remained the only party in opposition. This choice enhanced its public profile and led to its significant growth in the polls. In September 2022, FdI won the parliamentary elections with 26% of the vote and Giorgia Meloni became the leader of the first far right-led coalition government in Western Europe.

This book has not studied FdI's approach to Europe, partly because of its controversial status as a 'successor party'¹⁷ and partly because at the time of research, it appeared as an actor of limited relevance. However, early analyses of its positions suggest that its way of defining Europe is not too dissimilar from that of the MSI/AN and RN. Although FdI is on the whole significantly more critical of the EU than the MSI/AN ever was (and especially so between

---

¹⁵ Linda Basile and Rossella Borri, 'Sovereignty of What and for Whom? The Political Mobilisation of Sovereignty Claims by the Italian Lega and Fratelli d'Italia', *Comparative European Politics* 20, no. 3 (June 2022): 365–389, doi:10.1057/s41295-022-00273-w; Marianna Griffini, '"How Can You Feel Guilty for Colonialism? It Is a Folly": Colonial Memory in the Italian Populist Radical Right', *European Politics and Society*, 24, no. 4 (2023), 477–493, doi:10.1080/23745118.2022.2058753.

¹⁶ Davide Vampa, *Brothers of Italy: A New Populist Wave in an Unstable Party System*. (Cham: Palgrave Macmillan, 2023).

¹⁷ Gianfranco Baldini, Filippo Tronconi, and Davide Angelucci, 'Yet Another Populist Party? Understanding the Rise of Brothers of Italy', *South European Society and Politics* 27, no. 3 (2022), 385–405, doi:10.1080/13608746.2022.2159625.

2014 and 2019),[18] its approach to Europe is constructed through reference to the same concepts studied in this book. FdI has claimed attachment to a European civilization and has called for the construction of a confederal 'Europe of the Peoples'.[19] It has restated the necessity of defending national sovereignty in the EU and promoting the national interest in European institutions, and even insisted that Europe should become a strong global actor able to compete with the USA, Russia, and China.[20] In line with the MSI and RN, it has also frequently presented Europe as an endangered continent—although the dangers identified by FdI are more in line with those mentioned by other contemporary far-right parties and include 'gender ideology', 'Islamization', the 'great replacement', and EU bureaucracy.[21] FdI's leader Giorgia Meloni also used the European issue as a way to draw a link between the past and the present of her party, when in her book *Io sono Giorgia* (I am Giorgia) she recalled the heritage of the MSI/AN to assert her European credentials:

> For me, Europe has always been a hope. And I laugh when I hear people say that I allegedly lead an 'anti-European' party. My mind quickly goes back to my early years as an activist, to the slogans and the many songs that define the cultural baggage of the Italian right. Our older brothers imagined a strong and autonomous Europe [. . .] able to unite its people not with convoluted parameters or with a currency, but through the strength of its millenary tradition. With the fall of the Berlin wall, the world changed, we embraced our brothers in the East again [. . .]. Europe could have started breathing with two lungs again [. . .] and the European dream should have taken flight in that moment. But unfortunately, the opposite happened.[22]

Given the marked similarities between the language of FdI and that of the MSI/AN and RN, one could expect Europe to work as an ideological resource for FdI as well. While a more thorough analysis falls beyond the scope of this book, future research on the subject is well-warranted.

---

[18] Leonardo Puleo and Gianluca Piccolino, 'Back to the Post-Fascist Past or Landing in the Populist Radical Right? The Brothers of Italy Between Continuity and Change', *South European Society and Politics*, 27, no. 3 (2022): 359–383. doi:10.1080/13608746.2022.2126247.

[19] Fratelli d'Italia, 'Tesi Di Trieste', 2017, https://www.flipsnack.com/fratelliditalia/tesi-di-trieste.html. Fratelli d'Italia, 'Il Programma. Pronti a Risollevare l'Italia. Elezioni Politiche 25 Settembre 2022', 2022, https://www.fratelli-italia.it/programma/.

[20] Fratelli d'Italia, 'Tesi Di Trieste'.

[21] Fratelli d'Italia; Fratelli d'Italia, 'In Europa a Testa Alta', 2014, https://www.fratelli-italia.it/programma-europa/.

[22] Giorgia Meloni, *Io Sono Giorgia* (Epub) (Milan: Rizzoli, 2022).

References

Albanese, Matteo, and Pablo Del Hierro. *Transnational Fascism in the Twentieth Century: Spain, Italy and the Global Neo-Fascist Network* (London; New York: Bloomsbury Academic, 2016).

Baldini, Gianfranco, Filippo Tronconi, and Davide Angelucci. 'Yet Another Populist Party? Understanding the Rise of Brothers of Italy'. *South European Society and Politics* 27, no. 3 (2023): 385–405, 1–21. https://doi.org/10.1080/13608746.2022.2159625.

Basile, Linda, and Rossella Borri. 'Sovereignty of What and for Whom? The Political Mobilisation of Sovereignty Claims by the Italian Lega and Fratelli d'Italia'. *Comparative European Politics* 20, no. 3 (June 2022): 365–389. https://doi.org/10.1057/s41295-022-00273-w.

Bayer, Lili, Maia De la Baume, and Hannah Roberts. 'European Far-Right Leaders Fail to Tie the Knot'. *Politico*, December 2021. https://www.politico.eu/article/viktor-orban-marine-le-pen-jaroslaw-kaczynski-europe-far-right-parties-coalition/.

Beaudonnet, Laurie, and Henio Hoyo Prohuber. 'Being European, the Nationalist Way: Europe in the Discourse of Radical Right Parties'. *Party Politics*, March 2023, 13540688231161208. https://doi.org/10.1177/13540688231161209.

Cerrone, Joseph. 'Reconciling National and Supranational Identities: Civilizationism in European Far-Right Discourse'. *Perspectives on Politics* 21, no. 3 (2023): 951–966.

Charlemagne. 'Europe's Hard-Right Is Pitching Voters a Contradictory Fantasy'. *The Economist*, 2019. https://www.economist.com/charlemagnes-notebook/2019/05/18/europes-hard-right-is-pitching-voters-a-contradictory-fantasy. Last accessed 23 July 2019.

De Jonge, Léonie. 'The Populist Radical Right and the Media in the Benelux: Friend or Foe?' *The International Journal of Press/Politics* 24, no. 2 (2019): 189–209. https://doi.org/10.1177/1940161218821098.

Euronews. 'Europe's Far-Right Meets in Madrid for Two-Day Summit Led by Spain's Vox'. *Euronews*, January 2022. https://www.euronews.com/2022/01/29/europe-s-far-right-meets-in-madrid-for-two-day-summit-led-by-spain-s-vox.

Flood, Chris. 'Euroscepticism: A Problematic Concept'. UACES 32nd Annual Conference, 2002.

Flood, Chris, and Rafal Soborski. 'Euroscepticism as Ideology'. In *Routledge Handbook of Euroscepticism*, edited by Benjamin Leruth, Nicholas Startin, and Simon McDougall Usherwood (London: Routledge, 2018), 36–47.

Forchtner, Bernhard. 'Climate Change and the Far Right'. *WIREs Climate Change* 10, no. 5 (September 2019): e604. https://doi.org/10.1002/wcc.604.

Forchtner, Bernhard, and Balša Lubarda. 'Scepticisms and beyond? A Comprehensive Portrait of Climate Change Communication by the Far Right in the European Parliament'. *Environmental Politics* 32, no. 1 (January 2023): 43–68. https://doi.org/10.1080/09644016.2022.2048556.

Fratelli d'Italia. 'In Europa a Testa Alta', 2014. https://www.fratelli-italia.it/programma-europa/.

Fratelli d'Italia. 'Tesi Di Trieste', 2017. https://www.flipsnack.com/fratelliditalia/tesi-di-trieste.html/.

Fratelli d'Italia. 'Il Programma. Pronti a Risollevare l'Italia. Elezioni Politiche 25 Settembre 2022', 2022. https://www.fratelli-italia.it/programma/.

Glencross, Andrew. '"Love Europe, Hate the EU": A Genealogical Inquiry into Populists' Spatio-Cultural Critique of the European Union and Its Consequences'. *European Journal of International Relations* 26, no. 1 (2020): 116–136. https://doi.org/10.1177/1354066119850242.

Griffini, Marianna. 'How can you feel guilty for colonialism? it is a folly': colonial memory in the Italian populist radical right, *European Politics and Society*, 24, no. 4 (2023): 477–493.

Herman, Lise Esther, and James B. Muldoon. *Trumping the Mainstream: The Conquest of Mainstream Democratic Politics by the Populist Radical Right* (London; New York: Routledge, 2019).

Kessel, Stijn van, Nicola Chelotti, Helen Drake, Juan Roch, and Patricia Rodi. 'Eager to Leave? Populist Radical Right Parties' Responses to the UK's Brexit Vote'. *British Journal of Politics & International Relations* 22, no. 1 (2020): 65–84. https://doi.org/10.1177/1369148119886213.

Lorimer, Marta. 'What Do They Talk about When They Talk about Europe? Euro-Ambivalence in Far Right Ideology'. *Ethnic and Racial Studies* 44, no. 11 (2021): 2016–2033. https://doi.org/10.1080/01419870.2020.1807035.

Mammone, Andrea. *Transnational Neofascism in France and Italy* (Cambridge: Cambridge University Press, 2015).

McDonnell, Duncan, and Annika Werner. *International Populism: The Radical Right in the European Parliament* (London: Hurst, 2019).

Meloni, Giorgia. *Io Sono Giorgia* (Epub) (Milan: Rizzoli, 2022).

Moffitt, Benjamin. 'How Do Mainstream Parties "Become" Mainstream, and Pariah Parties "Become" Pariahs? Conceptualizing the Processes of Mainstreaming and Pariahing in the Labelling of Political Parties'. *Government and Opposition*, 2021, 1–19. https://doi.org/DOI:10.1017/gov.2021.5.

Puleo, Leonardo, and Gianluca Piccolino. 'Back to the Post-Fascist Past or Landing in the Populist Radical Right? The Brothers of Italy Between Continuity and Change', *South European Society and Politics* 27, no. 3 (2022): 359–383. https://doi.org/10.1080/13608746.2022.2126247.

Szczerbiak, Aleks, and Paul A. Taggart. *Opposing Europe? The Comparative Party Politics of Euroscepticism. Volume 2* (Oxford: Oxford University Press, 2008).

Tait, Robert. 'Far Right to Gather in Prague as Fears Grow of Rising Czech Populism'. *The Guardian*, December 2017. https://www.theguardian.com/world/2017/dec/15/far-right-conference-prague-czech-republic-populism-marine-le-pen.

Vampa, Davide. *Brothers of Italy: A New Populist Wave in an Unstable Party System.* (Cham: Palgrave Macmillan, 2023).

Williams, Benedicte. 'Electoral Strategy Trumps Political Ideology'. In *Varieties of Right-Wing Extremism in Europe*, edited by Andrea Mammone, Emmanuel Godin, and Brian Jenkins (Abingdon, Oxon: Routledge, 2013), 134–148.

Wolkenstein, Fabio. 'Christian Europe Redux'. *JCMS: Journal of Common Market Studies* 61, no. 3 (May 2023): 636–652. https://doi.org/10.1111/jcms.13400.

Zúquete, José Pedro. 'The New Frontlines of Right-Wing Nationalism'. *Journal of Political Ideologies* 20, no. 1 (2015): 69–85. https://doi.org/10.1080/13569317.2015.991492.

Appendix

Annexe 1: Corpus-building

Data collection

The main sources of this book consist of archival documents and various types of party literature. While archival resources represent the main source for the book, I also carried out six interviews with current and former members of the two parties, to gain a better knowledge of their inner workings. These included two former party leaders (RN and MSI/AN), a former MEP (RN), and three former regional councillors (RN). While their contributions are not cited, they provided valuable insights and relevant documentation on the parties of which they were (and in two cases still are) members.

Creating the corpus

The first step in the creation of the empirical corpus of this book consisted in identifying relevant sources. Data was collected through a mix of online and library research carried out in London, and archival research in Paris, Florence, and Rome. The aim of data collection was to build a corpus of documents in which the selected parties discussed 'Europe'. To do so, I first identified a number of general party sources, and then explored them thoroughly to build a corpus of documents which either centred exclusively on or discussed in some depth European issues. To avoid a common issue of 'Eurocentrism' in European studies, more general documents such as party programmes and congress motions were also included as to understand the overall place and relevance of Europe. Digital copies were made of relevant documents, so that they could be read and analysed in depth at a later stage.

Building a corpus for the Rassemblement National was a relatively straightforward process. The Rassemblement National is a party that has been reasonably successful and which has published a large number of documents. In addition, it has had its own publishing company (*Éditions Nationales*) which published a number of political books in its years of activity. Most Rassemblement National programmes were available directly online and accessible via a simple Google search, and those which were not immediately available could be retrieved from the Comparative Manifesto Project (MARPOR) and the Euromanifesto project database. In addition, the library of the London School of Economics had a number of primary sources available in book format. In this way, all programmes published between 1984 and 2019 were found, with the exception of the programme from 1993 which was retrieved at a later stage from Sciences Po Paris.

To complement this mainly electorally oriented corpus, I identified the need to draw upon additional party literature which would allow me to capture the non-electoral and internally directed dynamics of ideology and provide a more comprehensive view of 'Europe' in the RN's discourse. The opportunity to achieve this was offered by a two-and-a-half-month research stay in Sciences Po Paris, in which extensive use was made of the university's resources and of the documents available at the Bibliothèque Nationale de France. Thus, the initial corpus was enriched with articles and editorials from *Le National*, an early party magazine, *La Lettre de Jean-Marie Le Pen*, the official forthnightly magazine of the party between 1985 and 2008 (from 1995 and until it ceased publication in 2008 also known as *Français d'abord*), *Nations Presse Magazine*, a monthly publication aimed at supporting Marine Le Pen's campaign for the FN's presidency and her subsequent work as president of the party between 2010 and 2015, and a number of speeches retrieved from the BNF's 'Archives de l'Internet', which gave access to cached versions of the Rassemblement National's website. Finally, to cover the period in which no other non-electoral literature was available (2015–2019), I drew on further internet-based research, identifying relevant press releases, electoral material, and speeches from the Rassemblement National's website (https://rassemblementnational.fr/).

Building a corpus for the MSI/AN required more digging, but was greatly helped by the fact that many MSI archives have recently been digitalised, and that for most of its existence, the party had an associated daily newspaper, *Secolo d'Italia*, which made it possible to retrieve a large number of documents.

The starting point for corpus-building was the archive of the Fondazione Ugo Spirito—Renzo De Felice. The Fondazione Ugo Spirito—Renzo de Felice (from here on, FUS) was founded in Rome in 1981 following a donation by his wife of documents belonging to the late Ugo Spirito. The foundation has a large archival fund bringing together various MSI documents, including foundational documents, internal communications, congress motions, press reviews, etc. The first stage of this book's research was thus dedicated to sifting through the fund, identifying relevant documents—in particular, electoral material, speeches, reports, and party congress motions. This could be easily done online, as the archives of the Fondazione have been digitalized and made available on the website of the Italian Senate (https://patrimonio.archivio.senato.it). In addition, I spent two days in the offices of the FUS in Rome, exploring documents which had yet to be made available online. From this initial phase, I collected a number of party congress documents, as well as some relevant newspaper articles and reports.

Following this initial phase, my attention turned to the *Secolo d'Italia*, the party's official newspaper. The *Secolo d'Italia* provided additional resources, in particular editorials and articles discussing the MSI/AN's vision of Europe, party programmes, and congress documents. In fact, with the exception of the 'Fiuggi Theses', no other documents could be found online for AN. Microfilm copies of the *Secolo d'Italia* published between 1979 and 2009 were consulted in the library of the Università Cesare Alfieri in Florence, and relevant articles were saved in a digital form. While other forms of literature were considered (such as party magazines), there was no magazine comparable in terms of its relevance and continuity to *La Lettre* or even to *National Hebdo*, so the attention was mainly focused on the *Secolo d'Italia*. I also contacted the Fondazione Alleanza Nazionale to request any relevant documentation they may have on AN's positions on Europe, and requested the Euromanifestoes of AN from the Euromanifesto project. Finally, a trip to the Biblioteca di Storia Contemporanea in Rome and further research in the LSE Library resulted in the acquisition of three further programmatic books (two interviews with party leaders on Europe and the project of the Eurodestra, and an 'A to Z' of the principles of the MSI).

Overall, over 400 documents of various natures were collected, ranging between one and 187 pages. While there are some gaps in years (notably, there were no documents available for the RN between 1982 and 1984 or in 1996), the entirety of the period between 1978 and 2009 for MSI/AN, and 1978–2019 for the RN was covered. Note that this number of documents does not correspond to the entirety of articles published on Europe during the period but only a selection of the ones which upon a first read appeared more conducive to in-depth analysis. In particular, when making a decision on whether to make a copy or not, I privileged documents of an analytical nature or which expressed partisan positions, rather than merely descriptive ones discussing, for example, a new EU policy or the outcome of an EU summit. While the corpus is not exhaustive, the large number of documents provides a reasonable expectation that they could be considered representative of the parties' overall positions and discourse.

This initial corpus was read in depth and analysed, with the purpose of identifying common themes and threads across documents and across parties. A number of key documents were then selected for further in-depth analysis and brought together into a smaller sample of documents (26 MSI, 21 AN, and 71 RN—full list available in Annexe 2). The choice to analyse only a quarter of the documents was driven by both practical and theoretical considerations. Theoretically speaking, the preliminary reading of the documents, as well as previous research on these parties, highlighted the fact that they tended to display high levels of ideological intensity,[1] and often repeated the same points and ideas in different places. Thus, it was expected that analysing the whole corpus would not have produced significantly different results and that saturation would likely be reached even with a smaller sample. This was subsequently confirmed with the analysis, where the coding procedure stopped generating new codes before all documents had been analysed. In practical terms, given that the book relied on a form of qualitative analysis, investigating as a single researcher the entire corpus in full would have required conspicuous time investment for little added value.

In order to facilitate storage, I opted to code the purposive sample with NVivo. While NVivo has several functions that can be used to analyse a document—for example running word searches or seeking to identify patterns—in the case of this research it was mostly used as a filing system in which passages were highlighted and sorted into different 'codes'. Documents which were not already in a searchable PDF format had to be either transformed into searchable PDF files through OCR software or transcribed when OCR processes failed. This was the case for all MSI/AN documents and for a large portion of RN documents. Short documents (two pages or less) were transcribed in full. In the case of longer documents, these were transcribed in full only when the entire document was relevant. In the case of documents where only a part had been dedicated to Europe (e.g. in programmes where Europe only figured in the foreign policy section), only relevant sections were transcribed for analysis, although the documents were all read in full.

---

[1] Alexandre Dézé, 'Idéologie et Stratégies Partisanes: Une Analyse Du Rapport Des Partis d'Extrême Droite Au Système Politique Démocratique: Le Cas Du Front National, Du Movimento Sociale Italiano et Du Vlaams Blok' (Paris: Institut d'Etudes Politiques, 2008).

Annexe 2: Documents selected for in-depth analysis

List of analysed documents—Rassemblement National (71)

Year	Document name	Author	Type
1978	Programme 7e arrondissement	FN	Programme
1979	Plateforme de l'Union française pour l'Europe	FN	Programme
1981	Programme élections législatives	FN	Programme
1984	Les Français d'abord	Le Pen, Jean-Marie	Programmatic book
1985	Pour la France: programme du FN	FN	Programmatic book
1985	Immigration action ferme et résolue des élus FN au PE	FN	Article
1986	L'Europe, d'abord une volonté	Le Pen, Jean-Marie	Article
1986	L'avenir de notre Europe	Le Pen, Jean-Marie	Editorial
1987	Construire l'Europe de la Puissance	Mégret, Bruno	Unclear
1987	Jeunesse Nation Europe	Lang, Carl	Article
1988	Un nouveau pas vers l'Europe du tiers monde	Le Chevallier, Jean-Marie	Article
1988	Etre ou Disparaitre: Discours Le Pen Europe	Le Pen, Jean-Marie	Speech
1989	Passeport pour la victoire	FN	Pamphlet
1989	L'illusion du primat de l'économie ou l'Europe à l'envers	Pichon, Olivier	Article
1989	Pour Une Europe des Peuples	Le Pen, Jean-Marie	Editorial
1989	Euromanifesto	FN	Programme
1989	Les principes fondateurs de notre Europe	Mégret, Bruno	Article
1989	En avant pour les Européennes	Mégret, Bruno	Article
1990	Schengen ils l'ont fait	Salagnac, Catherine	Article
1991	Militer au Front	FN	Party guide
1991	Les échecs de l'Europe des douze	Le Pen, Jean-Marie	Editorial
1992	L'engrenage de Maastricht	Salagnac, Catherine	Article
1992	Notre Europe les patries contre Maastricht	Mégret, Bruno	Article
1992	Le serment de Reims	Le Pen, Jean-Marie	Editorial
1993	Sortons de cette Europe là	Le Pen, Jean-Marie	Editorial
1993	300 mesures pour la France	FN	Programme
1994	Ma vérité sur l'Europe	Le Pen, Jean-Marie	Interview
1994	Euromanifesto	FN	Programme
1995	Discours 1er Mai	FN	Speech
1995	Le contrat pour la France avec les Français	FN	Programmatic book
1997	17ème Fête des Bleu-Blanc-Rouge	Le Pen, Jean-Marie	Speech
1997	Programme	FN	Programme

Continued

Continued

Year	Document name	Author	Type
1998	Fête de Jeanne d'Arc du 1er Mai 1998	Le Pen, Jean-Marie	Speech
1999	Poursuivre notre mission pour changer d'Europe	Le Pen, Jean-Marie	Editorial
1999	Le Front National pour restaurer notre identité nationale face à l'Europe fédérale	NA	Dossier
2000	La Turquie et l'Union Européenne un mariage impossible	NA	Article
2000	Indépendance	Lang, Carl	Article
2001	Entretien avec Le Pen Jean-Marie	NA	Interview
2002	L'Europe des collabos	Lang, Carl	Article
2002	Pour un avenir français: le programme de gouvernement du Front National	FN/de Bouillon, Godefroy	Programme
2003	Au Parlement européen le Front National: le parti qui défend les français d'abord	Lang, Carl	Article
2003	Discours Le Pen Jean-Marie Conseil National du Front National	Le Pen, Jean-Marie	Speech
2004	Aucun bien n'est plus précieux que l'indépendance	Le Pen, Jean-Marie	Interview
2004	Quelle Europe/Pour défendre la France en Europe	Gollnisch, Bruno; Lang, Carl	Article
2004	Euromanifesto	FN	Programme
2005	Le discours du NON au référendum sur la Constitution européenne.	Le Pen, Jean-Marie	Speech
2006	Des plombiers polonais	Gollnisch, Bruno	Article
2007	Discours à Toulouse sur le thème de l'Europe	Le Pen, Jean-Marie	Speech
2007	Programme de Gouvernement de Jean-Marie Le Pen	FN	Programme
2008	Gollnisch A propos de l'Union Soviétique européenne	Gollnisch, Bruno	Speech
2009	Discours de Louis ALIOT lors de la Convention d'Arras	Aliot, Louis	Speech
2009	Euromanifesto	FN	Programme
2010	L'esprit du 29 mai	Le Pen, Marine	Speech
2011	Conseil National du FN—Le discours de clôture de Marine Le Pen	Le Pen, Marine	Speech
2011	L'autre Europe	Aliot, Louis	Editorial
2012	Notre projet: Programme Politique du Front national	FN	Programme
2012	Union européenne: vers le stade ultime de l'Union Soviétique Européenne ?	FN	Press release
2013	Appel de Marine Le Pen aux peuples d'Europe	Le Pen, Marine	Press release
2014	Non à Bruxelles oui à l'Europe des nations	Langlois, Marc	Article
2015	M. Schulz s'en prend à la Pologne/l'UE de plus en plus dictatoriale	Bay, Nicolas	Press release
2016	Sortir de l'Union européenne, une nécessité politique	Club Idées Nation	Blog post

Year	Document name	Author	Type
2016	Referendum aux Pays-Bas—lorsque les peuples parlent, l'Union européenne chancelle	Bay, Nicolas	Press release
2016	Discours Fréjus	Le Pen, Marine	Speech
2017	144 Engagements Présidentiels	FN	Programme
2017	Discours de Marine Le Pen à la Journée des élus au Futuroscope de Poitiers	Le Pen, Marine	Speech
2018	Discours de Marine Le Pen au Luc-en-Provence	Le Pen, Marine	Speech
2018	Discours de Marine Le Pen Fête des nations	Le Pen, Marine	Speech
2018	Discours de Marine Le Pen à Kintzheim	Le Pen, Marine	Speech
2019	Pour une Europe des nations. Manifeste pour une nouvelle coopération en Europe "L'Alliance Européenne des Nations"	RN	Programme
2019	Pour une Europe des nations et des peuples	RN	Programme
2019	Discours du 1er Mai, Metz	Le Pen, Marine	Speech

Movimento Sociale Italiano (26)

Year	Document name	Author	Type
1978	Intervista sull'Eurodestra	Almirante, Giorgio	Interview book
1978	Programma Eurodestra	MSI	Programme
1979	Programma Nazionale 1979	MSI	Programme
1979	XII Congresso Napoli 5–7 ottobre 1979	MSI	Congress motions (2):[2] Continuare per rinnovare (Almirante, Romualdi); Linea Futura (Rauti)
1979	Intervista sull'Europa	Romualdi, Pino	Interview book
1979	Programme Europee 1979	MSI	Programme
1980	Il MSI dalla A alla zeta	MSI	Pamphlet
1981	Atlantismo non servile	Romualdi, Pino	Article
1981	Le nostre radici	Romualdi, Pino	Article
1982	XIII Congresso—Roma, 18–21 febbraio 1982	MSI	Congress motions (3): Nuova Repubblica (Almirante); Spazio Nuovo '82 (Rauti); Destra '80 (Romualdi)
1983	Programma	MSI	Programme
1984	XIV Congresso—Roma 29 novembre–2 dicembre 1984	MSI	Congress motion (1)

Continued

---

[2] For further information on the number of votes received by each motion, see Marco Tarchi, *Dal MSI ad AN: Organizzazione e Strategie* (Bologna: Il Mulino, 1997), 62.

Appendix

Continued

Year	Document name	Author	Type
1985	L'Europa dei prefissi	Mantovani, Cesare	Article
1985	Ma la scelta è politica	Mantovani, Cesare	Article
1986	La Turchia e la Comunità Europea	Mollicone, Nazareno	Article
1986	Voglia d'Europa	Romualdi, Pino	Article
1987	Programma Politica Estera	MSI	Programme
1987	XV Congresso—Sorrento, 11–14 dicembre 1987	MSI	Congress motions (6): Andare Oltre (Rauti); Destra in movimento (Fini); Impegno Unitario (Servillo); Proposta Italia (Mennitti); Destra Italiana (Romualdi); Nuove Prospettive (Tremaglia)
1988	Alla logica della moneta opporremo storia e cultura	MSI	Article
1989	L'Europa riscopre le radici	Urso, Adolfo	Article
1990	XVI Congresso—Rimini, 11–14 gennaio 1990	MSI	Congress motions (6): Destra in movimento (Fini); Andare Oltre (Rauti); Impegno Unitario (Servillo); Proposta Italia (Mennitti); Nuove Prospettive (Tremaglia); Destra Italiana (Lo Porto)
1991	Tante incognite nel futuro dell'Europa	Petronio, Franco	Article
1992	Programma nazionale 1992	MSI	Programme
1993	La crisi politica travolge Maastricht	Gasparri, Maurizio	Article
1993	Nuova Europa e chi se ne è accorto	Toppi, Paolo	Article
1994	XVII Congresso—Roma, 28–30 gennaio 1994	MSI	Congress motions (1)

Note: Congress documents are counted as a single document; however, the number of Congress motions varies between the different congresses. The number and title of motions is specified in parentheses under the section 'Type'.

Alleanza Nazionale (21)

Year	Document name	Author	Type
1994	Alleanza Nazionale Programma Politiche	AN	Programme
1994	Alleanza Nazionale Programma Europee	AN	Euromanifesto
1995	Congresso Fiuggi, 25–27 Gennaio 1995	AN	Congress motion
1996	Destra vuol dire Europa	Tremaglia, Mirko	Article
1997	In Europa ci andremo da turisti	Malgieri, Gennaro	Article
1997	Euroconservatori Crescono	Respinti, Marco	Article
1998	Tesi conferenza programmatica di Verona	AN	Programmatic conference
1999	Manifesto elezioni europee	AN	Euromanifesto
2000	Valori ed idee senza compromessi—Manifesto dei valori	AN	Manifesto
2000	Rapporti più chiari con l'UE	Alemanno, Gianni	Article
2001	Tesi Seconda conferenza programmatica	AN	Programmatic conference
2002	Fini: vogliamo un'Europa dei popoli	Parlato, Lucilla	Interview
2002	E sarà patria anche la casa Europea	Chiggio, Rolando	Article
2002	Tesi II congresso: Vince la patria, nasce l'Europa	AN	Congress motion
2003	La via maestra per la nuova Europa	Armani, Pietro	Article
2004	Manifesto elezioni europee	AN	Euromanifesto
2005	Se il sogno Europeo diventa incubo	Selva, Gustavo	Article
2006	L'Europa straordinaria armonia fra diversità	Perdizzi, Riccardo	Article
2007	Una conferma europea per le tesi di AN	Alemanno, Gianni	Article
2008	Quest'Europa poco amata dagli europei	Carrino, Agostino	Article
2009	Mozione III Congresso	AN	Congress motion

References

Dézé, Alexandre. 'Idéologie et Stratégies Partisanes: Une Analyse Du Rapport Des Partis d'Extrême Droite Au Système Politique Démocratique: Le Cas Du Front National, Du Movimento Sociale Italiano et Du Vlaams Blok' (Paris: Institut d'Etudes Politiques, 2008).

Tarchi, Marco. *Dal MSI ad AN: Organizzazione e Strategie* (Bologna: Il Mulino, 1997).

Index

For the benefit of digital users, indexed terms that span two pages (e.g., 52–53) may, on occasion, appear on only one of those pages.

Akkerman, Tjitske, 31–32, 35
Aliot, Louis, 152–153
Almeida, Dimitri, 7–8
Almirante, Giorgio, 63–64, 89–91, 144
Alternative Fur Deutschland, 29–30 n 23, 79–80
Amsterdam Treaty, 99
Anderson, Ben, 114–115
Anfuso, Filippo, 60–61
Authoritarianism, 5–6, 38
  Authoritarian regime, 29–30

Beetham, David, 28
Berlusconi, Silvio, 39, 64–65, 174–175
Blot, Yvan, 41, 69–70
Bribesville
  See Tangentopoli
Brothers of Italy
  See Fratelli d'Italia
Brussels, 70–71, 94, 100–102, 123, 151–152, 172
  Bureaucrats, 101–102, 126–127, 151–152
Bulgaria, 69
Bureaucracy, 7–8, 94, 151–153, 175–176

Central and Eastern Europe, 61–62, 66–67, 69, 95–97
Chrysi Avgi, 29–30
Ciotti, Éric, 87–88
Civilization
  European, 7–8, 14–16, 47–48, 59–60, 63, 65–66, 68, 72–82, 91–92, 97, 119–120, 153, 159, 166, 175–176
  Western, 91, 117–118
Civilizationism, 78
Cold War, 7–8, 16–17, 124–125
Colonialism, 127
Common Agricultural Policy, 62–63, 145, 151–152
Common European Defense, 16–17, 92, 96–97, 144, 145–146, 153

Communism, 17, 117–119, 123–124, 127, 149, 157
  Anti–communism, 61–63, 115, 117–118, 131–132
Concept coding, 48
Consistency, 17, 34, 35–37, 49–50, 105, 106–107, 119, 126–127, 139–140, 155, 156–157, 159–160, 167
Cordon sanitaire, 88
Crosetto, Guido, 174–175
Czechoslovakia, 69

De Gaulle, Charles, 40–41, 142, 148
De Lange, Sarah, 32–33
De Vries, Catherine, 8–9
Decline, 68
  Demographic, 17, 115, 119, 121–122
  European, 89–91, 96–97, 119–121, 123, 150, 153
  National, 119, 123
Dédiabolisation (De-demonization), 26–27, 31–32, 42
Delanty, Gerard, 78, 80–81
Democracy, 26, 48–49, 87–88, 93–95, 99, 104–108, 126–128, 146, 147
Democratic deficit, 7–8, 94, 106–107, 158, 174
Discourse analysis, 14–16, 43–44, 46–47, 49
Draghi, Mario, 175
Dreux, 40–41

Eastern Europe
  See Central and Eastern Europe
Easton, David, 30–31
Edwards, Erika, 8–9
Elite, 5, 28–30, 47, 100–101, 115, 123, 130–132, 172
  See also political class
Elysée, 100
Emergency politics, 17, 114–116, 128, 132–133, 167

England, 63–64, 69
　See also United Kingdom
Enlargement (EU), 62–63, 66–67, 69, 72, 152
EU Convention, 64–65
Euro, 100–101, 151–152
Euroambivalence, 7–8, 170, 171
Eurocommunism, 89–90
Eurodestra (Euroright), 89–90, 129–130, 144
Euronationalism, 171–173
Europa Nazione, 60–61
Europe
　vs EU, 7–8, 14–15, 70–73, 168–169, 175–176
　of the Homelands, 148, 153–154
　Nation, 60–61, 147–148
　of the nations, 70–71, 153, 172–173
　of the peoples, 149–150, 153, 175–176
European Central Bank, 175
European Commission, 101–102, 119–120, 151, 152
European Constitutional Treaty, 49, 64–65, 146–147
European Economic Community (EEC), 45, 129–130
European Parliament, 9–11, 26, 47–48, 69–70, 127, 145–146, 151, 171–172
　Elections, 47, 49, 63–64, 89–90, 174–175
Europeanism, 61, 63–64, 75–76, 78, 142, 170–171
Europeanization, 15–16, 34–35, 43
Europeanness, 14–15, 59–60, 65, 66–67, 73, 75–80
Euroscepticism, 1–2, 6–10, 17, 78–80, 106–107, 167, 168–171
　Compromising, 78–79
　Hard, 7–8, 168
EUSSR, 81–82, 101–102, 152
Extreme right, 3–4, 26

Fascism, 25–27, 29, 29–30 n 29, 37–39, 58–59, 64–65, 87–88, 117–118
　Anti-fascism, 89–90
　Neo-fascism, 1, 39–40, 93–94
　Post-Fascism, 26–27, 39–40, 93–94
Federal Office for the Protection of the Constitution, 29
Fieschi, Catherine, 9–10
Fini, Gianfranco, 39, 64–65, 67–68

Fiuggi
　Congress, 39–40, 66–67 n 30
　Theses, 93–95, 117
Foreign policy, 16–17, 92, 95, 98–99, 142–143, 147–148
Forza Italia, 39, 64–65, 174–175
Forze Armate Rivoluzionarie, 63–64
France, 2, 37, 40, 63–64, 98–100, 103, 121, 123, 125, 127, 142–143, 150, 151, 154, 157–159, 166
Fratelli d'Italia (FdI), 17, 25–26, 39 n 64, 167–168, 174–176
Freeden, Michael, 44
　See also morphological analysis
Freiheitliche Partei Österreichs, 26, 43, 79–80, 170–171
Frexit, 71–72, 153
Front National, 1, 40, 42, 71
　See also Rassemblement National
Fronte Unitario d'Azione Nazionale (FUAN), 63–64, 92, 144
Fuerza Nueva, 89–90

Gasparri, Maurizio, 63–64, 92, 144
Gellner, Ernest, 4–5
Germany, 29, 62–64, 96–97, 142–143
Globalism, 99, 126–127, 157
Globalization, 41, 115, 120–121, 124–127, 142–143
Gollnisch, Bruno, 101–102
Great Replacement, 122 n 36, 175–176
Groupe Union Défense, 29–30 n 23

Halikiopoulou, Daphne, 8–9
Heinisch, Reinhard, 12
Homogeneization, 64–65, 72
Hooghe, Liesbet, 8–9

Identité, 70–71
Identity
　European, 16, 60, 63–67, 73, 74–75, 77, 78–80, 103, 153, 172, 173
　National, 7–8, 60, 63–64, 73, 74, 77, 173
Ideology, 2, 12–13, 15, 43–47, 72, 80, 105, 132–133, 139–140, 155
　Far right, 3–6, 8–9, 12, 17, 31–32, 37, 47, 60, 63, 65, 75–78, 81–82, 88, 102–103, 105–108, 115–116, 119–121, 123–124, 131, 140, 156, 166–167, 170–171

Ideological resource, 2–3, 12–17, 27–28, 34–37, 42–43, 47, 59–60, 75–76, 88, 105, 140, 156, 159–160, 166, 167–170, 176
Ignazi, Piero, 39–40
Immigration, 5, 17, 31, 36–37, 40–41, 59–60, 62–63, 74–75, 106, 115, 118–119, 118–119 n 19, 119–120, 122–123, 125, 127, 129–133, 151–154, 157, 172
Imperialism, 89–91, 104–105, 117–118, 123–124, 129, 142
Inserimento (insertion), 38
Iron Curtain, 64–65
Irredentism, 62, 96–97
Islam, 72, 115, 127, 172
  Islamization, 62–63, 73, 127, 176
  Islamism, 122–123, 127
Istria, 61–62
Italian Social Republic, 38, 60–61, 63–64
Italy, 2, 25–26, 37, 38, 60–64, 79–80, 93–94, 115, 142–143, 145, 146, 166, 168

Jacquot, Sophie, 34–35
Jobbik Magyarországért Mozgalom, 27–28, 31–32

La Lega/Lega Nord, 39–40, 43, 65, 132–133
La Lettre de Jean-Marie Le Pen, 74–75, 121, 123, 149–150
La Russa, Ignazio, 174–175
Lang, Carl, 153–154
Le Chevallier, Jean-Marie, 74–75, 122–123
Le Gallou, Jean-Yves, 41, 70–71
Le Pen, Jean-Marie, 40–41, 67–69, 72, 74, 96–97, 100, 101–102, 122, 149–151, 158
Le Pen, Marine, 26–27, 31–33, 42, 43, 71–72, 74–78, 87–88, 98–99, 101–102, 122–127, 129–131, 152–153, 168–169
Legitimacy, 11, 13, 15–17, 26–33, 43
  deficit, 15–16, 25, 26–27, 29–33, 43, 58, 75–76, 81–82, 87, 173
  Through boundary shaping, 127–133
  Through Europeanness, 75–81
  Through renewed commitments, 154–159
  Through shared narratives, 102–107
Liberal-democracy, 31, 38, 93, 128
Liberty, 2, 16–17, 44–45, 48–49, 88, 89–93, 96–99, 101–107, 116, 123–127, 129–132, 140–142, 150, 151–152, 154, 155–160, 166–167, 169, 170–171
  As autonomy, 16–17, 88, 89–99, 105–107, 117–118, 123, 151–152
  As power, 16–17, 88–93, 95–99, 103–104, 107–108, 117–118, 123–124, 126–127, 141–143, 147–148, 150, 159, 166–167
  As self-rule, 16–17, 88–89, 93, 96, 99, 100–108, 126, 151–152
Lisbon Treaty, 99

Maastricht Treaty, 7–8, 69–70, 99, 123, 125, 129–131, 145
  Referendum, 49, 69–70
Macron, Emmanuel, 42, 87–88
Mainstream, 1–2, 10–11, 15, 25–26, 29, 31–32, 78–79, 88, 95, 104, 105–108, 166–168, 174
  Right, 79–80, 105–106
  Parties, 8–9, 33–34, 38–39, 103, 105–106, 131–133, 174
Mainstreaming, 26, 31–35, 38, 39, 88, 103, 105–108, 114, 167
Martinelli, Olivier, 72
Marks, Gary, 8–9
Martinez, Jean-Claude, 69–70
Matignon, 100
McDonnell, Duncan, 11–12
Mégret, Bruno, 41, 97–99, 123–124, 150
Mélenchon, Jean-Luc, 87–88
Meloni, Giorgia, 168–169, 174–176
Mission
  European, 91–93, 95–97, 104, 125
Mitterand, François, 40–41
Moffitt, Benjamin, 128, 130–131
Mollicone, Nazareno, 62–63
Morphological analysis, 15–16, 43–46, 48, 60
  Adjacent concept, 44–45, 102–103, 116
  Core concept, 4–5, 44–45, 155–156, 158–159
  Perimeter concept, 44–45
  Peripheral concept, 44–45, 102–103
Movimento Sociale Italiano/Alleanza Nazionale, 1–2, 14–17, 25–26, 37–40, 42–43, 45–50, 59–79, 81–82, 87–97, 102, 103–105, 107–108, 115–121, 123–124, 127–133, 139–150, 155–157, 159–160, 166–168, 170, 172–176
Mouvement National Républicain, 41

Movimento Sociale Italiano–Fiamma Tricolore, 39
Mudde, Cas, 4–5, 7–8
Mussolini, Benito, 60–61

Nanou, Kyriaki, 8–9
National interest, 2, 17, 48–49, 81, 120–121, 140–148, 150, 151–152, 155–156, 158–160, 167, 168–173, 175–176
Nationalism, 4–6, 9–10, 17, 59–60, 63, 81–82, 102–103, 116, 155–156, 170–171
  civic, 78
Nativism, 4–5, 58–60, 75–76, 87, 102–103
Nice Treaty, 99
Normal pathology thesis, 31, 87–88
North Atlantic Treaty Organisation, 62–63, 90–91, 95, 117–118
Nouvelle Droite, 43, 68

Parti des Forces Nouvelles, 89–90, 121–122 n 33
Partij voor de Vrijheid, 79–80
Pathological normalcy, 87
Pocock, John, 80–81
Polarized pluralism, 38
Political class, 11, 31, 61–62, 69–71, 79–80, 95, 98–101, 119, 120–121, 123, 143, 145
  Establishment, 9–10, 33–34, 119
  See also elites
Politics of fear, 128, 130
Polyakova, Alina, 9–10
Popolo delle Libertà, 39, 47, 174–175
Populism, 5, 26, 33–34, 100–101, 123, 128, 130–131
Portugal, 62–63, 69
Pytlas, Bartek, 12

Radical Right, 3–4, 6, 31–32, 40
Rallo, Michele, 89–90, 144, 148
Rassemblement National (RN), 1–2, 5, 10–11, 14, 15–17, 26–27, 32–33, 40–43, 45–50, 59–60, 62–63, 68–82, 87–89, 94, 96–108, 115–116, 118–119 n 19, 119–133, 139–141, 149–160, 166–168, 170–173, 175–176
  See also Front National
Rauti, Pino, 39, 63–64, 90–91, 117–118, 118–119 n 19
Renan, Ernest, 69

Reungoat, Emmanuelle, 10–11
Romania, 69
Romualdi, Adriano, 142
Romualdi, Pino, 63–64, 89–92, 117–119, 129–130, 141–142
Rooduijn, Matthijs, 31–32
Russia, 89–90, 124, 175–176

Salvini, Matteo, 174–175
Secolo d'Italia, 62–63, 92, 119–121, 141–142, 146–147, 159
Second World War, 2, 25, 29–30, 42–43, 58–64, 70–71, 89–90, 117–118
Selva, Gustavo, 146–147
Single European Act (SEA), 69–99, 125
Smith, Anthony D, 4–5
Soviet Union, 8–9, 64–65, 116, 117–118, 123–125
  See also USSR
Sovereignty, 7–9, 69–72, 74–75, 98, 99–102, 104–107, 120–121, 123, 124–126, 151–154, 158–159, 168–169, 175–176
Spain, 62–64, 69
Startin, Nicholas, 11
Subsidiarity, 93–95, 105–106

Tangentopoli, 38–39
Technocracy, 143
  Technocratic, 70–71, 80, 94, 175
  Technocrats, 100, 120–121, 123, 151
Third Way, 90–91
Treaty on European Union (TEU), 104
Tremaglia, Mirko, 159
Turkey, 14–15, 62–63, 72–73, 76, 122–123, 152, 157

United Kingdom, 69
  See also England
USA, 17, 89–91, 96–99, 114–115, 117–119, 124–125, 127, 147–148, 150
USSR, 17, 89–91, 96–98, 117–118, 123–124, 147–148, 150, 172

Van Kessel, Stijn, 33–34
Vasilopoulou, Sofia, 8–9, 78–79
Verona Congress, 119–120
Vlaams Belang, 26–27, 31–32, 43, 79–80
von Coudenhove-Kalergi, Richard, 80

Wedge issue, 35–37

Werner, Annika, 11–12
West (the), 69, 119–122
Western Europe, 66–67, 146, 175
Wilson, Carole, 8–9
Wodak, Ruth, 128, 130
Woll, Cornelia, 34–35

Yalta agreements, 62, 89–91, 117–118
Yugoslavia, 61–62

Zariski, Raphael, 28–29
Zemmour, Éric, 32–33, 87–88